Achieving Quality Software

Achieving Quality Software

INCLUDING ITS APPLICATION TO SAFETY-RELATED SYSTEMS

Third edition

David J. Smith

BSc, CEng, FIEE, FIQA, FSaRS, MIGasE
Consultant,
Tonbridge, Kent, UK

With a Foreword by Dr Paul W. Banks

CHAPMAN & HALL

London · Glasgow · Weinheim · New York · Tokyo · Melbourne · Madras

Published by Chapman & Hall, 2–6 Boundary Row, London SE1 8HN, UK

Chapman & Hall, 2–6 Boundary Row, London SE1 8HN, UK

Blackie Academic & Professional, Wester Cleddens Road, Bishopbriggs, Glasgow G64 2NZ, UK

Chapman & Hall GmbH, Pappelallee 3, 69469 Weinheim, Germany

Chapman & Hall USA, 115th Fifth Avenue, New York NY 10003, USA

Chapman & Hall Japan, ITP-Japan, Kyowa Building, 3F, 2-2-1 Hirakawacho, Chiyoda-ku, Tokyo 102, Japan

Chapman & Hall Australia, 102 Dodds Street, South Melbourne, Victoria 3205, Australia

Chapman & Hall India, R. Seshadri, 32 Second Main Road, CIT East, Madras 600 305, India

First published as *Engineering Quality Software* by Elsevier Science Publishers Ltd, 1987

Second edition 1989 by Elsevier Science Publishers Ltd

Reprinted 1990 by Elsevier Science Publishers Ltd

Third edition 1995 by Chapman & Hall

© 1987 David J. Smith and Kenneth B. Wood, 1989 Elsevier Science Publishers Ltd, 1995 David J. Smith

Typeset in Times 10/12 pt by Acorn Bookwork, Salisbury, Wiltshire

Printed in Great Britain by T. J. Press, Padstow, Cornwall

ISBN 0 412 62270 X

A catalogue record for this book is available from the British Library

Library of Congress Catalog Card Number: 95-67909

Contents

Foreword

The rapid growth in use of programmable technology, in nearly all sectors of Engineering, is a well-known established trend and one which there is every reason to believe will continue into the foreseeable future. The drivers of this trend include cost, flexibility, rich functionality and certain reliability and safety advantages. However, as explained in this book, these advantages have to be carefully weighed against a number of disadvantages which, amongst other things, have fundamental implications for reliability and safety.

Ideally, a programmable system would be viewed as a fusion of hardware, software and user (or 'skinware'), operating under a set of environmental conditions. To date, such a unifying model does not exist and so hardware, software and human factors are still considered largely as three separate disciplines, albeit with certain interdependencies.

Established techniques are available which enable the engineer to develop systems comprising purely hardware components to a prescribed reliability and performance. Software, however, is fundamentally different in a number of ways, and does not lend itself to equivalent analysis. A major problem with software is its poor 'visibility', and consequently the great difficulty in understanding and predicting its behaviour in all circumstances. This results in the ever-present software design flaws, or 'bugs', which have plagued the software industry from its beginnings.

The growing use of software in safety-related systems has demanded that much more stringent software standards and methods are developed and employed. In recent years, through research and innovation, a number of powerful techniques and tools have been developed which greatly improve the software specification, design and test processes. These, together with traditional quality measures, have moved software development from 'black art' status to a respectable and rapidly developing engineering discipline – but one which won't mature for several years.

A further advance in recent times is in the general awareness surrounding software in safety-related applications. This is due largely to the concerted effort of learned institutions (such as IEE, IGasE and the Safety and Reliability Society) and government initiatives (for example the DTI's

Safety Critical Systems Club). Industry and academia are now working together in a positive and fruitful way.

On this positive note, it is tempting to speculate about the future, particularly in the context of safety-related systems. It seems certain that this trend of improving software engineering technology and practices will continue. Key to this will be the formal education and training of software engineers.

Schemes and courses are now in place to ensure that the 'new generation' of engineers receive the training and accreditation they will need to comply with stringent standards. The attitude of management and, indeed, the customer will need to be aligned with this new approach.

Another necessary factor will be the continued improvement of tools across the whole software design cycle. For example, tools supporting the use of formal methods will need to be more user-friendly, and be able to shield the user from a lot of the underlying mathematics. Finally, it is a reasonable bet to predict that object orientation, which enables the development of validated and readily reusable code, will continue to grow in popularity.

Dr Paul W. Banks

Preface

Engineering Quality Software was first published in 1987 and, due to the fast moving nature of the subject, was substantially amended in 1989.

Now, in 1995, so much has been developed by way of tools and techniques, guidance and standards, awareness of issues such as competence and accreditation and safety-related issues that a major update has become long overdue.

The subject of software quality and, in particular, its connection with the integrity of safety related systems has continued to accelerate in terms of both public and professional attention. At the same time, the tools and techniques available to the software designer and to the safety-related systems assessor have also continued to develop at the same rate.

One estimate of the UK demand for safety-related systems, having software control, was £350 million for 1991/92 which was thought to have doubled since 1987. A similar estimate of the Western European market put the figure at £1000 million.

The demand for competent designers and assessors has gone hand in hand with this expansion and the techniques, standards and guidance described in this third edition have become essential topics for software and safety-related engineers alike.

Topics which have been significantly expanded include:

- the safety life cycle;
- safety integrity levels;
- certification and competence;
- formal requirements;
- formal design methods;
- metrics.

This book reviews the current state of the art and, also, looks forward.

Acknowledgements

I am greatly indebted to Dr Paul W. Banks (both colleague and good friend) who has made a major contribution to this edition. He is largely responsible for Chapter 8 and has structured Chapter 9. Furthermore he has made constructive comments throughout the entire text and has contributed a useful Foreword. Paul is well known in the telecommunications and oil and gas industries as an expert in software development, and the book has benefited from his input.

I am also grateful to Dr Stuart Pegler, of British Gas R&T, for permission to use some of his illustrations in Chapter 12.

TA Consultancy Services have also been of assistance by contributing the MALPAS example, and associated explanation, for Chapter 11.

John Dixon, of Newcastle on Tyne, was instrumental in the development of the case study.

My thanks to them all.

PART ONE

The Background to Software Engineering and Quality

The first three chapters define the terms and background which are necessary for an understanding of the subject. Causes of failure, as well as the design cycle, are introduced and the basic software problems are outlined.

The meaning of quality in software   1

1.1 QUALITY – WHAT IS IT?

The popular perception of quality is somewhat subjective and still perpetuates the idea that the more elaborate and complex products somehow offer a higher level of quality than their humbler counterparts. There is, therefore, a temptation to equate sophistication, instead of simplicity of function, with good quality.

Traditionally quality has been defined as **conformance to specification** and it follows that failures arise when it is not met. This applies equally well to software and hardware although, for the former, the situation is often more complicated.

It follows that a good product requires not only this conformance but a good specification in the first place. This means that all the requirements have to be fully and unambiguously foreseen because, strictly speaking, failures cannot be acknowledged for functions which have not been specified in the first place.

Good products sometimes emerge despite inadequate specifications but this is usually the result of enlightened design and must be vigorously discouraged. On the other hand, a good specification is still no guarantee of an adequate product since the obstacles to achieving conformance are considerable. The following chapters address the techniques and tools which are currently available to maximize software quality.

The major problem with software is our lack of ability to foresee and define the numerous, and often complex, requirements. This includes complications which come from the combination of operating modes, input conditions and environments – especially in real-time applications. As systems become larger and more complex so the problem increases and often the result is prolonged negotiations, throughout design, test and even commissioning, to modify the original requirements.

Figure 1.1 illustrates the simple idea of measuring (i.e. 'testing') conformance against a specification as a means of demonstrating quality.

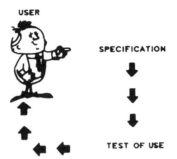

Fig. 1.1 Testing against specification.

Figure 1.2, however, introduces some complications which arise because:

- We have limited ability to foresee the requirements. The verification loop at the top of the diagram is the hardest of any of the 'tests' which arise. Firstly there is no higher document against which to

Fig. 1.2 The quality problem.

compare the requirements and secondly there is no way of guaranteeing that requirements have not been omitted.
- Our actual perception of the performance is limited. The validation loop is open ended in that however thorough a review of the software, it does not tell us how many faults remain.
- Test permits the demonstration of only a small sample of the code's possible permutations.

These difficulties are the substance of this book, which will concentrate on describing them and outlining the defences which are available.

The specification is only a statement of what the user perceives to be the field requirements and it is unlikely that it will cover all needs and eventualities.

The three main quality problems facing the software engineer are therefore:

1. verifying the requirements and establishing that there is no ambiguity, no omission and no error in the way that they have been stated;
2. validating the design which entails establishing that the code (in all its execution and real-time interface combinations) maps to the original requirements;
3. performing adequate tests despite the fact that extensive test times are only likely to permit a tiny fraction of the execution possibilities to be demonstrated.

A daunting task indeed!

1.2 SOFTWARE IS DESIGN

Thinking about the source of software failures (explored further in Chapter 2) is useful, at this stage. The traditional bathtub curve (Fig. 1.3) reminds us that hardware failures arise from three basic causes.

1. Early failures arise from an inherent population of defects due to design and/or manufacture and installation. The population slowly declines, thus demonstrating a decreasing failure rate.
2. So-called random failures result from variations in component strength and variations in stress.
3. Wear-out mechanisms which are physical.

Software cannot cause a failure for either of the latter two reasons. There is, therefore, an inherent population of logical features waiting for the appropriate conditions for them to be revealed as failures. This is analogous to the early failures group in the bathtub and these can **only** result from design.

Software faults are thus design faults and are not causally time related.

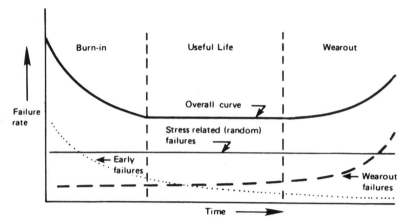

Fig. 1.3 The bathtub curve.

The rate at which they are revealed depends on the variety of ways in which the system is tested or used.

The remainder of this book will therefore concentrate on the design cycle and the activities which impact on software quality.

1.3 AN INTRODUCTION TO DESIGN

The electronic designers of the 1960s acquired their skills by a combination of imitation and practice. They were unwilling to document their methods and often worked alone. Although the skills and broad patterns of design were carried from task to task, two designs were seldom identical. In other words standardization was far from the norm in early electronic design.

The same approach to software, in the 1970s and early 1980s, led to poor design and error-prone code since the benefits of standard coding methods and standard packages of design were not encouraged.

The last 25 years have seen a radical change in approach to electronic hardware design. The size and complexity of electronic packages no longer permit such undisciplined methods. Circuit functions are obtained from proven packages and components which have become accepted as standards by electronic engineers.

Software design has started to undergo this transformation and is now often developed using proven structures and routines. Alas, this is still not the norm, but there are signs that the industry is moving in the right direction.

Lip service is certainly given to the newer methods (often called formal methods). They are varied and apply to various stages of the design, including the requirements stage itself. An engineering approach is therefore evolving and formalized methods are certainly recognized as necessary to assure quality software.

Traditional quality methods in software design have resulted in a 'checklist' approach. This is discussed later in the book and, indeed, Appendix 1 offers substantial examples. There are, however, pros and cons to this approach which are also explained. In essence checklists are open-ended suggestions and provide no means of quantifying the quality of the software in question.

Hence, the modern methods (so-called formal methods) involve a more mathematical approach so that reviews can be more quantitative. Mathematical proofs of correctness and the validation of code semantics can never be perfect but at least offer a more formal quality assurance method than before.

The key areas are:

- Formal specification: The use of mathematically based and even automated methods for translating requirements into design.
- Design methodologies: Libraries of reusable software packages. Proofs of correctness and validation of code may be largely automated.
- Test: Test specifications may be automatically generated by the design tools. Test beds will be more and more powerful and will be automated.

1.4 QUALITY VERSUS TIMESCALES AND COST

It would be well to look at the cost of failures during software design. Figure 1.4 illustrates two main points.

Firstly, the cost of revealing and correcting failures is lower, the earlier

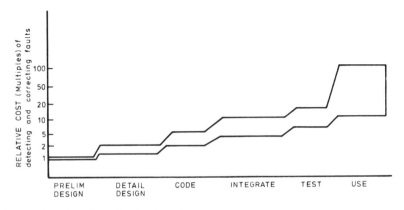

Fig. 1.4 Cost benefits of early detection.

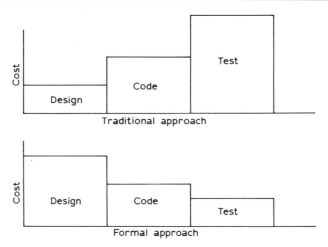

Fig. 1.5 Costs for traditional and formal approaches.

that it takes place. Pennies spent during the early design stages therefore reap greater dividends than pounds wasted on diagnosis and costly modification later on.

Secondly, the variation in cost from one fault to another increases as one progresses through the design. This is because any fault discovered during the development of the functional specification will incur roughly the same amount of effort to correct. On the other hand, a fault which is discovered during test may involve as little as one module of code but may extend to the whole hierarchy of design documents.

Nevertheless, the temptation is usually to save time and money during the specification and early design stages of a project. Schedule and commercial pressures provide an incentive to jump into the coding stages before the design is mature and, in any case, the coding stage is usually the most attractive to designers. This is because it is perceived to be the most creative stage and is seen to lead to a tangible output.

A more formal approach involves holding back from coding and investing resources in the requirements and design stages which are explored in Chapters 8 and 9. It is now well proven that this will lead to an overall quicker and less costly design – would that everyone agreed!

Figure 1.5 compares the distribution of costs between the traditional and more formal approaches. Committing more resources to early design simplifies the coding process and substantially reduces the number of faults which need to be revealed during test. The total cost and schedule is thus reduced.

2.1 ADVANTAGES AND DISADVANTAGES OF PROGRAMMABLE SYSTEMS

A programmable system is any piece of equipment or device which, having a computer architecture (i.e. arithmetic and logic capability plus a memory and a means of sequencing stored instructions), relies on those stored instructions in order to function. This is called a Von Neumann architecture and applies to the vast majority of computers and to what is currently known as programmable electronics.

The set of logical commands is usually referred to as the software. It is merely binary 0s and 1s within the machine but takes various forms of alphanumeric coded commands at the programmer level. It is important to understand that these commands are only the expression of 'design' or 'problem solution' which the programmer has developed from some initial requirement. It is really, therefore, the entire hierarchy of documents, as well as the code, which should be described as the software.

The design cycle, explained in this chapter, and the document hierarchy, discussed in Chapter 7, will make clear what is involved.

The term programmable electronic system (PES) is often used in place of computer. This has arisen out of their use in control and safety systems. Indeed, control and safety functions have long been implemented using programmable equipment which embraces a number of levels of processor architecture ranging from the simple to the complex. In the past they tended to be classified as:

- *Mainframe computing.* Systems with very large numbers of terminals supporting a variety of concurrent tasks. More often than not they are used for data-processing applications such as banking and seat reservation systems.
- *Minicomputing.* The distinction between minicomputing and mainframe has become blurred due to the rapid increase in size, speed and

facilities of the former. They are often used for process monitoring and control.

- *Microprocessing*. Again, there is a blurring between this category and the minicomputer but microprocessors are typically stand-alone machines. They are used, however, for real-time control as well as off-line computing purposes.

In view of the many and diverse real-time applications it is necessary to expand this simple view into a more refined description of processor types. Mainframe and minicomputing falls into category (f) below. Categories (b) and (c) are examples of microprocessing whereas (d) and (e) introduce equally important programmable architectures at a lower component level. Category (a), whilst not strictly a programmable architecture, has to be considered since many of the software quality problems still occur with this type of design.

(a) Simple stored sequence control where a memory contains a number of commands providing a sequence of control outputs. These steps are accessed by hardwired circuitry. Branching decisions are not possible since the traditional central processing unit (CPU) architecture is not present.

(b) Programmable logic controllers (PLCs) which are processor-based having simple instruction sets. They are commonly used in industry and tend to be of rugged design. They involve fewer commands than normal branching software and are tailed to control applications. There are many such devices, and languages include simple ladder logic, configurational languages and others including basic branching instructions. Since the possibility of compiler-related errors exists, evidence should be sought of extensive field experience and safe operation.

(c) Proprietary microprocessor controllers which are embedded microcomputers in a bus-related architecture with a high degree of standardization and thus better proven experience.

(d) Devices not incorporating a CPU but nevertheless having programmed hardware, for example, applications-specific integrated circuits (ASICs) and field-programmable gate arrays. Their design involves the use of hardware description languages which are functionally little different from conventional high-level programming languages and so are susceptible to similar problems.

(e) Embedded microprocessors, where a large-scale integration (LSI) device having a CPU architecture is used to provide functions within custom built circuitry. Due to the high package density, the programming is usually carried out at machine level. For this reason, the testability of the software is poor and the quality more difficult to verify.

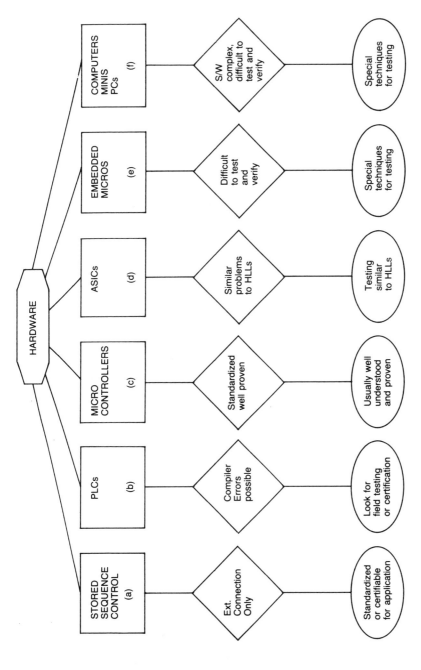

Fig. 2.1 Processor types.

(f) Computers involving CPU architectures on a larger scale to the above and having more powerful processing and storage capability. They are likely to be used for applications where simultaneous data and control flows are required. The applications software is likely to be complex and thus difficult to verify. Distinctions have become blurred but this category includes PCs, minicomputers and workstations.

Figure 2.1 shows the above categories and summarizes the picture. Real-time applications have expanded more than any use of computing in the last decade. They include:

- *communications.* telephone signalling, mobile radio and telephony, telemetry;
- *domestic.* appliance control and timing, security, utility metering;
- *energy and petrochemical plant.* process control and safety systems (e.g. shut down, fire detection), power and pressure and flow optimization;
- *transport.* fuel optimization, auto landing, road and rail signalling;
- *health.* diagnostics, prosthesis control, body monitoring, blood analysis, surgery;
- *industry – manufacturing.* robotics, process data gathering, process control, stock control;
- *commerce.* word processing, calculations, elevators, graphics, mail, banking systems, dealing systems, cash dispensing, electronic payment, personnel access control.

There are clearly advantages to be had from the faster and more sophisticated controls available from PESs. There are, however, disadvantages and a comparison is necessary at this stage.

2.1.1 Functional and reliability advantages

- Less hardware (i.e. fewer devices) for any given function due to the high levels of integration and the fact that many functions can be programmed into a single device.
- Fewer device types and therefore easier familiarity with the hardware design options.
- A consistent architecture which leads to a more consistent approach to the design and the need for fewer spares.
- Modifications and reconfigurations are simpler because they can often be carried out by changes to the software.
- Running logs can be kept of real time and calculated data. This facilitates maintenance planning.
- Self-test (auto-test) can be carried out at frequent intervals by software routines. This enables dormant faults to be revealed more quickly, thus improving reliability and availability.

2.1.2 Safety-related advantages

- Permits more remote control thus removing human operators from hazardous areas.
- Provides more sophisticated process interlocks thus reducing the probability of hazardous failures.
- Monitors process parameters to give timely warning of potential hazardous trends.
- Provides early warning diagnostics by logical analysis of real-time conditions.
- Provides centralized displays and graphics (on visual display units (VDUs)) which greatly reduce the probability of human error in plant control. Remember that the majority of major plant-related incidents (Piper Alpha, Bhopal, Three Mile Island, etc.) involve some element of human error.

2.1.3 Reliability and safety disadvantages

- Software is difficult to 'inspect' for inherent faults. There is no parallel to the hardware technique of 'failure mode analysis' where failures of component parts are assessed for their potential to cause some defined system level failure. There is no equivalent mapping with software. Lines of code do not, of themselves, have a failure potential.
- It is harder to impose standard approaches to software design. By its nature, software development is an intellectual exercise and much as the earlier electronic designers enjoyed a certain freedom of expression the same has been the case with programmers.
- Software changes are harder to control than hardware changes since they involve documentation, software storage media and the code itself. There is less visibility and the task of control is that much harder.
- It is not easily possible to predict software failure rates. This is addressed in Chapter 15.
- Exhaustive testing is impossible because the number of permutations of execution path is nearly always too high to allow more than a fraction of a percent of coverage. With real-time systems the problem is worse due to the additional permutation of input and output conditions.
- There is a greater susceptibility of redundant systems to exhibit common mode failure due to the common software in the various redundant channels. Diverse software, although some defence, is no panacea, as is discussed in Chapter 13.
- External corruption of stored data and stored program instructions adds to the failure possibilities.

2.2 SOFTWARE-RELATED FAILURES

It is necessary to define failure, and some other related terms. Unlike hardware failures, software-related failures do not involve a physical change causing an item to stop functioning. Software-related failures are the result of errors, arising from various types of fault, which do not always become evident immediately. Unlike the hardware 'bathtub curve' (Chapter 1) there is no wear-out feature whereby failure rate increases due to degradation. Furthermore, there are no constant failure rate failures due to the random interaction of stresses and component strength. There is only a population of inherent faults (bugs) which decreases as they are revealed.

Figure 2.2 illustrates the terms fault/error/failure.

Faults occur in hardware and in software. Software faults (often called bugs) are design related and do not necessarily result in failures. A long time may elapse before that portion of code is executed (if at all) under the appropriate conditions (e.g. inputs, output, internal loading, timing) for the fault to propagate.

A fault may propagate to an error. This is the condition whereby there is some wrong state – an incorrect data value or an instruction is incorrect; the CPU is pointing to the wrong instruction in the program. This may arise when the execution of the program allows the fault to cause the error. There is still no failure.

The error may propagate to become a failure unless some error

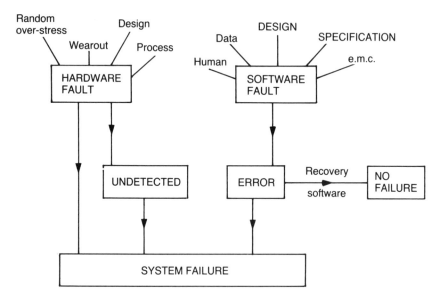

Fig. 2.2 Fault, error, failure.

recovery feature of the code allows it to be detected and rectified (Chapter 13). A failure, just as with hardware, is when the system fails to perform its desired function.

This is different from the propagation of hardware faults which either lead directly to system failure or, in the presence of redundancy/diversity, remain dormant until coincident faults exist.

2.3 CAUSES OF FAILURE

Faults can be caused at all stages in the design cycle including the requirements specification itself. Evidence suggests that the majority of errors (over 60%) are committed during the requirements and design phases whereas barely 40% occur during coding. That is not to say that coding is not a part of design but that it is only the final activity in a much larger process.

The more complex the system the more will faults tend to arise out of ambiguities and omissions in the specification stages. The major sources of faults are:

1. *The requirement specification*
   - Incorrect requirements due to:
     —Model not a good fit to the physical situation.
     —Incorrect document cross-references.
   - Inconsistent or incompatible requirements
     —Conflicting requirements widely separated in the documentation.
     —Conventions not consistent.
   - Requirements illogical.
   - Requirements unclear.
   - Requirements omitted.
2. *From the design*
   - Unstructured approach to the design breakdown (e.g. detail addressed too soon).
   - Lack of proper reviews.
   - Lack of change/configuration control.
   - Specification was misunderstood.
3. *From coding*
   - Semantic errors involving incorrect use of statements.
   - Logical errors in translating the design into code.
   - Detailed syntax errors which escape detection by the compiler.
   - Poor data validation (e.g. no default conditions after a data input.
   - Variables not initialized or used incorrectly.
   - Insufficient arithmetic accuracy for the application.
   - Type mismatch (e.g. string used as a variable).
   - Residual errors in compilers.

Chapters 7–13 will describe the tools and techniques available to minimize the above types of fault.

2.4 THE NEED FOR A DESIGN LIFE CYCLE

The life cycle is an essential model for the application of all the techniques in this book. It fulfils two important roles.

Firstly, it provides a hierarchy of design which progresses from the requirements forwards (or downwards) through successive layers of design to the code itself. The concept is that each stage is achieved before moving onto the next. In that way each stage should reflect the requirements of the preceding stage until code is created to match the original requirement.

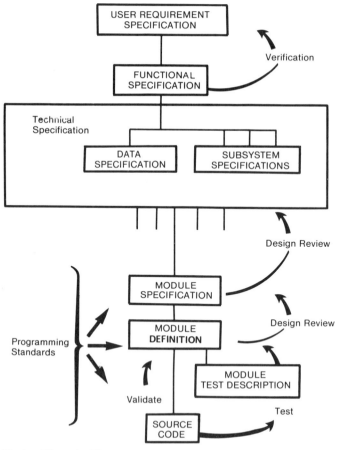

Fig. 2.3 Design life cycle (1).

Secondly, it provides a framework for the quality activities, which include reviewing each stage against the preceding stage for correctness. Thus, there is an opportunity for corrective action and a measure of confidence to proceed to the next stage.

Figure 2.3 shows one of the many versions of the life-cycle concept.

This version draws attention to the need for verification at each stage. Notice that the requirements phase is part of the design cycle since it is very much a part of the design. It is really the design base from which everything else follows and against which its correctness is compared. As we have seen already it is an important source of faults.

The feedback loops shown in Fig. 2.3 introduce the various names of the review activities at each stage. In one sense they are all design reviews. They differ, however, in the techniques used which need to be appropriate to the stage in the design cycle.

Design review of specifications in natural language may well involve a comparison of statements and a search for ambiguity whereas, on the other hand, the validation of code may involve mathematical techniques.

Textual review of the requirements specification is the hardest review and the one most likely to be ineffective. The problem stems from the fact that the user may not know fully what is required and may have difficulty in formalizing a specification which can be translated into a design. However good the requirements specification there still remains the difficulty that there is no higher level of documentation against which to review it. Chapter 10 will address some detail of the various review stages.

Test is, of course, included as yet another form of review wherein code is actually executed and the results compared with a predetermined test specification.

The cycle has been presented in many forms and Fig. 2.4 shows another version which emphasizes the sequence of activities.

Assuming for the moment a satisfactory set of requirements, the next stage is to produce a functional specification (Fig. 2.3). This is part of system design (Fig. 2.4) and the purposes of each of the document levels will be explained, in detail, in Chapter 7.

From here on there is design iteration down to module level after which elements of the system are integrated together. Review, and test, when appropriate, is carried out against the higher-level specifications.

Finally, acceptance takes place against a predefined specification. Acceptance usually concentrates on demonstrating the functional aspects of the product, rather than reviewing transparent design details.

Designing is thus the process of breaking down a requirements specification into a logical hierarchy of successive descriptions resulting eventually in program code.

The design cycle is an excellent concept. It is well known, however, that the temptation to jump to the coding stage is strong, often resulting in the

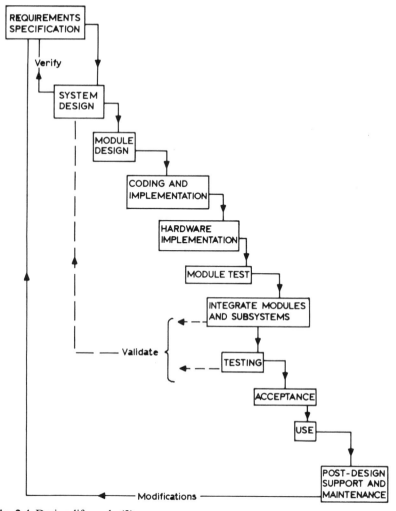

Fig. 2.4 Design life cycle (2).

need to reverse engineer the intervening levels of design and documentation after the event.

The serious penalty that follows is that the documentation is then based on the code, and any reviews, as described above, will consist of meaningless comparisons whose outcomes are prejudged. The effectiveness of the software quality techniques will thus be severely compromised.

Nevertheless, the design-cycle concept is the very basis of the guidance and information in this book. It has to be taken seriously and implemented for every software design.

3.1 SAFETY-RELATED APPLICATIONS

Many of the applications of programmable equipment are those which involve carrying out safety functions. Examples are fire and gas detection apparatus, shut-down and control systems in process plant, medical electronics, aircraft controls, machine-tool control, nuclear plant and weapons-systems control. The consequences of failure are often severe.

There has been a great deal of discussion, and some confusion, concerning the terms **safety-critical** and **safety-related**, which have tended to be used synonymously. The former has tended to be used where the hazard leads to fatality whereas the latter has been used in a broader context. There have been many definitions which differ slightly as, for example:

- Some distinguish between multiple and single deaths.
- Some include injury, illness and incapacity without death.
- Some include effects on the environment.
- Some include system damage.

However, the current consensus distinguishes them as follows:

- Safety-related systems are those which, singly or together with other safety-related systems, achieve or maintain a safe state for equipment under their control.
- Safety-critical systems are those which, on their own, achieve or maintain a safe state for equipment under their control.

The difference relates to the number involved and the term **safety-related application** implies a control or safety function wherein failure or failures could lead to death, injury or environmental damage.

For the remainder of this book the term **safety-related** will be used in the sense that any programmable system is safety-related where a failure, singly or in combination with other failures/errors, could lead to a death, injury or environmental damage.

A piece of equipment, or software, cannot be excluded from this safety category merely by identifying alternative means of protection. This would be to prejudge the issue by describing the safety integrity in terms of the number of levels of protection. A formal safety integrity assessment would still be required.

3.2 SAFETY INTEGRITY LEVELS

3.2.1 The need for safety criteria

It is important to remember that risk is described by two measures:

- the frequency of the event;
- the consequences of the event.

The former may be described in terms of frequency, rate or the mean time between events. The consequences are often described by the number of potential fatalities. These measures need to be established during the assessment.

One's perception of risk is usually influenced by the consequences. Thus, loss of property is more acceptable than personal injury which, in turn, is more acceptable than a fatality. Furthermore, multiple fatalities are generally considered less acceptable than single fatalities. It is necessary to take account of such perceptions when setting risk criteria.

Some typical frequency levels for different levels of severity are shown in Table 3.1. It should be noted that the perception of acceptable risk varies according to the severity of the consequence and the degree to which the exposure is voluntary. There is, in addition, an emotive element based on one's ability to understand the risk. An example is the relative fear of a nuclear incident compared with one associated with oil and gas.

There is also a qualitative approach, not involving rates and frequencies, which involves ranking and grouping the risks according to severity. This is described in section 3.2.2.

The usual approach to risk targets is to decide to which of the following three categories it belongs:

1. The risk is so great that reduction must be undertaken.
2. The risk is so small as to be acceptable.
3. The risk is between the above two categories and risk reduction should be undertaken, having regard to the cost, until it is as low as is reasonably practicable (ALARP).

Since there is no such thing as zero risk, the cost of risk reduction has to be balanced against the potential benefit. What constitutes a level of

Table 3.1 Typical risk frequency levels

Frequency of risk per annum	Example	Perception
10^{-7}	Lightning	Single fatality, generally perceived as acceptable
10^{-7}	Nuclear	Involuntary, multiple fatalities, some perceive as unacceptable
10^{-7}–10^{-6}	Gas	Users are voluntary, one or few fatalities, generally perceived as acceptable
10^{-7}–10^{-6}	Rail	Users are voluntary, one or few fatalities, generally perceived as acceptable
10^{-5}–10^{-4}	Chemical	Voluntary, multiple fatalities (employee) borderline perception of acceptability
10^{-4}	Road	Voluntary, usually single fatalities, perceived as unacceptable but tolerated

safety as far as is reasonably practicable at any time is ultimately determined by the courts.

The achievement of an acceptable level of system safety integrity for a software based system can only be judged by assessing the system against some tolerable target risk. The target may be established as a result of:

- incident data which establishes an accepted norm;
- overall national risk figures;
- theoretical assessments of the system.

The software can then be linked to the system safety integrity. The question then arises as to which aspects can be quantified and which can only be addressed in a qualitative manner.

3.2.2 Quantified risk assessment and safety integrity levels

Safety integrity is often defined as the probability of a safety-related system performing the required safety functions under all the stated conditions within a stated period of time.

The question arises as to how this may be assessed and/or demonstrated. This involves a combination of two complementary approaches:

1. Quantified assessment
   At the higher levels of safety integrity a quantified approach is usually needed. A numerical prediction is carried out using probability models

and/or simulation techniques and the results compared with the required integrity level. Reliability prediction is well established as a means of predicting the frequency of hazardous failures. Techniques such as fault-tree analysis, block-diagram modelling, cause–consequence analysis and simulation are well described in the reliability literature and take account of:

- hardware failure rates;
- human error rates;
- levels of equipment redundancy;
- repair intervals;
- common mode failure rates.

In the case of programmable equipment, only the hardware failure rates can be quantified since there are, as yet, no universally accepted criteria for predicting software failure rates. Thus, total system reliability cannot be quantified, but only certain elements.

2. Safety integrity levels

An emerging International Electro-technical Commission (IEC) international standard adopts the concept of safety integrity levels for safety-related systems. The method is to rank the hazardous failures into safety integrity groups and to provide, for each group, specific requirements in the form of configuration rules and other contributors to risk reduction and hence to safety integrity. Table 3.2 shows target figures (which are currently under review) for four safety integrity levels of which level 1 is the lowest and level 4 is the highest. This is in order to permit higher levels to be defined, should it become necessary, without disrupting the existing figures. They refer to the total of random hardware, systematic and human factor related failures.

Some types of failure (e.g. hardware random failures) can be quantified, in which case the quantified approach may be used. Other features can only be addressed qualitatively and judgement will have to be applied as

Table 3.2 Safety integrity levels

Safety integrity level	High demand/continuous mode of operation (Dangerous failures/yr)	Demand mode of operation (Probability of failure to perform design function on demand)
4	$>= 10^{-5}$ to $< 10^{-4}$	$>= 10^{-5}$ to $< 10^{-4}$
3	$>= 10^{-4}$ to $< 10^{-3}$	$>= 10^{-4}$ to $< 10^{-3}$
2	$>= 10^{-3}$ to $< 10^{-2}$	$>= 10^{-3}$ to $< 10^{-2}$
1	$>= 10^{-2}$ to $< 10^{-1}$	$>= 10^{-2}$ to $< 10^{-1}$

to which defences are applicable at each safety integrity level. It is understood that engineering judgement will be needed to establish the measures
needed at each level.

Software failure rates cannot easily be quantified and it therefore lends
itself to the approach which links specific measures to safety integrity
levels.

Chapters 7–13 (Part 3) provide generic guidance on equipment configuration and software quality. Ideally the configuration guidance and
software quality methods would be associated with specific safety integrity
levels. In other words a checklist ought to evolve so that specific techniques and measures will be called for at each safety integrity level. The
higher the level, the more stringent would be the requirements. It is
intended that this type of guidance will develop in time.

The IEC international standard (described in section 5.2.3) and the civil
avionics standard (described in section 5.2.10) come the closest to this at
the present time in that they recommend specific measures for specific
safety integrity levels. The civil avionics standard uses the term 'criticality
levels'.

3.3 THE SAFETY LIFE CYCLE

In Chapter 2, the concept of a design life cycle was developed. It was seen
that this systematic approach is necessary in order to provide a basis for
progressive development of the software and to allow the review process
to take place.

It is useful to broaden this life-cycle idea in order to describe a framework for the overall safety process (from the first consideration of risk,
through design and implementation, to eventual field data collection).

Figure 3.1 shows the safety life-cycle model as proposed in the IEC
guidance (see Chapter 5).

The design cycle complements the safety life cycle by describing more
detail within the design process. The following is a brief amplification of
the steps in the cycle.

- *Concept*: This involves developing a level of understanding of the
  safety-related system and its environment.
- *Overall scope definition.* This involves defining the boundary of what is
  described as the safety-related system. It also involves laying down the
  scope of the hazard and risk analysis to be carried out.
- *Hazard and risk analysis.* To identify the hazardous events. To identify
  the combinations and sequences of events leading to the hazardous
  failure modes. To determine the frequencies where applicable.
- *Overall safety requirements.* To develop a safety requirements

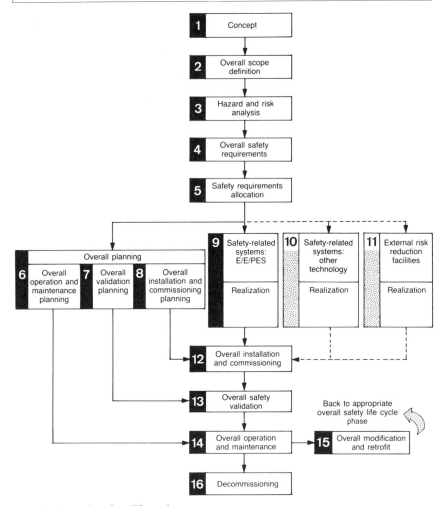

Fig. 3.1 Overall safety life cycle.

specification, with the regard to the safety integrity requirements for the safety-related system, and external risk reduction features in order to achieve the required level of safety.

- *Allocation of safety requirements to designated safety-related systems.* To allocate target safety requirements and external risk reduction measures to the designated safety systems. It is at this stage that the safety integrity levels are allocated to the safety-related systems and to external risk-reduction facilities.

- *Overall operation and maintenance strategy.* To lay down a plan, and a safety management system, to ensure that the required safety is implemented and maintained.

- *Overall validation planning.* To lay down an overall specification for validating that the safety requirements are met.
- *Realization.* Creating the actual safety-related systems.
- *Overall installation.* To install the overall safety-related systems and external risk reduction facilities.
- *Overall safety validation.* To validate that the safety requirements meet the safety specification.
- *Overall operation and maintenance.* To operate and maintain the combination of safety-related systems in accordance with the strategy and to achieve the required safety.
- *Overall modification and retrofit.* To ensure that the safety-related systems and external risk reduction measures remain adequate after modification.
- *Decommissioning.* To ensure that the safety-related systems and external risk reduction measures remain adequate during decommissioning.

For each phase of the safety life cycle it is beneficial to define:

- objectives for the stage;
- specific requirements of the stage;
- a scope;
- defined inputs (e.g. measures, documents, assessments);
- defined outputs or deliverables needed to comply with the requirements (e.g. calculations, assessments, judgements).

PART TWO

Guidance, Legislation and Liability

The next three chapters provide a review of the current published standards and guidance and place them in the context of the legal scenario and current attitudes to competence.

Legislation and liability | 4

The introduction of laws concerning product liability, and the development of legislation concerning safety and major industrial hazards, has had a considerable impact on the software designer. Failures and their consequences, arising from software errors, are covered by such regulations as much as those from any other cause.

The implementation of much of the legislation involves the Health and Safety Executive and it will therefore be useful to give a brief outline of the way in which it operates.

4.1 THE HEALTH AND SAFETY EXECUTIVE

The Health and Safety Executive (HSE) was set up under the authority of the Health and Safety at Work Act 1974 and is administered through the Department of Employment. It is the executive and operating branch of the Health and Safety Commission (HSC) and carries out HSC policy. The HSE is made up of inspectorates which operate within the civil service structure.

The HSE headquarters develops policy and provides specialist services. There are 20 area offices, each of which manages direct enforcement activities in a specific geographical area. To deal with matters affecting whole industries the HSE has set up a number of national interest groups (NIGs). A principal inspector in one of the 21 areas is responsible for HSE participation in each NIG and is the HSE specialist for that industry. General enforcement duties such as hygiene, machine guards, working conditions, etc. are handled mostly by factory inspectors.

Plant design and its operation and maintenance are also monitored by factory inspectors to ensure that both existing and proposed installations are fit for purpose and properly operated.

Major hazards, affecting employees or the public, are the concern of specialist inspectors or by specialists from the Major Hazards Unit. Section 4.4 expands on the Control of Industrial Major Accident Hazards (CIMAH) regulations.

Plant operators are required to demonstrate, by using formal hazard assessment techniques (see Chapter 3), the possible ways in which a plant can fail and the nature and extent of any consequences for the public or for employees. If any of the failures can cause injury, major damage, or death then the probability of the event must be calculated.

This type of hazard assessment is used by the HSE to establish consultation zones around hazardous installation. Planning authorities are required to consult with the HSE when addressing applications for development within those zones.

It is acknowledged (as discussed in Chapter 3) that there is no such thing as zero risk, and therefore the law requires that risks are reduced 'as low as is reasonably practicable' (ALARP). This involves weighing the cost of risk-reduction measures against the benefits to employees and the public. Ultimately, what constitutes ALARP can only be determined in the courts.

4.2 THE HEALTH AND SAFETY AT WORK ACT 1974 AND EC LEGISLATION

Modern safety legislation, in the UK, is currently dominated by the Health and Safety at Work Act 1974. Although hardly recent, it is important legislation which imposes responsibilities on everyone.

Section 1 sets out general duties for every employer to ensure, as far as is reasonably practical, the health, safety and welfare, at work, of all employees.

Section 2 goes into detail as to how these duties can be discharged.

Section 3 concerns the duty of employers to conduct undertakings so as not adversely to affect the health or safety of persons other than employees.

Section 6 is very important in that it imposes strict liability in respect of articles produced for use at work, although the Consumer Protection Act actually extends this liability to all areas. It is very wide and embraces designers, manufacturers, suppliers, hirers and employers of industrial plant and equipment. This is an area of criminal law since failure to observe these duties is punishable by fine or imprisonment. Compensation, on the other hand, is dealt with in civil law.

Other main duties can be summarized as:

- design and construct products without risk to health and safety;
- provide adequate information, to users, for safe operation;
- carry out research to discover and eliminate risks;
- make positive tests to evaluate risks and hazards;
- use safe methods of installation;
- use safe (proven) substances and materials.

Concessions are:

- It is a defence that a product has been used without regard to the relevant information supplied by the designer.
- It is a defence that the design was carried out on the basis of a written undertaking by the purchaser to take specific steps sufficient to ensure the safe use of the item.
- One's duty is restricted to matters within one's control.
- One is not required to repeat tests upon which it is reasonable to rely.

Everyone concerned in the design and provision of an article is responsible for it. Directors and managers are held responsible for the designs and manufactured articles of their companies and are expected to take steps to assure the safety of their products. Employees are also responsible and the 'buck' cannot be passed in either direction.

The recommendations given in the software-related documents, described in Chapter 5, are for the most part state-of-the-art guidance rather than legal requirements. Nevertheless, the Health and Safety at Work (H&S@W) Act requires us to address such guidance since to ignore it could be construed as not taking all reasonable steps to assure safety. That does not mean that all guidance must be followed blindly. What it does mean is that it should be addressed and that there should be a reasoned justification for proceeding in an alternative way.

In 1989–90 the EC agreed to a framework of directives that will eventually replace the H&S@W Act. These directives are more prescriptive and detailed than the H&S@W Act but nevertheless mirror its provisions by placing general duties on both employees and employers for all work-related activities. Many of these were to be implemented by the beginning of 1993.

The H&S@W Act meets the majority of the EC requirements and it is therefore the HSC's intention to implement them with little disruption to the existing UK framework.

The specific directives currently cover:

- the overall framework;
- the workplace;
- use of work equipment;
- use of personal protective equipment;
- manual handling;
- display screen equipment.

4.3 CIVIL LIABILITY

Product liability is the liability of a supplier, designer or manufacturer to a customer for injury or loss resulting from a defect in that product.

There are reasons why this has become a focus of attention. In 1985 the EC published a directive which led to national legislation. Secondly, during the 1980s, there was a wave of actions in the United States resulting in spectacular awards for claims involving death and personal injury. By 1984 sums awarded in these cases had exceeded $1 000 000. Changes in the UK became inevitable and the Consumer Protection Act reinforced the application of the principle of strict liability which will be explained in section 4.3.2.

The widespread application of computer control and safety systems leads to the possibility of personal injury or damage in the event of software-related failure. Under these circumstances there is potential civil liability which includes suppliers of computer control equipment and the programmers and designers concerned.

This may arise under a number of legal regimes.

4.3.1 The general law

Contract law

This is largely governed by the Sale of Goods Act 1979, which requires that goods are of merchantable quality and are reasonably fit for the purpose intended. Privity of contract exists between the buyer and seller which means that only the buyer has a remedy for injury and loss and only against the seller. However, in consumer contracts, exclusion clauses are void so that the seller cannot avoid liability. A contract does not have to be writing and may be inferred from the existence of a sale.

Common law

The relevant part of common law, in this context, is the tort of negligence, for which there is the remedy of damages. Everyone has a duty of care to his neighbour, in law, and failure to exercise reasonable precautions with regard to one's skill, knowledge and the circumstances constitutes a breach of that care. A claim for damages for negligence, in common law, is therefore not restricted by privity of contract but is open to anyone affected. The onus, however, is with the plaintiff to prove that:

- The product was indeed defective.
- The defect was the cause of the injury in question.
- This was foreseeable and that the plaintiff had failed in this duty of care.

Statute law

The main statutory Acts are:

- The Sale of Goods Act 1979:
  Goods must be of merchantable quality.
  Goods must be fit for purpose.
- Unfair Contract Terms Act 1977
  Exclusion of personal injury is void.
  Exclusion of damage liability is valid only if it is reasonable.
- Consumer Protection Act 1987
  Imposes strict liability.
  Replaced the Consumer Safety Act 1978.
- Health and Safety at Work Act 1974 (Section 6)
  See above.

Thus, prior to the Consumer Protection Act 1987 there was a form of strict liability, but:

- Privity of contract excluded 3rd parties in contract claims
- There was an onus to prove negligence unless there was actually breach of contract
- Exclusion clauses involving death and personal injury were void.

4.3.2 Strict liability

The concept of strict liability hinges on the idea that liability exists for no other reason than the existence of a defect. This is the keystone of the Consumer Protection Act 1987. Neither breach of contract nor negligence is required in order for one to incur responsibility. Thus, a manufacturer or seller will be liable for compensation if a product causes injury.
 In this context the word defect includes:

- Manufacturing: impurities, foreign bodies, production fault, installation fault.
- Design: not fit for purpose, inherent safety hazard in the design.
- Documentation: lack of warnings, inadequate operating or maintenance instructions.

4.3.3 The Consumer Protection Act 1987

In 1985, after nine years of discussion, the European Community adopted a directive on product liability and member states were required to put this into effect before the end of 1988. The English and Scottish Law Commissions each produced reports in 1977 and a Royal Commission document (*The Pearson Report*) was published in 1978. All of these recommended forms of strict liability. The Consumer Protection Bill resulted in the Consumer Protection Act 1987, which established strict liability as already described.

The Act provides that a producer is liable for damage caused wholly or partly by defective products which include goods, components and materials but excludes unprocessed agricultural produce. The word 'defective' is defined as not providing such safety as people are entitled to expect, taking into account the manner of the marketing, instructions for use, the likely uses and the time at which the product was supplied. Death, personal injury and damage (other than to the product) exceeding £275 are included. The consumer (plaintiff) has to prove that the defect caused the damage but no longer has the onus of proving negligence. There are some defences which include:

- The state of scientific and technical knowledge at the time was such that the producer could not be expected to have discovered the defect – known as the 'development risks' defence.
- The defect results from the product complying with the law.
- The producer did not supply the product.
- The defect was not present when the product was supplied by the manufacturer.
- The product was not supplied in the course of business.
- The product was in fact a component part in the manufacture of a further product and the defect was not due to the component.

In addition, the producer's liability may be reduced by the user's contributory negligence. Furthermore, unlike the privity limitation imposed under contract law, any consumer is covered as well as the original purchaser.

The Act sets out a general safety requirement for consumer goods and applies it to anyone who supplies goods which are not reasonably safe having regard to the circumstances pertaining. These circumstances include published safety standards, the cost of making goods safe and whether or not the goods are new.

4.3.4 Insurance

Product liability has had a considerable effect on insurance:

- an increase in the number of claims;
- higher premiums;
- the creation of separate product liability policies;
- involvement of insurance companies in defining quality standards;
- contracts which require the designer to insure the customer against genuine and frivolous consumer claims.

Some critical areas are:

- All risks: this only means all risks as specified in the policy. It is important to check that one's requirements are met by the policy.
- Comprehensive: means little more than the above.
- Disclosure: the policyholder is bound to disclose any information relevant to the risk. Failure to do so, whether asked for or not, can invalidate a claim. The test of what should be disclosed is described as 'anything the prudent insurer would wish to know'.
- Exclusions: the Unfair Contract Terms Act 1977 does not apply to insurance so one should read and negotiate accordingly. For example, defects related to design might be excluded and this would considerably weaken a policy from the product liability standpoint.
- Prompt notification of claims.

Premiums are usually expressed as a percentage of turnover and cover is divided into three areas:

1. product liability – cover against claims for personal injury or loss;
2. product guarantee – cover against the expenses of warranty and repair;
3. product recall – the expenses of recalling defective products.

4.4 MAJOR INDUSTRIAL HAZARDS

Since the 1960s, the development of the process industries has resulted in large quantities of flammable and toxic substances being stored and transmitted which, in the event of accident, could affect the public. Society is becoming increasingly aware of these hazards as a result of such incidents as:

- Flixborough (UK) 1974: 28 deaths due to an explosion involving cyclohexane;
- Seveso (Italy) 1976: unknown number of casualties due to a release of dioxin;
- San Carlos Holiday Camp 1978: around 150 deaths due to an accident involving a propylene tanker;
- Bhopal (India) 1984: over 2000 deaths due to a release of methyl isocyanate;
- Chernobyl (USSR) 1986: unknown number of casualties due to the melt-down of a nuclear reactor;
- Piper Alpha (UK) 1988: 167 deaths due to a fire on an offshore platform.

Although none of these well-known major incidents, which have shaped current legislation, have involved software failure, they have stimulated the perception that errors in software could lead to similar accidents.

In fact, media attention has been drawn to Sizewell B, a Swedish aircraft accident, the London Ambulance Service software and a hospital radiotherapy dosing problem, all of which have been associated with concerns over software errors.

Following the Flixborough disaster the HSC set up the Advisory Committee on Major Hazards (ACMH) which made various recommendations concerning notifications of hazards.

Owing to a general lack of formal controls within the EC, a draft European Directive was issued in 1980. Delays in obtaining agreement resulted in this not being implemented until September 1984. The HSC introduced, in January 1983, the Notification of Installations Handling Hazardous Substances (NIHHS) regulations. These required the notification of hazardous installations and that assessments be carried out of the risks and consequences.

The 1984 EC regulations were implemented, in the UK, as the Control of Industrial Major Accident Hazards (CIMAH) regulations, 1984. They are concerned with people and the environment and cover processes and the storage of dangerous substances. A total of 178 substances were listed, with the quantities of each which would render them notifiable. In these cases a safety case (nowadays called safety report) is required which must contain a substantial hazard and operability study and a quantitative risk assessment. The purpose of the safety report is to demonstrate either that a particular consequence is relatively minor or that the probability of its occurrence is extremely small. It is also required to describe adequate emergency procedures in the event of an incident. The latest date for the submission of safety reports is three months prior to bringing hazardous materials on site.

There have been two subsequent amendments to the CIMAH regulations (1988 and 1990) which have refined the requirements, added substances and revised some of the notifiable quantities.

Following the offshore Piper Alpha incident, in 1988, and the subsequent Cullen enquiry, the responsibility for UK offshore safety was transferred from the Department of Energy to a newly formed department of the HSE. Equivalent requirements to the CIMAH regulations are now applied to offshore installations and the latest date for submitting cases was November 1993.

Quantification of frequency, as well as consequences, in safety reports is now the norm and the role of human error in contributing to failures is attracting increasing interest. Emphasis is also being placed on threats to the environment.

The CIMAH regulations will be replaced by a further directive on the Control of Major Accident Hazards (COMAH). Although similar to CIMAH, the COMAH requirements will be more stringent including:

- provision of information to the public;
- demonstration of management control systems;
- identification of 'domino' effects;
- details of worker participation.

4.5 THE EC SOFTWARE DIRECTIVE

This concerns copyright protection of computer programs (i.e. software) and had to be implemented in national laws before 1 January 1993. Since any too precise definition of a computer program would be likely to become quickly out of date, a loose definition is used. The term 'preparatory design material' is therefore currently taken to include flow charts, design structures, formal requirements languages and so on.

As with conventional copyright law it is the form of the software which is protected and not the underlying idea/principle. In practice the borderline between an idea and its expression in software terms is not always clear. The ideas underlying a piece of software can often be so closely connected with the way in which they are expressed that protection of one actually confers protection of the other.

Ownership of the rights is with the writer and not the person or organization commissioning the work. It is therefore important to take this into account in contracts for subcontracted software. Employees are, however, another matter – in that case the ownership is with the employer.

The issue of 'decompilation', that is to say analysing the object code to reveal the underlying logic, is a problem area. It was acknowledged that a certain amount of decompilation would be necessary in order to develop other programs to work in conjunction with the purchased program. In practice it would be unlikely that a designer would know which parts of the program meet that criterion, in which case it would be very difficult to meet the directive.

5 | Current standards and guidelines

Both the software and safety-related industries have discovered, over the years, that the use of standards can lead both to economies and to ensuring that particular requirements are universally understood. In just the same way that manufacturers of mechanical piece parts must have standards, in order that both their products meet the customers' requirements, so must the software industry ensure the compatibility of its tools and products. A proliferation of languages, operating systems, environments and validation tools may lead to diversity and choice but it also minimizes portability and inter-operability.

As a result standards and guidelines have been developed, in this area, for over ten years. This chapter outlines the contents of the major documents which impact on software quality and, also, its safety-related applications.

There are a number of ways in which standards evolve. The first is the recognition, by an industry sector, or professional group, that common methods or tools will lead to efficiency. Another is the imposition of quality or safety features resulting from professional or even public awareness of a need. Standards need to be regularly reviewed in order to maintain their relevance and to keep them in step with evolving technology.

5.1 GENERIC QUALITY SYSTEMS

This section addresses quality management systems but not those specific to software. Many of the software-quality documents (section 5.2) are based on the precepts of these generic quality-management systems which are briefly outlined.

There are various quality management systems which have been developed over two decades. There is, of course, a high degree of overlap since many are based on earlier standards.

The term 'quality management system' means the set of procedures which describes how design, manufacture and test are controlled and how defects are followed up and remedied.

This was recognized in the 1970s and since then various standard systems have evolved which encompass both the design and manufacture of items. More recently, the two additional areas of the provision of services and the writing of software have been included to the 'quality world'.

The principle, however, is always the same. One defines how the business is to be run and controlled and then sets about implementing procedures and audits to ensure conformance to the methods which have been laid down.

Quality management systems were first called for in the defence industry but have since spread to the provision of commercial and consumer goods.

In the 1960s the North Atlantic Treaty Organization (NATO) produced the allied quality assurance publications (AQAP) procedures. They shifted the emphasis from simple inspection and test to control, by the supplier, of his own organization with audit surveillance from the purchaser.

In the early 1970s, the UK Ministry of Defence (MOD) introduced the AQAP standards into industry in a commercially enforceable and anglicized form known as Defence Standards 05-21, 05-24 and 05-29. These were quality management systems ranging from 05-21 (which covered contracts requiring design as well as manufacture) through 05-24 (for manufacture alone) to 05-29 which was a simple system involving inspection and test only.

The need for a national system was seen and, by the late 1970s, the British Standards Institute (BSI) had produced BS 5750 Parts 1, 2 and 3, which were really the AQAP/05 requirements under a BSI heading.

There followed various guidance documents which elaborated on the BS 5750 requirements and, in 1987, it was updated and reissued.

The European response has been to publish much the same requirement as the ISO 9000 series of quality management standards.

Table 5.1 provides a summary of the standards and shows their equivalence. The six columns refer as follows:

1. *Country*. Country or body which requires the standard.
2. *Overall quality management*. Usually a standard, in the same numbering series as the rest, which describes the overall management strategy and organization needed to support the remainder of the requirements.
3. *System for design, manufacture, installation and servicing*. Usually the highest standard in the series which covers the activities involved in

Table 5.1 Summary of current standards

Country	Overall quality management	System for design and manufacture	System for production, installation	System for inspection and test	Guidance documents
Europe	ISO9000	ISO9001	ISO9002	ISO9003	ISO9004
UK*	BS5750 (Part 0)	BS5750 (Part 1)	BS5750 (Part 2)	BS5750 (Part 3)	BS5750 (Part 0)
NATO*		AQAP1	AQAP4	AQAP9	AQAP2&5
UK MOD*		05-21	05-24	05-29	05-22&25
USA	ANSI	ANSI	ANSI	ANSI	ANSI
	ASQCQ90	ASQCQ91	ASQCQ92	ASQCQ93	ASQCQ94
USA Defence		MIL-Q-8958A	MIL-1-45208A		
CANADA	CSAZ299,0-86	CSAZ299,1-85	CSAZ299,2-85	CSAZ299,4-85	CSAQ420-87
GERMANY	DIN ISO9000	DIN ISO9001	DIN ISO9002	DIN ISO9003	DIN ISO9004
Former USSR		40.9001-88	40.9002-88		

*Superseded by ISO standards

design and development as well as the procurement, manufacturing and test phases.

4. *System for production, installation.* Similar to the above but without design and development. In other words, products are produced to a drawing without any aspect of modification or design response to a customer's functional requirement.

5. *System for inspection and test.* A simple standard where customers rely on inspection and test, at the vendor's premises, as a verification of conformance.

6. *Guidance documents.* The above standards are usually supported by explanatory, amplifying guidance which spells out the systems in more detail.

5.1.1 BS EN ISO 9000 Series (and BS 5750)

The 1994 changes to ISO 9000, whilst significant, are not radical and do not alter the overall approach.

The paragraph numbers of ISO 9002 now line up with ISO 9001. The following notes therefore apply to both standards with the exception of those items referring to design.

In practice most of the changes will involve activities which organizations conforming to ISO 9000 will have already implemented as part of their interpretation of the existing standard.

The main thrust is to sharpen up the requirements. Some specific areas are:

- management review;
- preventive action;
- statistical methods.

The following paragraph numbers are from the standard:

*4.1 Management Responsibility
*4.4.1 Quality Policy
Now states that it must be relevant to the expectations and needs of customers.
*4.1.2 Organisation
Responsibilities of quality-related staff to be documented. Sharpens up the need to identify resource-related difficulties and requires the management representative to report on the fitness of the system.
*4.1.3 Management Review
Defined intervals now required.

*4.2 Quality System

A cross-referenced hierarchical system of manual and procedures. Documentation to be appropriate to the skills involved.

*4.3 Contract Review

Clarifies need for documented procedures and that tenders and verbal orders are included as well as amendments to contracts.

*4.4 Design Control

The accent is, again, on documenting requirements. Design inputs are expected to take account of statutory requirements. Design review is now compulsory (at least one) and should involve all functions. Design outputs also require specific review. The distinction between validation and verification is made. There is now a requirement for design validation (e.g. prototype test, trials) to establish fitness for use.

*4.5 Document Control

A general clarification which includes electronic as well as hard documents.

*4.6 Purchasing

No substantial change.

*4.7 Purchaser Supplied Product

Re-titled Control of Customer Supplied Product.

*4.8 Product Identification and Traceability

Allows any suitable identification.

*4.9 Process Control

No substantial change.

*4.10 Inspection and Testing

No substantial change.

*4.11 Control of Inspection, Measuring and Test Equipment

Test software now included.

*4.12 Inspection and Test Status

No substantial change.

*4.13 Control of Non-Conforming Product

Documentation now a clear requirement.

*4.14 Corrective and Preventive Action

A distinction between corrective and, longer-term, preventive action is drawn.

*4.15 Handling, Storage, Packaging and Delivery

Now clearly requires documented procedures at all stages.

*4.16 Control of Quality Records

Accepts electronic records.

*4.17 Internal Quality Audits

No substantial change.

*4.18 Training

No substantial change.

*4.19 Servicing
Now added to 9002. Documented procedures required.
*4.20 Statistical Techniques
Confirms need to establish procedures for statistical methods when required.

5.2 SOFTWARE QUALITY STANDARDS AND GUIDELINES

These documents refer specifically to the quality and safety of the software design, with its documentation and code, rather than addressing system quality or system safety.

5.2.1 TickIT: Guide to Software Quality Management System Construction and Certification

This guide, based on ISO 9001 (EN 29001), was prepared by the British Computer Society (BCS) under contract to the UK DTI. Its purpose is to relate the ISO 9001 generic quality standard to the specific area of software design. There are five sections:

1. an introduction;
2. the application of ISO 9001 to software;
3. a purchaser's guide;
4. a supplier's guide;
5. an auditor's guide.

TickIT is a formal certification status which can be obtained over and above ISO 9001. Certain bodies obtain the accreditation, from the National Accreditation Council for Certification Bodies (NACCB), to award TickIT.

The document relates the life-cycle activities to the ISO 9001 paragraphs. It develops the quality-planning activities as seen to be needed by the purchaser and suggests a type of 'quality life cycle' for the supplier. The auditor's guide provides a checklist approach to the ISO 9001 requirements as applied to software.

One of the appendices deals with performance standards for auditors.

5.2.2 UK HSE Guidance Document: Programmable Electronic Systems in Safety Related Application

Although published in 1987, the 'HSE Guidelines' have very much dominated the assessment of safety-related programmable equipment for nearly a decade. It is the HSE's intention to adopt the proposed IEC international standard (see section 5.2.3) when finalized.

These guidelines were developed from a draft as early as 1984 which, in turn, arose from a booklet *Microprocessors in Industry* published by the HSE in 1981.

Second-tier (less generic) guidance was encouraged by the HSE and the IGasE, EEMUA and UKOOA documents, also described in this chapter, followed in that spirit.

The document was published in two volumes, with the detailed technical substance given in the second volume:

- Vol 1: *An Introductory Guide*
- Vol 2: *General Technical Guidelines*

Volume 2 outlines the assessment strategy against three characteristics:

1. the configuration;
2. the hardware reliability;
3. the systematic, including software, safety integrity.

It addresses a number of basic configurations of control and safety system using programmable and non-programmable elements. Three principles are given for assessing the configuration. In summary these are:

1. The combined number of programmable and non-programmable safety systems shall not be less than the number of conventional systems traditionally used.
2. No single hardware failure in a PES shall cause a hazardous failure mode.
3. No single software failure shall cause a hazardous failure mode.

The configurations described in the document can be summarized as in Fig. 5.1. (a) which shows the concept of a PES safety system whereby a single hardware or software failure can cause the hazardous failure in the process. This fails to meet two of the above criteria.

(b) represents the concept whereby both a non-programmable and a PES element impinge on the process, but in such a way that a failure of at least one programmable and one non-programmable element would be needed for the hazardous failure in the process. This usually meets all of the above criteria.

(c) Here the idea of replicated PES, but with diverse software, is shown. For the hazardous failure to occur in the process at least two 'different' software failures would be needed. This offers some degree of protection but is not a panacea (see Chapter 13).

The document goes on to address software quality and describes methods of hardware safety and reliability analysis such as fault-tree and failure-mode analysis.

There are over 20 pages of checklist questions covering similar questions to the checklists in this book.

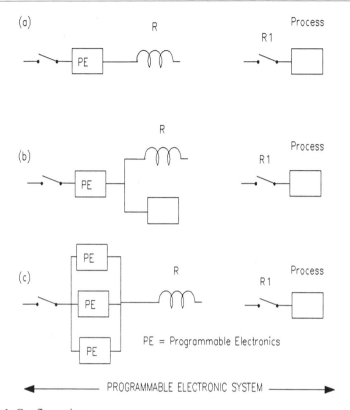

Fig. 5.1 Configurations.

The use of checklists carries both advantages and disadvantages:

- They provide an *aide-memoir*e so that essential features are not overlooked.
- They should not be used slavishly but as a menu from which to select the pertinent areas for the system in question. They should therefore be used only by experienced assessors.
- They constrain lateral thinking by giving the impression of being exhaustive.

5.2.3 IEC International Standard – Functional Safety: Safety-related Systems Part 3

Currently in draft, this International Electrotechnical Commission (IEC) standard is one of three parts:

1. Part 1: *General Requirements*;

2. Part 2: *Requirements for Electrical/Electronic/Programmable Electronic Systems*;
3. Part 3: *Software Requirements*.

Part 3 is the specifically software-related part of the standard. It covers most aspects of software quality:

- safety requirements specification;
- identify safety functions related to the software and assign a safety integrity level;
- develop the software safety requirements;
- design, develop and test software having regard to the quality plan, life cycle and integrity level;
- integrate the software and hardware;
- validate the software;
- apply the standard to software maintenance and modification.

The software safety and development life cycles are central to the document and these are similar to those shown in Chapters 2 and 3. An attempt has been made to relate specific activities and techniques to the safety integrity levels by assigning 'recommended', 'highly recommended' and other classifications to the techniques at each level. Each of the techniques is described in some detail.

5.2.4 *UK MOD Interim Defence Standard 00-55: The Procurement of Safety Critical Software in Defence Equipment*

This superseded the MOD 00-16 guide to achievement of quality in software. 00-55 is far more stringent and is currently seen as the most demanding of the standards in this area. Whereas the majority of the documents described here are for guidance, 00-55 is a standard and is intended to be mandatory on suppliers of 'safety critical' software to the MOD. It is unlikely that the majority of suppliers are capable of responding to all of its requirements but the intention is that, over a period of time, industry migrates to its full use.

It deals with software rather than the whole system and its major requirements include:

- the non-use of assembler language;
- the use of static analysis;
- a preference for formal methods;
- the use of a safety plan;
- the use of a software quality plan;
- the use of a validation plan;
- an independent safety auditor.

5.2.5 *UK Defence Standard 00-16: Guide to the Achievement of Quality in Software*

This was published in 1980 and is now superseded by 00-15 (above). It is a comprehensive outline of the software quality activities as they existed at the time.

There are three major areas of guidance and ten appendices which feature checklists for each major software activity. The three areas are:

1. Pre-contractual activities: This addresses the establishing of requirements and overall life-cycle planning.
2. Codes of practice: This section identifies the areas where standards are needed (e.g. documentation, configuration management, design review, test and subcontracted software).
3. Software quality procedures: Here the activities are listed and described.

The appendices provide detail on pre-contractual activities, software-quality planning, design and programming techniques, documentation, configuration management, design review, test, trials, transfer to customer and subcontracted software.

5.2.6 *IEE: Guidelines for the Documentation of Software in Industrial Computer Systems* (currently at Edition 2, 1990)

This document was prepared by the Institution of Electrical Engineers (IEE) Computing Standards Sub-committee and first published in 1985.

It provides a thorough guide to the purpose and content of the major types of document needed for the hierarchy, from requirements through to acceptance.

Section 1 – Introduction to the guidelines – draws attention to the range of software system types, covering:

- fixed program systems (e.g. event loggers);
- limited variability systems (e.g. PLCs);
- full variability systems (e.g. real-time control systems using a high-level language).

Throughout the guidelines the type and size of each document applicable to each of the above types are addressed.

The software life cycle is briefly introduced together with the associated areas of documentation.

Section 2 – User requirements specification – provides a thorough template for writing requirements specifications using the traditional free expression. This section includes:

- a description of the purpose of a requirements specification;
- its objectives and structure and the need for unambiguous measurable requirements;
- operating requirements (e.g. consoles, inputs, outputs, graphics, alarms, safety, security, timing, printing);
- interface requirements (e.g. electrical, logical, human, digital/analogue, series/parallel);
- environmental requirements;
- attributes (e.g. availability, repair times, documentation, adaptability).

Section 3 – Functional specification – provides an overview of the specification which follows from the user requirements specification and describes how the system will meet these requirements. The outline covers:

- a description of the purposes of a functional specification;
- its structure;
- system functions (e.g. control functions, malfunction response, data to be stored, operating procedures, safety and security);
- system interfaces (e.g. human, data, real time, I/O, communications);
- system attributes (e.g. reliability configuration, maintenance and support facilities);
- design and test constraints (e.g. language, test methods, quality plans, design tools to be used).

The essential difference between the user requirements and functional specifications is that the latter describe features and parameters whereas the former state more generalized requirements.

Section 4 – Software system specification – covers the hierarchy of design documents including a mention of the module level. Modules of code are referred to as programs. The section describes the specification in the following hierarchy and gives a description of each level.

- system structure – the breakdown into subsystems;
- subsystem structure – the breakdown of subsystems into program modules;
- data – inputs, outputs and databases;
- functions and relationships – functional features and information flow.

The module level of code is not emphasized as strongly as in Chapter 7 of this book.

Section 5 – System acceptance testing – describes the means by which the supplier demonstrates that the requirements of the functional specification have been met. The following documents are described:

test philosophy – the overall scope, range and types of test;
test plan – a schedule of activities;
test specifications – detail of each test;

test logs – a record of all events;

test summary – a summary of test failures;

commissioning report – an overall summary including any modifications carried out;

certificate of acceptance – a formal contractual acceptance document.

Section 6 – Post-installation documentation – outlines the operating and maintenance documents but also includes development documentation (drawings, listings, etc.) and general contractual documents (licences, warranty, ownership, etc.). The quantity of post-installation documentation will vary considerably between fixed program, limited and full variability systems.

Section 7 addresses the purpose and implementation of configuration control.

Section 8 provides a glossary and bibliography.

5.2.7 IGasE: IGE/SR/15 1994 Programmable Equipment in Safety Related Applications

IGE/SR/15 was published in 1989 under the title *Use of Programmable Electronic Systems in Safety Related Applications in the Gas Industry*. It was decided to revise SR/15 in the light of developments and it was felt that the document should become more prescriptive rather than merely listing alternative approaches.

There are substantial enhancements.

- *Safety life cycle.* Since the emerging European guidance documents, which will eventually become standards, are based on the concept of a safety life cycle, SR/15 was amended to harmonize.
- *Risk assessment.* As part of the safety life cycle, assessment of risk in order to implement a suitable integrity of design is emphasized. Emerging guidance draws attention to two approaches. One is quantified risk assessment (QRA) and is widely applied in the gas industry. It involves establishing a quantified target for specific incidents and then carrying out probabilistic studies to establish if proposed designs are compatible with that target. The other is the integrity-levels approach which is now included. SR/15 now identifies these alternatives, although it seems that the gas industry has tended to adopt the former (QRA) approach.
- *Formal methods.* This phase is commonly used in referring to two areas of development. One is the techniques for validating code in order to establish the degree to which it reflects accurately the underlying specification. The main technique is known as static analysis, for which computer tools are available. During the late 1980s and early

1990s the gas industry acquired and used these tools. SR/15 now describes the techniques and explains the benefits and the limitations of their use.

SR/15 now describes the current state of the art of mathematical methods and outlines the benefits and the difficulties associated with them.

- *Competence*. SR/15 now addresses this area and draws the distinction between the 'responsible engineer' and areas of specific competence in the use of tools and/or techniques.
- *Applications*. The application section has, where possible, been made more prescriptive in its recommendation of design configurations. A section on metering and data logging has been included since an increasing number of these devices are being designed around programmable elements.
- *Assessments and checklists*. Formal assessment of the integrity of safety-related systems has become commonplace in the industry. SR/15 now states positively that such assessments should be undertaken rather than describing assessment as a mere possibility. As an aid to assessment a comprehensive set of checklists has been included.

5.2.8 *EEMUA: Safety Related Programmable Electronic Systems*

The Electronic Equipment and Materials Users Association (EEMUA), also in response to the HSE guidelines, published a second-tier document which covers:

- relevant standards;
- definition of terms;
- assessment of application requirements;
- qualitative assessment of safety-system applications;
- general design considerations;
- design specification;
- changes and modifications;
- design-environmental aspects;
- testing and commissioning;
- operation and maintenance.

5.2.9 *BS EN 61131-3 1993 Programmable Controllers* (Part 3, *Programming Languages*)

BS EN 61131 is in four parts. Part 1 is general information, Part 2 is equipment requirements and tests, Part 4 is user guidelines.

Part 3 concerns programming languages for programmable controllers.

It is a highly detailed technical description of the types of PLC language discussed in Chapter 12.

It addresses common elements of languages such as printed characters, data types and representation, variables, program organization, sequential function charts and configuration elements.

Textual languages and graphical languages are then covered in detail, including methods of formal specification.

5.2.10 *RTCA DO-178B/(EUROCAE ED-12B) – Software Considerations in Airborne Systems and Equipment Certification*

This is a very detailed and thorough standard which is used in civil avionics to provide a basis for certifying software used in aircraft. Drafted by a EUROCAE/RTCA committee, DO-178B was published in 1992 and replaces an earlier version published in 1985. The qualification of software tools, diverse software, formal methods and user-modified software are now included.

It defines five levels of software criticality from A (software which can lead to catastrophic failure) to E (no effect). The standard provides guidance which applies to levels A to D.

The detailed listing of techniques (67 pages) covers:

- systems aspects: including the criticality levels, architecture considerations, user modifiable software;
- the software life cycle;
- software planning;
- development: including requirements, design, coding and integration;
- verification: including reviews, test and test environments;
- configuration management: including baselines, traceability, changes, archive and retrieval;
- software quality;
- certification;
- life-cycle data: describes the data requirements at the various stages in the life cycle.

Each of the software quality processes/techniques described in the standard are then listed (10 pages) and the degree to which they are required is indicated for each of the criticality levels A to D.

5.2.11 *DIN VDE 0801 (Germany) – Principles for Computers in Safety-related Systems*, January 1990

This standard grew out of the TUV handbook: *Microcomputer in der Sicherheitstechnik*. Whereas the handbook was targeted towards system architectures, the standard is more software oriented.

5.2.12 EWICS TC7 Documents

The European Workshop on Industrial Computer Systems (EWICS) was set up as an EEC funded group of committees of which TC7 was a major activity. TC7 addressed safety, security and reliability of industrial real-time computers. The main outputs have been:

Book 1, in 1988, which included six papers on:

- development of safety-related software;
- hardware for safe computer systems;
- verification and validation guidelines;
- documentation guidelines;
- verification and validation techniques;
- requirements specification.

Book 2, in 1989, which included five papers on:

- guidelines for design of computer systems for safety;
- guidelines for assessment of safety and reliability of critical computer systems;
- a questionnaire for system safety and reliability assessment;
- guidelines on software quality assurance and measures;
- guidelines on the maintenance and modification of safety-related computer systems.

Book 3, in 1990, intended as a directory which assessed a number of techniques used in software development. It included six sections on:

- introduction;
- safety analysis (e.g. fault trees, event trees, failure mode analysis);
- fault avoidance;
- fault detection;
- failure detection;
- failure containment.

In addition there have been a number of conference proceedings.

5.2.13 Some other documents

Some of the following documents are now very old but they played a significant part in the development of software quality and are included for the sake of completeness.

The EEA guides

Between 1978 and 1985, the Electronic Engineering Association (EEA), 8 Leicester Square, London, published four guides in the area of software-quality assurance. They were one of the earliest attempts to address this need and are worthy of continued mention. They are:

1. *Guide to the Quality Assurance of Software (UK)* – 1978
   The activities and controls are described for each of the then life-cycle phases (design documentation, planning, implementation, evaluation and test, post-design).

   Extensive checklists dealing also with quality planning and subcontracted software are also provided.

2. *Establishing a Quality Assurance Function for Software (UK)* – 1981
   The sections consist of the following: the need for software quality; the software quality functions; responsibilities; personnel; standards; tools; life cycle; compendium of standards.

3. *Software Configuration Management (UK)* – 1983
   Highlights the differences between hardware and software configuration management. It includes the following: specification boundaries; changes; subcontract; management; items to be controlled at each stage of the life cycle; automated change control systems (pros and cons).

4. *A Guide to the Successful Start-up of a Software Project (UK)* – 1985
   Intended for managers with little prior knowledge, it covers the following: guidance on information needed and its sources; customer requirements; planning; programmes; schedules; configuration management; documentation standards.

The STARTS guide

Software Tools for Application to Real Time Systems (STARTS) was a guide prepared by the National Computing Centre under DTI sponsorship. The guide was prepared using teams drawn from industry and emphasized tools and methods then available. It covered:

- project management;
- configuration management;
- project support environments;
- requirements definition and design;
- verification, validation and testing.

Also published was the *STARTS Purchaser's Handbook* which harmonized the procurement practices and the software requirements to be placed on suppliers. It outlined best practice in specifying, purchasing and maintaining real-time systems and indicated the level of software engineering which purchasers should expect from their suppliers.

IEEE (USA) Software Engineering Standards

The Institution of Electrical and Electronics Engineers (IEEE), USA, has developed, over a number of years, an extensive set of standards to enhance communication between software engineers and to provide guidance on the types, formats and content of software documents as well as on the activities in the design cycle. These standards, whilst being detailed, are nevertheless generic in that many organizations would need to tailor them to their specific needs. That having been said, they are strongly recommended.

The standards available at the time of writing are:

610.12	*Glossary of Software Engineering*
730	*Standard for Software Quality Assurance Plans*
828	*Standard for Software Configuration Management Plans*
829	*Standard for Software Test Documentation*
830	*Recommended Practice for Software Requirements Specifications*
982.1	*Standard Dictionary of Measures to Produce Reliable Software*
982.2	*Guide for the Use of IEEE Standard Dictionary Measures to Produce Reliable Software*
990	*Ada as a Program Design Language*
1002	*Standard Taxonomy for Software Engineering Standards*
1003.1	*Information Technology – Portable Operating System Interface.* Part 1 *System Application Program Interface (C language)*
1003.1-1988/INT	*Interpretations for Portable Operating System Interface for Computer Environments*
1003.2 Volumes 1 and 2	*Standard for Information Technology Portable Operating System Interface. Part 2 Shell and Utilities*
1003.3	*Standard for Information Technology Test Methods for Measuring Conformance to POSIX*
1003.5	*Standard for Information Technology POSIX Ada Language Interfaces. Part 1 Binding for System Application Program Interface*
1003.5 INT	*Standards Interpretations for IEEE Standard 1003.5-1992*
1003.9	*Standard for Information Technology POSIX FORTRAN 77 Language Interfaces.* Part 1 *Binding for System Application Program Interface*
1008	*Standard for Software Unit Testing*
1012	*Standard for Software Verification and Validation Plans*
1016	*Recommended Practice for Software Design Descriptions.*
1016.1	*Guide to Software Design Descriptions*
1028	*Guide for Software Reviews and Audits*
1042	*Guide to Software Configuration Management*

1045	*Standard for Software Productivity Metrics*
1058.1	*Standard for Software Project Management Plans*
1061	*Standard for a Software Quality Metrics Methodology*
1062	*Recommended Practice for Software Acquisition*
1063	*Standard for Software User Documentation*
1074	*Standard for Developing Software Life-cycle Processes*
1209	*Recommended Practice for the Evaluation and Selection of CASE Tools*
1219	*Standard for Software Maintenance*
2003.1	*Standard for Information Technology Test Methods for Measuring Conformance to POSIX Part 1 System Interfaces*

The IECCA Guide to the Management of Software-based Systems for Defence, 3rd Edition

The Inter-establishment Committee on Computer Applications (IECCA) was set up in 1968 and is an MOD body. Its purpose was to address real-time computing and, in particular, the evaluation of CORAL 66 and Ada compilers as well as the development of MASCOT (see Chapter 9). It included:

- system life cycle;
- potential problems and risks;
- management techniques;
- MOD policy for real-time systems;
- impact of procurement policies.

UK MOD JSP188: Requirements of Software in Military Operational Real-time Computer Systems (UK)

This was a joint services publication (1980) which describes (in the same manner as the IEE document in section 5.2.6) the hierarchy of documents. The definitions were somewhat different, referring to levels. Level 1 was the functional specification; level 2 describes the tasks, data structure and interconnections; level 3 described the internal function of processes by flow charts; level 4 was the module documentation and code.

ElektronikCentralen: Standards and Regulations for Software Approval and Certification (Denmark)

This was published in 1984 and reviews software quality in the safety-critical area. Sources of failure, and defences against them, are described in some detail.

Guidelines for the Nordic Factory Inspectorates

ElectronikCentralen prepared a report which was to be the guidance for systems containing microprocessors. The guidelines contained design recommendations and checklists. Safety assessments were called for covering the following steps:

- defining the system boundary;
- hazard analysis;
- specifying the safety requirement;
- identifying safety critical systems;
- analysing those safety critical systems;
- certification criteria;
- change management.

CEC collaborative project

This was a European-funded project to publish a set of guidelines together with a review of the documents in the PES area.

US Department of Defense Standard 2167: Defense System for Software Development

This is a 90-page document (1985) containing a lot of detail about software quality methods at that time. The sections were:

- definitions;
- general requirements (design-cycle, organization, subcontracting, etc.);
- detailed requirements (two or three pages on each aspect of the life-cycle);
- coding standards.

And even more documents

- *Software for Computers Important to Safety for Nuclear Power Plant*: Supplement to IEC 880.
- *Medical Electrical Equipment Incorporating PESs*: IEC (TC62/WG2).
- *Safety-related Software for Railway Signalling*, Tech Spec 23, 1991: Railway Association UK.
- *Safety-related PESs for Railway Signalling*, Tech Spec 24, 1992: Railway Association UK.

5.3 SPECIFICALLY SAFETY-RELATED STANDARDS AND GUIDELINES

Some safety-related documents are addressed at safety-related equipment irrespective of whether it contains a programmable element. The IEC 65A

(Secretariat) document, described here, is of that type. Nevertheless since, in practice, the vast majority of safety-related systems do rely on software, the documents have been included here.

5.3.1 *IEC International Standard – Functional Safety: Safety-related Systems*, **Parts 1 and 2**

These combine what were previously known as the Working Group 9 and Working Group 10 documents. It will provide a generic standard for functional safety for all applications areas.

The concepts of safety life cycle and safety integrity levels (described in Chapter 3) are central to the standard.

Within the UK the comment process is being handled by the BSI.

Part 3 is the specifically software part of this document.

5.3.2 *UK MOD Interim Defence Standard 00-56: Hazard Analysis and Safety Classification of the Computer and Programmable Electronic System Elements of Defence Equipment*

Whereas 00-55 addresses the software this document encompasses the entire 'safety-critical' system. It calls for hazard and operability studies (HAZOPS) to be carried out on systems and subsystems of safety-related equipment supplied to the UK MOD.

There are tables to assist in the classification and interpretation of risk classes and activities are called for according to their severity.

Responsibility for safety has to be formally defined as well as the management arrangements for its implementation.

It is intended that 00-56 harmonizes with RTCA DO-178B/ (EUROCAE ED-12B) and that it should be compatible with IEC 65A Secretariat – functional safety – safety-related systems.

5.3.3 *UKOOA: Guidelines for Process Control and Safety Systems on Offshore Installations*

Currently (1994) in draft, this United Kingdom Offshore Operators Association (UKOOA) guide offers guidance for control and safety systems offshore. The sections cover:

- the role of control systems in hazard management;
- categorization of systems (by hazard and application);
- system design;
- equipment design;
- operation and maintenance.

There is an appendix addressing software in safety-related systems.

5.3.4 *Safety Related Systems, Guidance for Engineers*, The Hazards Forum. Available from IEE

Originally published, by the IEE, as the Safety Related Systems Professional Brief, this has been revised and published under the umbrella of the Hazards Forum.

The document is for professional engineers involved in the specification, development, assessment, maintenance or operation of safety-related systems.

Its purpose is to provide a concise overview of the matters, concerning safety-related systems, of which they should be aware. It is intended only as an overview and as a pointer to where further information can be obtained.

Major items addressed are:

- safety life cycle;
- liability and legal matters;
- competence;
- code of practice;
- definitions;
- substantial references.

Certification and competence

6

It is a theme of this book that the difficulties in validating the correctness of software far outweigh those of proving the integrity of hardware. Indeed, the failure of an aircraft's programmable flight control system is of such great importance that the question of certification has long been of concern.

A safety-related system is unlikely to be commissioned into service until the user is satisfied that it is as safe as is reasonably practicable.

The purpose of certification is, therefore, to provide objective evidence that a system has been developed and implemented in accordance with some accepted practice.

A key feature in certification is that of independence and the best method of achieving it is via third party assessment.

There has been attention given to this matter by government, industry, academia and professional societies such as the Institution of Electrical Engineers and The Safety and Reliability Society. In 1993 the UK Department of Trade and Industry (DTI) published a report on safety certification in the information technology (IT) sector and is anxious to establish a certification framework. The UK MOD 00-55 standard (described in Chapter 5) goes some way towards the idea of system certification by calling for formal third party assessment.

Certification of people, as well as systems, is also an issue. Both the Guidance on Safety Related Systems for Engineers, published by the Hazards Forum, and Guidelines on Risk Issues, published by the Engineering Council, draw attention to the need for activity in this area.

The UK Health and Safety Executive (HSE) is currently (1994) encouraging work towards the development of criteria for persons involved in safety-related systems.

6.1 CERTIFICATION OF SYSTEMS

Implicit in the concept of certification is the need for an objective standard against which to certify. Certification is thus a written statement that a system meets the criteria in question. This can take a number of forms as, for example:

- certification against a standard;
- certification against a guideline;
- certification of fitness for purpose.

The latter is harder to achieve because it is to some extent open-ended. The first two, on the other hand, can more easily be verified but provide a confidence which is only as good as the standard or guidance against which the system has been 'measured'.

Despite numerous guidelines (Chapter 5) there is still a shortage of standards suitable for certification purposes. This is because the requirements would need to be highly prescriptive, rather than open-ended, for a standard to lend itself to this purpose.

The production of standards, however, is a costly business. The evolution of the MOD Standard 00-55 has been estimated to have cost £1M and the aviation standard DO178B six times that figure. It is likely, therefore, that standards will arise from national rather than product- or sector-specific funding. One advantage of such single generic standardization is that it discourages proliferation of standards and creates consistency across sectors of industry.

The DTI propose a hierarchy of five areas of certification, namely:

1. *Overall system safety.* Involves interfaces of systems, people and organizations. The hardest to define.
2. *Integrated electromechanical systems.* Addresses more specific safety system elements and includes assessment.
3. *Component type-approval.* Conformance to specification only, because the effect of component behaviour cannot be considered in isolation.
4. *Processes.* Simple quality management certification but will incorporate their application to risk.
5. *Personnel.* Involves competence in respect of specific tasks (see below).

One particular system of accreditation is TickIT, which applies to software quality management systems. In much the same way as a quality management system can be certified to ISO 9000 (BS 5750), the TickIT scheme applies the same principles to the production of software. The guide is described in Chapter 5. Organizations should ideally be TickIT certified. This will provide a high degree of assurance that processes are well defined and under control and that, also, there is some commitment to the state of the art of a changing technology.

To date, in the UK, accreditation has generally been managed by the DTI although TickIT is administered by DISC (a part of BSI).

The National Measurement Accreditation Service (NAMAS), part of the National Physical Laboratory (NPL), has approved the Electrical

Research Association (ERA) as a test service for safety-related software. It is intended to apply the requirements of emerging International Electrotechnical Commission (IEC) and industry-specific standards.

A DTI sponsored project known as Framework for Evaluation of Safety-Critical Objects (FRESCO) is seeking to improve the process of assessing safety-related products by providing some standardization of approach. Currently assessment organizations approach the task from differing viewpoints and the project will address:

- procedures to be followed by assessors;
- common assessment criteria;
- assessor qualifications and skills.

6.2 CERTIFICATION OF PEOPLE

Accreditation of management systems and of products has been mentioned above but interest is equally strong in measuring the competence of individuals. Any measurement of competence leads inevitably to the question of accreditation.

In many professions, and even in some trades, it has long been obligatory to obtain a licence to practise. These are often legal requirements with severe penalties for misrepresentation (e.g. doctors, pilots, solicitors). As a consequence it has been necessary for each profession to develop the specific conditions which need to be satisfied by those seeking certification of competence. The engineering profession has long been conspicuous for its failure to impose such restrictions on practitioners and, at this time, anybody is free to design or implement a programmable safety-related system.

Nevertheless, interest is now being shown in some system of certification, at least for engineers involved in safety-related systems (and their software).

For many years software designers and computer programmers have been drawn from a variety of disciplines and often trained from scratch with no specific educational requirements having been identified.

The average software-design team, or data-processing department, has its sprinkling of graduates from various disciplines as well as those with no formal qualifications. The skill which unites them is the ability to interpret problems in a way compatible with the computer.

In earlier days programmers were often mathematicians who had learnt the intricacies of the hardware architecture which was programmed in machine code. Gradually high-level languages appeared and the need for in-depth knowledge of the hardware disappeared. Ability to code, debug and test became predominant although the documentation nearly always followed after the event.

A mathematical training is no doubt still useful in programming the solution to a scientific equation and an accounting background is useful when designing sales ledger software. Nevertheless the primary ability is in translating the problem, via the design cycle, into a programming language. On the surface, therefore, it would seem a simple matter to define a set of skills in order to define competent software designers. This is, unfortunately, not the reality.

Understanding the different problems over the whole life cycle have improved the understanding of the need for a suitable software-engineering qualification. The structure of the qualification syllabus should therefore be based on the design life cycle. The draft postgraduate syllabus, proposed by the IEE, for safety-related systems is in fact based on the safety life cycle described in Chapter 3.

Essential software-engineering skills must take account of the overall system aspects as well as the software element itself. They include:

- *Discrete mathematics.* To tackle more formal specification methods and to use formal verification techniques.
- *Formal design methods.* To produce a well-structured, readable and testable design.
- *Formal validation and test methods.* To verify, during design, the system being developed.
- *Hardware knowledge.* Sufficient understanding of hardware architectures to aid overall system understanding.
- *Regulatory matters.* Including guidelines, standards, legislation and their development as they constrain system design and validation.

It is becoming increasingly difficult to differentiate between safety-related requirements and software requirements. This is due to the proliferation of software into safety-related systems. The tendency is, rightly, to emphasize the system aspects rather than to treat software in isolation. As a result guidance on safety-related issues is likely to be valid for software design regardless of whether it is safety related.

The draft postgraduate syllabus considered by the IEE safety critical system group is thus highly relevant. In summary, it covers the safety life cycle in a modular approach which includes:

- safety concepts and terminology, including safety integrity levels, risk perception, safety life cycle etc.;
- hardware architectures and equipment;
- risk and reliability assessment technology, including human error (which warrants a full module) and common cause failures;
- aspects of audit, validation and verification;
- legislation, regulatory framework, insurance, liability, guidance and standards;

- professional responsibilities including competence and safety management;
- design methodologies throughout the life cycle;
- language issues including formal methods, metrics, modelling and maintenance;
- software operation and maintenance.

Any process of certification must take account of the useful life of the competence to which it refers. Appropriate arrangements for retesting and recertification in order to ensure the currency of the competence are needed.

Until a fully qualified software engineer, with the appropriate knowledge and skills, is available the industry must rely upon the experience-specific skills currently available.

Only through a process of qualification and certification can the software process be established as a profession in its own right. This requires that industry, academia and the professional bodies agree upon and implement a cohesive approach, hopefully based upon the above.

Only through a totally professional software engineering discipline will the industry advance.

6.3 COMPETENCE

Currently the term competence implies a subjective judgement of a person's knowledge and the ability to apply it in a specific context. Competence in one area does not necessarily imply the ability to transfer it to another. Some skills are transferable (e.g. the use of high-level language to translate comprehensive design documents into code) whereas others (e.g. the use of a particular validation tool from one high-level language to another) may not.

The term 'competence' is also applied at many levels covering the skills specific to the management. A specific skill would be the ability to write requirements in VDM (see Chapter 8) whereas a more general skill would be the ability to manage a safety-related control system design project.

The former is easier to measure because it can be defined in terms of testable elements of knowledge and ability. It follows then that this is the type of competence which might more easily lead to certification. The latter, on the other hand, relies on a combination of judgements which may not be measurable except in hindsight.

The term 'competence' is frequently used with the implication that only the best possible response in any situation will suffice. Upon reflection this would exclude all but the top few in any profession. The judgement given during the Abbeystead explosion enquiry is useful. In summary it defined competence as that average level of skill which can be expected from the average member of that profession having the necessary experience and training.

The HSE initiative (in collaboration with the IEE and BCS) proposes a joint study of the qualification, training and experience required by engineers working on safety-related systems. The object of the exercise is to establish criteria for determining the competence of practitioners.

The IEC draft standard (*Functional Safety – Safety-related Systems*) calls for 'appropriate' training, knowledge, experience and qualifications for the task in hand. A number of competency factors are listed. It nevertheless remains for industry to develop and implement the use of specific and measurable criteria.

The problem will not be solved in a single initiative and the most likely way forward is the gradual implementation of modules of education, training and measured experience which will enable an initial system of partial licensing to be set up. More comprehensive accreditation may then follow in time.

6.4 THE SOFTWARE ENGINEER

The development of the software industry has been rapid and has involved many changes. A factor which has remained constant, however, has been its reliance on the programmer.

The programming task is largely one of problem solving and, for many years, programmers have been recruited from a variety of disciplines or have been trained from scratch with no particular educational requirements having been identified.

Anyone with a logical aptitude, and a little training, can write a computer program. The proliferation of computing at home and in schools bears witness to that. However, a program which meets the modern requirements of usability and maintainability requires additional skills to those required for simple coding.

This is not always appreciated by managers who, themselves, may have received little formal software training. Promotion may well have been on the basis of speedy coding whereas the skills required are of a different nature.

The software engineer, as distinct from the traditional programmer, will need to be able to:

- challenge and establish user requirements;
- verify those requirements;
- assess, choose and use design methods (Chapters 8 and 9) suitable for the project;

- plan and implement reviews and tests (Chapter 10);
- choose tools (e.g. validators, compilers);
- be aware of software and safety-related standards and guidance;
- be team-oriented rather than motivated by personal achievement.

Awareness of the various problems throughout the design cycle has sharpened the view that properly qualified software engineers are needed. Many of the skills can be learnt in mid-career but some (as for example the formal methods in Chapter 8) are likely to be available only from the newer generation of software graduates.

The transition from an industry of programmers to one of software engineers cannot, therefore, be instantaneous. It will evolve as do other disciplines.

Three features of need to be defined when planning and structuring software-engineering training.

1. the knowledge required (e.g. methods, standards, tools);
2. skills which should be defined in behavioural terms (e.g. ability to translate a design requirement into a given formal method, ability to use and interpret the outputs of a particular software-validation tool);
3. attitudes such as team-based motivation, commitment to the software-quality philosophy, etc.

6.5 THE WORKING ENVIRONMENT

There is a wide variation in performance, both in terms of speed and error rate, amongst programmers and software engineers. This is one reason why predictions of schedule and cost (Chapter 15) are seldom accurate. Some relevant factors are:

- *Peer effects.* It has been found that people working closely together demonstrate less variation in performance than the norm. In one experiment randomly paired programmers worked together on specific design tasks. The performance variation of a pair was 1.2:1 whereas the variation across the group was 5.6:1.
- *Speed and error rate.* It has been found that speed of programming does not necessarily imply a high error rate. Studies have shown that the highest error rates are associated with average speed programmers and engineers whereas both the very fast and the very slow generate fewer errors.
- *The workplace.* Criticisms of noise, lack of privacy, interruptions to concentration and of general ambience are fairly common. Studies tend to show that the better performers are those in the better-perceived working environments.

PART THREE

Achieving Software Quality

The next seven chapters cover the basis of software quality techniques, including the modern methods.

The traditional approach | 7

7.1 QUALITY AND THE LIFE CYCLE

In Chapter 2, the design life cycle was described as a model against which to map quality activities. This was expanded, in Chapter 3, to take account of the activities called for in safety-related application of software.

There is nothing new in the idea of software quality. It has evolved from the hardware quality activities of inspection and test of system elements and components against defined standards. Hardware quality is usually achieved (although perhaps not entirely) by bringing together conforming parts and materials and by using proven processes.

The design of software, on the other hand, is not an equivalent situation. Simple conformance of program modules to some specification is little or no guarantee of failure-free performance when the modules are brought together. In other words although it is possible (and necessary) to validate each module of code against its specification the interrelationship of the coded modules is far more subtle than is the case with pieces of hardware.

It is extremely important to realize that a very large number of faults involve the interaction of hardware and software and that they can only be prevented (or corrected) by a system approach.

Currently, quality systems concentrate on establishing the existence of standards and controls and seek, by means of audit, to verify that they are applied.

Software quality activities could be said to fall into two categories:

1. specification, documentation and programming disciplines (and associated tools) which reduce the probability of faults being committed during design;
2. activities which attempt to identify and remove faults. They are disciplines (e.g. review and test) which do, in addition, help to reduce the probability of faults being committed.

The main activities are:

- *documentation controls*. This includes document standards, and configuration control. The life-cycle models, shown in Chapter 2, bear a close resemblance to the structure of the documentation. This chapter will therefore deal with structure and control of software/ system documentation. Since documentation is the only visibility to software this is the vital cornerstone of software quality. Without it the remaining activities and techniques will fail.

- *Programming standards.* Rules for the structure of the code and use of languages and compilers constitute another ingredient in minimizing faults. This aspect is also dealt with in this chapter.
- *Design review.* These are comparisons of various stages of the design with higher levels of documentation. They are the feedback loops described in Chapter 2. Chapter 10 deals with the structure and conduct of reviews as they apply at different parts of the life cycle.
- *Test.* A test and integration strategy is needed which builds up from module testing to ultimate system test. This is also addressed in Chapter 10.
- *Fault-tolerant design.* There are many techniques for making a system tolerant to software faults. This involves ways of detecting and correcting errors before they propagate to become failures. Chapter 13 outlines these.
- *Failure feedback.* The more structured and formal the system of failure recording and feedback, the faster will be the reliability growth which arises from the modifications to remove them.

7.2 QUALITY MANAGEMENT, ORGANIZATION AND PLANNING

The role of quality management is to monitor conformance to procedures and standards by means of:

- establishing quality plans;
- quality management reporting;
- participating in reviews (Chapter 10);
- audit.

In some cases software quality is operated as a separate activity from the existing hardware quality. This tends to be the case in organizations whose skills are traditionally hardware related and which have evolved products with programmable features.

This can lead to a blinkered approach wherein problems/failures are classified as 'hardware' or 'software' when in fact the solution may be found in a compromise or solution involving both.

There are two approaches to software quality organization. One is the centralized quality department approach and the other is the project quality function. The latter has the advantage of flexibility to project needs and can bypass the traditional structure facilitating speedy reporting.

In any case (separate or otherwise) there has to be an identifiable organizational responsibility for software quality. Titles are not all-important but the tasks and responsibilities are. In a small organization it may be necessary for some quality activities to be assigned to people who combine the responsibility with other roles.

There should be a quality manual and a structure of procedures as called for in ISO 9001 (Chapter 5). It must be remembered that the production of software is a design and not a manufacturing activity. Thus ISO 9001 (BS 5750 Part 1) is the appropriate quality management standard and **not** ISO 9002 (BS 5750 Part 2).

One problem which arises from defined quality department structures is that quality is often seen as a 'box'. This leads to barriers between quality and other staff and the concept that quality is the responsibility of the quality department can be bred. Quality must be accepted as everyone's responsibility and as part of the working practice.

Total quality (TQ) and 'quality circles' initiatives help considerably in this respect since they encourage all team members to own the problems and to participate in finding solutions.

A quite separate issue is the quality plan. Whereas the quality manual and procedures describe controls and procedures at a generic company level, the quality plan is specific to a development or project. It will draw on specific procedures from the quality management system but will combine these with features specific to the customer or project.

The quality plan must embrace:

- a list of the deliverables;
- a list of tools/environments to be used;
- how, when and by whom reviews are to be carried out;
- what standards, procedures and codes of practice will be applied;
- where possible a documentation hierarchy for the project (this will evolve with the design);
- arrangements for quality control of subcontractors;
- methods of failure reporting;
- the test strategy and control of testing;
- extent of customer involvement in quality;
- customer acceptance criteria for the project.

One standard for quality plans is ANSI/IEEE STD 730-1984 (*Standard for Quality Plans*).

7.3 DOCUMENTATION HIERARCHY

It is tempting to proceed very quickly to the coding stage when only a part of the design has been conceived. Indeed commercial pressures sometimes make this almost inevitable.

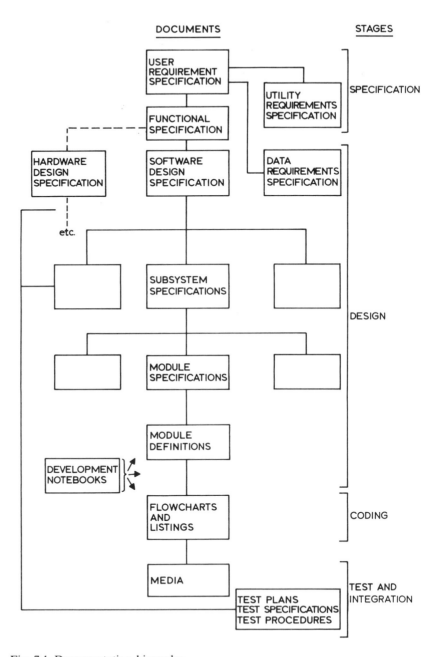

Fig. 7.1 Documentation hierarchy.

Nevertheless it is absolutely vital that a structure (hierarchy) of documentation is created which follows the design cycle through from requirements to the actual coded modules.

This will vary, according to the size and complexity of the product, from a complex hierarchy of specifications, as shown in Fig. 7.1, to a few pages consisting of:

- a functional specification;
- some design text and diagrams;
- the program listing (i.e. lines of source code).

In the more complex systems a structured hierarchy is essential in order to proceed with a 'top-down' approach whereby the requirement is decomposed from the user requirement, through the levels of design, to the code.

This top-down approach is generally favoured since it treats the system as a whole (both hardware and software) and not as piecemeal components which can be the result of a 'bottom-up' approach.

The author's experience is that the most common deficiency in software design is the lack of this hierarchy and that this inevitably leads to serious design problems, delays and many more failures during test and commissioning. In addition to the structure and partitioning of information inherent in a document hierarchy, the main requirements are that:

- it provides sufficient detail;
- it is up to date;
- it is understood by everyone;
- it provides traceability;
- safety-related elements are easily identifiable.

The key documents are:

User requirements specification

This describes the functions to be performed by the system. It should be complete and unambiguous and should be quantitative wherever possible in order to facilitate the assessment of whether the requirements have been met.

Since the user requirements specification is a formal contractual document it is important that its preparation is a thorough and painstaking process involving all interested parties. A good structure is described in the IEE document (see section 5.2) and includes:

- An overview providing a perspective of the system within the plant or total environment in which it is to be employed. It should indicate the overall objectives of the system.

- System requirements setting out in full detail the requirements as they relate to the operating requirements.
- System interfaces outlining how it is required to communicate with the world. This includes both human and electrical/data interfaces.
- System environment which covers all the features which would affect the hardware and software design.
- System attributes describing and listing the parameters which constrain the design.
- Test considerations including diagnostic requirements which will affect operation and maintenance.
- A commercial section addressing licensing, etc.

Ideally the user requirements specification should be a precontractual document since it specifies what the contract will provide. In practice, however, it may well be subject to negotiation and change after the contract has been established, in which case both parties must carefully evaluate the performance, cost and schedule implications.

Functional specification

The functional specification takes the requirements of the user specification and describes the actual processing functions which are to be carried out in order to achieve those requirements. It will address language, memory requirements, databases, the partitioning of the system into subsystems, inputs, outputs, interface communications, data flow, etc.

The important difference between the functional specification and the user requirements specification is that whereas the latter states **what** is required, the former describes **how** it will be achieved in terms of functions. It is usually prepared by the supplier in response to the user requirements specification and, once agreed, becomes a part of the contractual documentation against which acceptance will ultimately be reviewed.

During the detailed process of generating the functional specification, deficiencies and ambiguities in the user requirements specification will arise. These must be negotiated and documented as mentioned above.

Software-design specification

Once the software and hardware functionality has been separated, one can proceed to consider the software aspects separately. This proceeds in a top-down manner until subsystem or module specifications are derived, according to size and complexity. Whereas the functional specification addresses the externally apparent functions of the system, the software-design specification addresses the way in which those functions will be implemented in software.

Subsystem specification

If the system is small enough it may be possible to do without subsystem specifications and to move directly to module specifications. In large systems, however, subsystems will ultimately consist of modules and the subsystem specification will describe the functions of the subsystem, the data flow between modules and the interfaces to the other subsystems.

A typical subsystem specification would commence with a brief (one-paragraph) description of the subsystem function. For example:

The graphics subsystem receives inputs of the status of fire and gas detection devices. It processes this data to construct mimics of zones and their fire and gas alarm status. This information is passed to the VDU subsystem.

The specification will carry on to describe how the subsystem is decomposed into modules and what procedures they carry out. Interfaces to other subsystems may be described by means of data flow diagrams.

There will also be a breakdown of the subsystem into modules (basic coded units) together with a brief description of each module. A statement concerning the operating system, memory requirements and hardware environment would also be included.

Module specification

Modules are the building blocks of the hierarchy since they contain the basis of the eventual code. A module of code should be concerned with a single function that can be easily perceived by a single person. G. J. Myers wrote 'Write a sentence describing the purpose of the module. If the sentence is a compound sentence, containing a comma or more than one verb, then the module is probably more than one function.'

The module specification describes:

- inputs and outputs to the module;
- how it integrates to other modules and databases;
- its function;
- secondary functions (e.g. error handling);
- performance criteria (e.g. execution time).

An estimate of the quantity of source code may sometimes be given at this stage. A figure of 100 lines is regularly quoted as a target maximum.

Depending on the project, and the high-level language being used, pseudo code, decision tables, flowcharts and state diagrams are all techniques which might be used. The programming standard will outline and provide rules and standards for those techniques which can be used in the project.

Module definition

The module definition is a more detailed level of design than the module specification. It involves the actual coding of the module specification and addresses the testing and performance of that module. It includes:

- the module specification;
- source code listing;
- test specification;
- test procedure;
- test results.

This package then constitutes a total description of the module and its design and test history.

At a lower level of detail the standard lists the contents of the module definition package and the requirements for outward referencing to other specifications. It requires the following to be included:

- files belonging to the module;
- files accessed by the module;
- complementary explanation to enhance the code, which should not detract from the requirement that code should contain adequate comment;
- diagrams to describe data flow, flow charts, etc., as applicable;
- timing calculations (e.g. execution, disk access, CPU time);
- notes of any compiler problems;
- error-handling philosophy;
- test requirements (e.g. harnesses, simulators, hardware);
- inspection/walk-through records;
- modifications.

Again it will state the documentation numbering conventions for the project and will give rules for format legibility.

The test description is part of the module definition package and includes a requirement for the following to be described:

- the item to be tested;
- the tests to be carried out;
- the hardware required;
- the test results;
- a summary of the results;
- a summary of the errors;
- a summary of any modifications;
- diagnostic details as they arise from the debug process.

Utility requirements specification

This should contain a description of the hardware requirements including the operator interfaces, hardware memory requirements, processor hardware, data communications hardware and software support packages.

User manual

This is an essential document since it is often the only visibility that the user has to the functions of the software. It must be readable and contain adequate, but not excessive, detail.

The user manual must form part of the test programme in order to verify that the software actually performs in the way that the manual describes.

Development notebooks

It is an excellent thing for each designer to have a development notebook – a looseleaf file containing written notes, listing, changes, correspondence, etc. This can be an invaluable aid to diagnosis during testing when the reasons for certain lines of code or some changes have become blurred in one's memory. Furthermore, with the turnover of design staff it is possible that the person in question may not be available when problems arise.

Requirements matrices

These provide a graphical system of cross-referencing between specifications as well as a method of checking off each requirement against the test specifications.

7.4 CONFIGURATION CONTROL

When developing a system it is vital that the state of the design at specific points is uniquely identifiable. In other words, a snapshot of the design which lists all the documents and media, by issue number, is required at regular intervals. This is often referred to as a **baseline**. In the event of disaster this enables the design to be retrieved at least to the state of the previous baseline.

Configuration management, which applies to hardware, software and documentation, plays a vital role because it allows control to be exercised over the baselines and the changes which represent the move from one baseline to another.

Thus, a baseline forms a reference point in the overall work schedule, whose four main functions are:

1. a reference point for progress measurement;
2. a basis for subsequent development and control;
3. a reference point for measuring quality;
4. a recovery point.

The selection of baseline points is arbitrary but, in practice, tends to coincide with project milestones (e.g. functional spec, start of functional test). The key point is that during system development baselines can be related to the design cycle.

Some basics include:

- Software identification is achieved by ensuring that name, version, date and inspection level are maintained both in the software itself and on the media labels.

		AB/089	BL1	BL2	BL3	BL4	BL5	BL6
Requirements spec		100	1.0	2.0	2.0	2.0	2.0	2.0
Functional spec		200	1.0	2.0	2.1	2.1	2.0	2.1
Hardware tech spec		300		1.0	2.0	2.0	2.0	2.0
Software tech spec		400		1.0	2.0	2.0	2.0	2.0
subsystems–SUPYS		410				1.0	2.0	2.0
	INIT	420				1.0	2.0	2.0
	FULLCHECK	430				1.0	2.0	2.0
	DOFOREVER	440				1.0	2.0	2.0
Modules–	ADDRESS	441				1.0	2.0	2.0
	DETDIAG	442				1.0	2.0	2.0
	DETFIRE	443				1.0	2.0	2.0
	CLOCK	444				1.0	2.0	2.0
	DISPSTAT	445				1.0	2.0	2.0
	CHKKEY	446				1.0	2.0	2.0
	REPORT	447				1.0	2.0	2.0
Quality plan		900	1.0	2.0	2.0	2.0	2.0	
TestSpecs–	MOTHER Bd	911					1.0	2.0
	CPU Bd	912					1.0	2.0
	I/O	913					1.0	2.0
	COMMS	914					1.0	2.0
	PSU	915					1.0	2.0
	I/O CPU	921					1.0	2.0
	COMMS/CPU	922					1.0	2.0
	FUNCTIONAL	931					1.0	2.0
	I/O LOAD	932					1.0	2.0
	MARGINAL	933					1.0	2.0
	MISUSE	934					1.0	2.0
	ENVIRONMENT	935					1.0	
EPROM–XYZ							1.0	–
PROM–ABC							–	1.0

Fig. 7.2 Document master index.

- Document identification includes title, reference number, version, date, page number (sequentially and not renumbering for each section).
- A master index is maintained which lists and uniquely identifies all items which define the configuration of each baseline. Figure 7.2 shows a typical master index which describes the baselines (up to baseline 6) in the case study in Part 6.

All of this leads to

- modifying the software;
- modifying the hardware;
- reporting discrepancies;
- disposal of documents and media;
- keeping secure masters;
- modification approval;
- labelling documents and media;
- segregating non-conforming items.

It is vital to ensure that changes are formally documented and controlled, particularly since there is no visible change to the software media (tapes, disks, PROMs). Any hardware change can render the software incompatible, therefore the build state of the two must be carefully controlled. A PROM containing the incorrect issue of software, even though only a single statement may have been changed, can cause a system to malfunction. This may well be a hazard in a process control or safety system.

Figure 7.3 shows a typical outline of a change system which co-ordinates both documentation and media.

The library/bureau function may well provide a focal point for this configuration and change control. Other library functions are:

- storage and identification of media and documents;
- build state records;
- spare copies and security;
- audit reports;
- codes of practice;
- test documents.

A good rule is that a document first becomes subject to configuration control once it is used by another person. The library then takes control by checking completeness and format and provides a unique identity and issue status.

Media should have visible labelling containing serial and issue status and this information should also be present in the software itself – that is to say, written on to the disk, encoded on the tape leader, programmed into specific locations of the PROM.

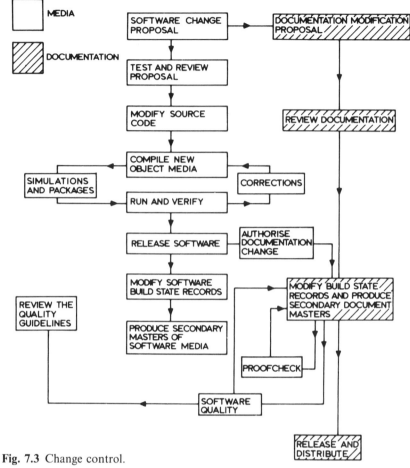

Fig. 7.3 Change control.

Arrangements for secure storage are important and 'insurance copies should be made weekly (or even daily) for storage in a different location. Banks provide this function and many organizations make use of the facility.

Whilst it is possible to perform these tasks manually they are better done with computerized tools since this minimizes the opportunity for error. For example, a tool may automatically change the issue number of a document when it has been changed. Several tools are available which assist in the management of not just source and object code but the documents which support them. The essence of these tools is that they minimize human access to the objects under control and therefore maintain control of them. In this way complete visibility of any changes to baselines is provided. Their main features are:

- automation of the library function for both software and documentation;
- control of access to library databases;
- secure version and change control;
- a record of versions and releases;
- assurance that documents stay in step with software changes;
- enablement of past versions to be accurately generated.

Some current automated tools, on the market are:

- AllChange from Intasoft Ltd;
- CHANGEMAN from EDS;
- Lifespan from BAeSEMA Engineering.

Some CASE tools contain configuration management tools as part of the total package.

7.5 PROGRAMMING STANDARDS

The purpose of coding standards is to define the language, methods, rules and tools which are to be used.

7.5.1 General rules

The human brain is not well adapted to retaining random information; hence standardized rules and concepts substantially reduce the probability of error.

A standard approach to creating files, polling output devices, handling interrupt routines, etc., constrains the programmer to use proven methods.

A further step in that direction is the use of standard subroutines to perform common functions within the system. Re-inventing the wheel is both a waste of time and an unnecessary source of error. Examples are:

- extended memory addressing (EMA) buffer management;
- EMA table access;
- system error routines;
- commonly used data structures.

The undisciplined use of GOTO statements in high-level language is dangerous and leads to difficulties in understanding the functions when reading source code. This is often referred to as spaghetti code. Modern block structured languages often contain no GOTO statement.

The avoid data corruption, the use of globals should be minimized so that modules can only access data local to their subsystem. Where global data (e.g. EMA buffers, system data) is required standard subroutines must be used for access.

A good guide to module size was given in Section 7.3 (G. J. Myers quotation). However, the ultimate criterion is its ability to convey to the reader a grasp of the function.

7.5.2 Structured programming

If the design has been well structured, then the coding activity should, after reading the module specification, be almost routine. Structured programming uses the concepts of:

- sequence (i.e. a sequential list of instructions);
- selection (e.g. IF–THEN–ELSE);
- iteration (e.g. DO WHILE).

Flow is generally down the page (i.e. no spaghetti!). Simple modules will have an entry at the top and exit at the bottom. Note, however, that the important concept of 'information hiding' requires multiple entry points.

The following light-hearted example, in a sort of pseudo code, illustrates the difference between structured and unstructured approaches.

Unstructured	*Structured*
⟨embark⟩	⟨embark⟩
begin	**begin**
get in boat;	get in boat;
reach for bags;	reach for bags;
if bags in reach **then goto** 'out'	**if** in reach **then**
again: shout for help;	put bags in
if help comes **then**	**else**
begin	begin
take bags;	**while** no one around **do**
	shout for help;
goto 'out';	take bags;
end;	put bags in boat;
goto 'again';	**end**;
'out': put bags in boat;	sailaway;
sailaway;	**end**.
end.	

Looking at the two examples it can readily be seen that the same problem has been tackled in two ways. In the unstructured case it is necessary mentally to add lines and arrows to perceive the loops. In the structured case the flow is always forwards. Note that, in the structured case, no **goto** statement is present.

7.5.3 Describing the modules

Earlier in this chapter it has been emphasized that the design objective is to arrive at well-defined modules. There is no prize for complexity. There are several methods for developing the module on paper.

Flow diagrams are a method of graphical representation which emphasize flow of control. They are less popular now as a result of more formal block structured languages.

Hierarchical diagrams provide a breakdown by task and then detail as illustrated in Fig. 7.4.

Warnier diagrams use both horizontal and vertical dimensions, and Fig. 7.5 shows the equivalent to Fig. 7.4 in Warnier form.

Structured box diagrams, sometimes known as Nassi–Shneiderman diagrams, are another format and the same task is shown again in Fig. 7.6.

Pseudocode uses English language statements as illustrated in the 'embark' example above.

7.5.4 Software coding standards

In addition to the module definition standard, a software programming standard will extend to the actual production of code. Thus, constraints and guidance are extended to the very bottom of the design hierarchy.

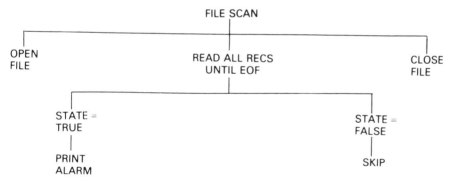

Fig. 7.4 Hierarchical diagram.

Fig. 7.5 Warnier diagram.

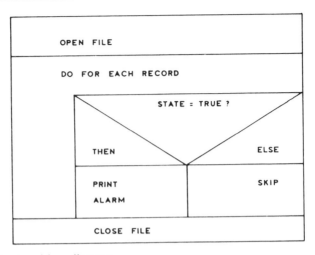

Fig. 7.6 Structured box diagram.

In the ideal case of a project specific standard the following will be included:

- A description of the computing environment including the operating system.
- The language and compiler (including version number).
- Details of compiler evaluation (see Chapter 9).
- Conditions under which the use of machine code is permitted (e.g. time-critical functions).
- Editing facilities.
- Rules for limiting the use of globals.
- The precise meaning of such terms as module, subsystem and routine and their functional boundaries.
- Header contents (e.g. name, date, issue, author, amendment history, calling sequence of module, synopsis of module, input and output parameters, data and globals accessed, messages passed to and received by the module, etc.).
- General advice on coding strategy.
- Rules for layout of the block structure and conventions for use of upper and lower case type (see Fig. 7.7). This includes the use of spaces, indented nesting, pagination, etc.
- Rules for the use of specific commands (e.g. limits on use of **goto**, use of simple **if** conditions, absence of dangling **then** or **else** commands).
- Rules within loops (e.g. entry, exit, forbidden commands within the loop).

```
begin
  while not key do
    if entry allowed then
    begin
      for: i = 1 to n do
      check (access, i, result);
      If result does not = true then
      error exit else
        set access;
    end;
    If entry denied then
    begin
      report entry (access-code, code);
      raise alarm (code);
      If time>18 then
      begin
        remote dial (code);
        lock all;
      end;
    end;
  end-do;
end
```

Fig. 7.7 Sample of block-structured code.

- Code template examples for regularly used sections of code (see Fig. 7.8).
- Algebraic rules (e.g. $A/B*C$ means $(A/B)*C$, not $A/(B*C)$).
- Naming conventions referenced to the technical specification.
- Advice on commenting and spacing as an integral part of the code which should describe rather than reproduce it.

```
Package QUEUE is
  type Q is limited private
  procedure ADD (PQ; in out Q; X: in INTEGER);
  procedure REMOVE (PQ: in out Q; X: out INTEGER);
  function EMPTY (PQ: in Q) return BOOLEAN:
private
  Q-S: constant:=100;
    type INTV is
      array (INTEGER range<>) of INTEGER:
    type Q is record
      Q-VEL: INTV (1..Q-S);
      FRONT: INTEGER range 0..Q-S:=0;
      BACK: INTEGER range 0..Q-S:=0;
    end record;
end QUEUE:
```

Fig. 7.8 A code template. This template has an Ada package header which makes it available for use as a template outside the package.

- Rules for subroutines relating to single entry and exit at top and bottom.
- Specific rules on the use of **goto**, such as obtaining project authorization, forward branching, commented destination.
- Error return conventions.
- Language facilities not to be used.
- Exception handling rules.

7.6 AUDIT

This involves an assessment of the controls used in the design and management process and an evaluation of their effectiveness. The systems and guidelines (Chapter 5) provide a basis for the audit and, in most cases, offer checklists as an aide memoire against which to examine an organization.

There are advantages and disadvantages in the use of checklists. On one hand they provide a means of ensuring that each question is remembered and thus enable the auditor to select the most appropriate questions. Furthermore, the checklists can be revised and updated as additional lessons are learned and thus one is always presented with the total of previous experience.

On the negative side, however, there is a temptation to expect yes/no answers and this can lead to a false view of the situation. In most cases it is the reason for the answer rather than the answer itself which provides the real information. For example, 'Is a high- or low-level language being used?' has no right or wrong answer. The reasons given for the answer are, however, of great importance.

7.6.1 Objectives of the audit

- To establish, by reviewing the techniques described in this book, that there is adequate control over the software design process.
- To establish that standards are being used for the documentation and production of the software.
- To assess, aided by the checklists, the comprehensiveness of the controls and the integrity of the product.
- To seek evidence that the standards are being applied and periodically reviewed.
- To establish that there are adequate controls over test and integration.
- To establish that there is a real capability, on the part of the team, to implement the requirements into a system.
- To establish that strict configuration controls exist.
- To establish that there is control over bought-in software.

7.6.2 Planning the audit

It can be seen, from the contents of this book, that the number of potential questions which could be addressed is vast and, for that reason, it is essential to plan the strategy of an audit. Since it will not be possible to address every feature that affects software quality it will be prudent to select a sample based on the critical features of the product and any known problem areas experienced by the designer. The following information must be available in order to formulate a plan:

- *Vendor details.* The range of products and services. A summary of any approvals which he has from other customers or authorities. The management and quality structure. The names of executives responsible for design and quality. The main customers. The number of employees in hardware and software design, test, quality, etc. The existence of any standards such as BS 5750.
- *Product details.* The requirements specification. A functional summary and environmental details. The range of hardware with type and quantity of memory. The language used. The current stage of development.
- *Audit team and schedule.* A list of persons involved with their areas of responsibility. In determining the skill requirements, the program language and equipment type are relevant.
- *Documentation summary.* A complete list of specifications such as are described in this chapter. Prior knowledge of the documents and their structure will allow more time to concentrate on evaluating their use and the state of the project. A list of documents should be prepared and a perspective of the hierarchy obtained by preparing a large chart. Any documentation standards or guidelines should be studied thoroughly.
- *Checklists.* A copy of the appropriate checklists from the previous chapters. These can be marked up to indicate the sample of questions which have been decided upon for the audit.

7.6.3 Implementing the audit

Include the vendor's quality organization in the documents and insist on a quality manual and quality plan. Look for evidence that these are not simply for show. There is a tendency at present to pay lip-service to software quality and often procedures are more advocated than practised. Look for hard evidence of their application.

The first aim should be to review the documents vertically to establish that requirements are fully and correctly reflected down through the specifications to the code modules. Module definitions should be audited for conformance to coding standards, layout, cross-referencing and functional performance. It will probably be necessary to take samples, in which case:

- Establish how long is to be spent on the activity and thus how many modules are to be audited.
- Allow adequate time for study of the requirements and functional specifications. This should not be skimped in order to include a few more modules.
- Choose a sample of modules having regard for the critical functional areas of the equipment. The sample need not be random.
- Choose a sample of change notes and trace each through the system.

Review with the project manager the areas which you intend to audit and examine the schedule for timing of design reviews and tests. The audit is unlikely to be a single activity but spread over the various design-cycle activities. In the early stages the specifications can be audited. Later the coded modules can be examined, followed by the design review and inspection/walk-through activities and eventually test and integration.

In an audit which extends over more than one day it is a good idea to present the problems daily to the vendor for discussion. For example, each day's findings could be copied to the vendor at 4.00 p.m. and jointly reviewed at 10.00 a.m. the next morning. In this way timely remedial action can be initiated on the spot.

The sequence should be:

1. plan;
2. establish schedule of activities with vendor;
3. prepare checklists, specifications and standards;
4. audit;
5. initiate remedial action with vendor;
6. prepare audit report.

An important feature is that each and every deficiency should be written down and agreed, at the time, by everyone involved. All deficiencies must be based on factual evidence.

7.6.4 The audit report

When the audit is spread over a long period interim reports should be prepared after each visit. At the end of the audit a full report is required consisting of:

- persons involved and their roles;
- each of the checklists;
- written report on each audit item;

- list of deficiencies and remedial action agreed;
- actions taken and modifications which resulted;
- summaries of design reviews;
- an overview and recommendations (no more than one page).

Appendix 1 provides sample checklists which the user can develop and add to from experience.

7.7 SOFTWARE REUSE

It is frequently assumed that the reuse of software, including specifications, algorithms and code, is not only economical in terms of project time savings but will, since the item is proven, lead to less failures than if the software were developed anew. There are reasons for and against this assumption.

Reasonable expectations of reliability, from reuse, are suggested by:

- The reused code or specification is proven.
- The item has been subject to more than average test.
- The time saving can be used for more development or test.
- The item has been tested in real applications environments.
- If the item has been designed for reuse it will be more likely to have stand-alone features such as less coupling.

On the other hand:

- The reused item is being used in a different environment and, thus, undiscovered faults will be revealed.
- If the item has been designed for reuse it may contain facilities not required for a particular application. The additional complexity may well result in lower reliability.
- The item may not be ideal for the application and other items may thus have to be changed.
- Problems may arise from the internal operation of the item not being fully understood.

No particular correlation between reuse and software reliability has currently been demonstrated.

8 | Formal methods in requirements

'Send reinforcements – we're going to advance'
'Send three and fourpence – we're going to a dance'

8.1 THE SCOPE OF FORMAL METHODS

The term 'formal methods' has been much used and much abused. It covers a number of methodologies and techniques from the mathematical statement of requirements through formalized design methodologies (Chapter 9) to the automated validation of code (Chapter 11). Thus, formal methods can be applied throughout the life cycle.

In the context of this chapter, however, the term is used to describe a range of mathematical notations and techniques applied to the rigorous definition of system requirements which can then be propagated into the subsequent design stages. The strength of formal methods is that they address the requirements at the beginning of the design cycle. One of the main benefits of this is that formalism applied at this early stage may lead to the prevention, or at least early detection, of incipient errors. The cost of errors revealed at this stage is dramatically less than if they are allowed to persist until commissioning or even field use. This is because the longer they remain undetected the more serious and far reaching are the changes required to correct them.

It has already been stated that the requirements specification is a major source of failures. If the programmer has been directed to solve the wrong problem, or if the requirements are incomplete or ambiguous, then even error-free code will still lead to system failures in use.

Especial interest in these methods has been generated in the area of safety-related systems in view of their potential contribution to software and system quality and thus to the safety integrity of systems in whose design they are used.

Formal methods are equally applicable to the design of hardware and software. In fact they have been successfully used in the design of large-scale integration electronic devices as, for example, the Viper chip produced by RSRE in Malvern, UK. In this chapter, however, the emphasis is on their use in software design.

Nevertheless, it should always be borne in mind that establishing the correctness of software, or even hardware, alone is no guarantee of correct system performance. Hardware and software interact to produce a system effect and it is the specification, design and validation of the system which matters. This system-wide view should also include the effects of human beings and the environment.

The potential for creating faults in the specification stage arises largely from the fact that it is carried out mainly in natural language. On one hand this permits freedom of expression and comprehensive description but, on the other, leads to ambiguity, lack of clarity and little protection against omission. The user communicates freely in this language which is not readily compatible with the formalism being discussed here.

A number of techniques have been developed to replace natural language with a mathematical language. Being mathematically based, the problems of ambiguity, inconsistency and (to some extent) omission are greatly reduced. User requirements can be captured in a precise and concise way.

The potential benefits are considerable but they cannot be realized without properly trained people and appropriate tools.

Formal methods are not easy to use. As with all languages, it is easier to read a piece of specification than it is to write it. A further complication is the choice of method for a particular application. Unfortunately, there is not a universally suitable method for all situations.

8.2 WHAT ARE FORMAL METHODS?

An important feature of a formal method is that it permits each stage of design to be checked against the previous stage(s) for consistency and correctness. They do not, however, assist greatly in design and development. In other words, their formalism assists in backwards checking but does not substitute for the creative input necessary to progress the design forwards to the next stage. Figure 8.1 illustrates this difference.

There are three main types of Formal Method:

1. data-oriented;
2. process-oriented;
3. state-oriented.

8.2.1 Data-oriented methods

This group includes model-based notations such as VDM and Z, which define a system in terms of a set of permissible operations on a data

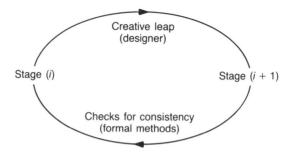

Fig. 8.1 Value of formal and creative steps.

structure. Specifications are explicit system models, and this accounts for their appeal and relative popularity. Secondly, there are the algebraic notations, such as OBJ, which enable system definition in terms of hierarchies of data types. Each data type includes a list of operations which are matched to the various instances of parameter lists under that data type. Data-oriented methods provide no means of modelling concurrency, state or time.

8.2.2 Process-oriented methods

Here the emphasis is placed on defining processes and how they interact. Examples of these methods include communications sequential processes (CSP) and calculus of concurrent systems (CCS). Processes are defined in terms of 'external' events, algebraic derivation of results and a description of the possible sequences of events for the process. Processes work together by sharing events and interchanging data. These methods do not provide the means for structuring data as specifications.

8.2.3 State-oriented methods

The best-known example in this class is the Petri-net (see also section 8.4.6). Petri nets provide a means of defining and reasoning about the states of a system. In essence, the system is expressed as a graph of possible states and the rules for transitions between the states. Time may be explicitly included, and used to define the actions of a real-time system. There is no means within the graphical notation for defining processes or data structures.

8.3 CURRENT METHODS

The following seven methods are not the only requirements languages but, in this continuously developing area, they represent the main ones in current use. The section on VDM is somewhat fuller than for the other methods in order to provide a deeper appreciation of at least one method.

8.3.1 Vienna development method (VDM)

This method stems from development carried out by IBM in Vienna. It is a rigorous mathematically based method which allows specifications to be stated in a mathematical form. VDM provides a formal notation and a variety of reasoning techniques suitable for many applications.

Although it has been emphasized that there is no universally suitable method, it can be said that VDM is probably the most widely used. Examples range from compiler development to process control systems.

VDM is model-based in that systems are described by means of concepts which can be clearly mapped onto the problem. This includes the use of sets, data objects and operations/functions which manipulate this data.

In some cases one can use the existing well-known sets such as integers, whereas a particular problem might require the invention of a special set. For example, the colours red, amber and green might be defined as a set for the purposes of a software system for controlling traffic lights. This would be expressed, in set notation, as:

$$colour = \{red, amber, green\}$$

In this simple case the VDM notation would be the same.

VDM encourages a top-down approach because it employs abstract data types which need to be progressively translated (decomposed) into specifics.

As is often the case with advanced techniques, the optimum benefit is obtained by a selective use. In other words VDM might sensibly be applied to a critical (and highly logical) aspect of a system. For example, in a safety system the critical voting and decision-making process would lend themselves well to the technique. Blanket use, at present, would be prohibitively costly and, as mentioned, it is not suitable for handling time-related aspects of system behaviour.

There is currently a British Standards committee which is working towards an ISO standard for VDM. This will probably further promote VDM as a definitive syntax when it becomes available.

An example of VDM is given here and is based on the case study in Part 5 of this book. It sets out to describe the requirements for fire detection within a zoned area. Figure 8.2 shows the concept of zones containing detectors. It highlights various features which this formal approach forces us to address, and then to describe explicitly.

This is modelled in VDM below. Note that the specification has been

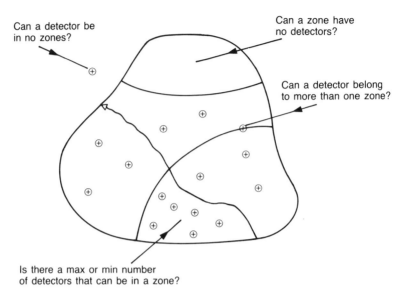

Can a detector be in no zones?

Can a zone have no detectors?

Can a detector belong to more than one zone?

Is there a max or min number of detectors that can be in a zone?

Fig. 8.2 Zones containing detectors.

simplified slightly and that some notation has been omitted, the aim being to convey the essence without becoming bogged down in notation. The general approach is to 'abstract' away from the specific idea of zones with detectors to the more general concept of sets of objects. The next step is to specify the properties in this abstract form (which at this point could relate to many 'real-world' situations) and finally to 'instantiate' (i.e. restrict) the sets to being zones and the objects to being detectors.

In the example, the specification is built in five stages:

A – Two sets are said to be disjoint if they have no elements in common.

$$is-disj : \text{set of } X * \text{set of } X \rightarrow B$$

This notation is used to define the form of the inputs and outputs of *is-disj*. The inputs are two sets and the output is Boolean. For simplicity the equivalent statements are omitted from later set constructs. The meaning of this construct is as follows:

$$is-disj\ (S_1, S_2) \triangleq \text{ if } S_1 \cap S_2 = \{\} \text{ then true else false}$$

i.e. 'the two sets, S_1, S_2, are disjoint' is defined as the set intersection $S_1 \cap S_2$ being empty. The disjoint set concept enables the analyst to state, unambiguously, the understanding that a detector can only reside in one zone.

B – Zones, and associated detectors, have been abstracted to sets of objects.

The overall area requiring fire protection comprises multiple zones and is therefore a 'set of sets'. This is depicted by the contents within the thick contour in Fig. 8.2 and is denoted by SS (for super-set). The next specification statement states that all the sets within this super-set are 'pairwise' disjoint. It does this by taking all combinations of pairs of sets, and uses *is-disj* to define them as being disjoint:

$$is-prdisj \ (SS) \triangleq \forall \ S_1, S_2 \in SS \ \cdot$$

$$S_1 = S_2 \ \lor \ is-disj \ (S_1, S_2)$$

This means the super-set SS is pairwise disjoint if, for all sets S_1, S_2 within the super-set, the sets are either the same or ($\lor$) *the sets are disjoint.*

The term '$S_1 = S_2$' within this definition may seem a little perverse but relates to the fact that in choosing S_1 as a first element of a pair, it is 'put back in the bag' and could be chosen again.

C – The introduction of the notation of a partitioned set of sets.

The pairwise disjoint construct may not seem useful in itself but it is a handy building block for the concept of set partition:

$$\{P \in set \ of \ (set \ of \ X) \ | \ invp(P)\}$$

This defines the set of partitions, P. Each partition is an element of the super-set (i.e. set of sets) and the set of partitions satisfies the properties *invp(P)*:

$$invp(P) \triangleq \{\} \notin P \ \land \ \bigcup P = X \ \land \ is-prdisj \ (P)$$

invp(P) means: a partition cannot be the empty set; the main union of partitions embraces all elements; partitions are pairwise disjoint. By referring again to Fig. 8.2, it is clear that this addresses three of the four questions relating to detectors and zones. A review with the user will identify whether the analyst's understanding is correct. The fourth question, which concerns the number of detectors in any particular zone, is inserted during the instantiation which follows.

D – Instantiation

The set of zones is:

$$\{Z \in Set \ of \ (set \ of \ detector) \ | \ invp(Z) \ \land$$

$$Card(Z) \geqslant 3\}$$

Card(z) refers to the cardinality (or number of detectors) in any particular zone. The analyst has defined this to be at least 3, to allow for failure and maintenance, and the definition of the fire condition which is given below. Again, this will need to be reviewed and discussed with the user/customer.

Consider a 'simple detector', that is one which can only be in one of two states:

$$DETVAL : DETECTOR \rightarrow B$$

In this model, fire detected maps to TRUE and no-fire maps to FALSE.

E – The fire- and gas-detection system applies the following rules:

1. **Alarm** but not **fire** (i.e. ring bell but do not trigger executive action)

$$\exists! D \in Z. \; DETVAL (D) = TRUE$$

which means there is one and only one detector in any particular zone exhibiting the fire condition.

2. **Fire** so ring bell and trigger executive action

$$(\exists D_1, D_2 \in Z \wedge D_1 \neq D_2).$$
$$DETVAL (D_1) = DETVAL (D_2) = TRUE$$

which means there are two distinct detectors in the same zone exhibiting the fire condition.

To summarize, the example illustrates how formal methods (in this case VDM) can be used to give an unambiguous definition of zones within a fire- and gas-detection system. This is then built upon to give a definition of alarm and fire conditions.

8.3.2 Z

The Z notation is, in some respects like VDM, a language using a model-based approach. It is also based on set theory and first-order predicate logic. It makes use of a 'schema' as one of its key features. This consists of a number of named objects with well-defined relationships between them. In computing terms this arrangement provides a syntactical unit from which the whole specification can be built.

Great emphasis is placed on readability and Z specifications are embedded into natural language documents in order to aid under-standing.

An example of a 'schema' might be a database consisting of people's names against each of which is stored a telephone number.

It might be described as follows:

DBtelephone

---

known: P NAME
phone: NAME → PHONE

---

known = dom phone

Two components of this schema are the set of *known* names known to the database and the partial function *phone* which records the telephone number against certain names. As an example:

known = {Smith, Banks, Souch}
phone = {Smith → 01 123 1234, Banks → 01 234 2345, Souch → 01 345 3456}

From this we can then go on to describe events which might happen.

Schemas can be used to describe all aspects of a system (i.e. the states it can occupy, the transitions it can make and, as we transform the specification into design, the relationship between one view of a state and another.

8.3.2 OBJ

OBJ is a language for writing and also for testing requirements which are best expressed in algebraic terms. It is compatible with the concepts of object orientation. This means that systems are modelled in terms of the 'objects' that make them up, rather than the processes which are carried out.

To explain this further let us return to the detector aspects of the case study. The model-based approach views the whole detector and its inputs and the logic applied to the voting as an entity. The object-oriented approach, however, would break the system down into definable objects (e.g. detector, voter). The inner workings and interface properties of each object therefore have to be thoroughly and unambiguously defined. System design can then be achieved by bolting together the various objects. This is analogous to hardware design where the inner architecture of an integrated circuit is far less important to the designer than a precise electrical definition of its performance, viewed as a black box.

8.3.4 Communicating sequential processes (CSP)

CSP is an approach for the specification of concurrent systems, that is to say systems requiring simultaneous functions (e.g. robots).

A system is modelled as a network of independent processes. Any two processes can communicate only if they are both ready – when they are suspended for a synchronized transfer of data. This interchange is known as a rendezvous. Processes are viewed as operating asynchronously but obviously have to suspend themselves while waiting for a rendezvous.

In addition to concurrency, CSP is a valuable tool for specifying distributed systems. Distributed systems, which may or may not involve concurrency, are complex systems involving two or more processors.

8.3.5 Controlled requirements expression (CORE)

This is an analysis method originated by systems designers and BAe, consisting of a set of formal techniques for gathering and structuring requirements information.

It is a graphical technique whose features have been derived from other widely used specification methods. The notation can be used both for requirements and for design.

The CORE method consists of a number of steps, each of which must be completed for each level of decomposition. These stages are:

- problem definition;
- viewpoint analysis;
- tabular collection;
- data structure diagrams;
- isolated viewpoint action diagrams;
- combined viewpoint action diagrams;
- non-functional requirements;
- system constraints;
- completion.

The technique has been in use for some time but needs automated support when used for large systems.

8.3.6 Input output requirements language (IORL)

IORL is a language which uses graphics and tables. It was aimed at engineers so that they could express system performance characteristics and algorithms.

The highest level is the schematic block diagram (SBD). SBDs are rectangular boxes that identify all the principal system components and the data interfaces which connect them together.

In IORL the designer must maintain the distinction between control flow and data flow. SBDs are decomposed into further levels of SBD as far as is feasible. Each SBD is generated as a separate document.

The predefined process diagram (PPD) is used to describe the detailed flow logic of a single process. It is used to improve the readability of the specification, to allow identification of dependent components and to enable the specification to be presented in a hierarchical manner.

A computed-aided systems design (CASE) tool is available which uses the IORL requirement language to express software specifications. IORL uses blocks and icons to create flow and timing diagrams. Parameter tables accompany the diagrams.

8.3.7 Higher-order logic (HOL)

HOL is another model-based method. It is worthy of mention because it has some very rich features for specifying complex systems. Its flexibility has led to its use in both hardware and software design.

8.4 TOOLS AND SUPPORT

The introduction of formal methods requires both appropriately trained personnel and supporting tools.

The skills are basically mathematical in nature but will not necessarily have been acquired from a conventional mathematical education. Appropriate courses are therefore needed and it must be remembered that the lead time for acquiring proficiency in the techniques is not insignificant. It may well be necessary to phase their introduction with the help of consultants whilst the organization acquires the appropriate experience and culture.

Each of the methods described in sections 8.4.1–8.4.4 require the support of complementary tools. Although each of the tool types is described as a separate entity, in practice they are available as tool sets for each of the languages. They come as packages which typically include the configuration management and library functions.

The individual tools include the items given in sections 8.4.1–8.4.4.

8.4.1 Documenters

These are the 'word processors' of the language being used. They contain the language set of the method as, for example, the symbols used in the VDM example above.

8.4.2 Syntax checkers

These process the specification documentation (produced by the above documenter) for testing the correctness of the syntax of the statements written in the language in question. This is much the same as the function performed by a compiler which performs similar checks on procedural coding languages.

8.4.3 Theorem provers

Whereas the above two tools are to do with the notation itself, theorem provers actually test the reasoning and logical assertions made in the statements which have been written. In other words they address the semantics of the specification much as the static analysis tool (described in Chapter 11) examines the semantics of procedural code.

The human mind is not well adapted to lengthy and repetitive checks and comparisons. It is therefore in this area that the strength of these theorem provers is felt. Without them the use of formal methods would hardly be practicable.

8.4.4 Animators

These effectively 'execute' the specification to enable one to 'test' the outcome of the statements made. They are therefore excellent for two particular reasons:

1. Helping the user to revisit and review the requirements for completeness and accuracy.
2. Assisting in specifying acceptance test criteria at an early stage.

8.5 AUTOMATED DESIGN

Ultimately the whole design process, from requirements specification to coding, will be automated. This is the dream and it will, no doubt, come to pass in a decade or so.

Figure 8.3 illustrates the concept.

8.6 ADVANTAGES AND LIMITATIONS

There are a number of advantages, most of which are inherent to the methods themselves. On the other hand there are some difficulties which are primarily a result of the currently immature state of their development.

8.6.1 Strengths

Because they are mathematically based the results are concise, unambiguous, and can be tested for internal consistency and enable proofs of cor-

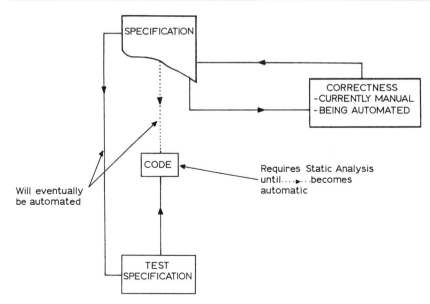

Fig. 8.3 An automated design cycle.

rectness. This is of great benefit in revealing inconsistencies between parts of the system.

There is the potential, eventually, to translate directly from requirements to code.

They force a deeper consideration of the system requirements by offering abstraction above the programming level. They point to a clear understandable design and give insight into the principles to be followed.

They can handle hardware as well as software.

They can offer the possibility of verification to show mathematically that the design satisfies the specification.

8.6.2 Weaknesses

The methods are not easy to use. The mathematics is not trivial and there is, at present, a shortage of skills and experience in this area.

The costs of training and support tools are significant and the use of formal methods has the effect of front-loading projects. Unless management are fully committed to this technology the support and funding of these methods is likely not to be forthcoming.

The methods are currently less than fully mature and thus they cannot provide a fully verified design, although it must be said that the situation is improving rapidly.

There is, as yet, a shortage of hard evidence to provide justification for their use. This is largely because of confidentiality and commercial considerations.

Typically they are only applied to critical parts of a project, due to lack of support tools.

There is no guarantee of correct application of the tool or method.

They tend to ignore machine and hardware limitations.

8.6.3 Guidance

These methods need to be applied at system level rather than focused on either hardware or software design alone.

It is probably better to introduce them in a modest way to start with in order to master each stage before attempting the next. In this way drawbacks will not necessarily cause unacceptable waste of time and money and the confidence to move forward will remain.

Choose established methods for which there are already adequate supporting tools.

Do not stint on the cost of training. Unless the appropriate skills are thoroughly mastered the initiative will almost certainly fail.

Formal methods in design | 9

9.1 WHAT IS THE DESIGN PROCESS?

Software design is the process which translates the requirements specification into a detailed representation of a software system. Good software design is essential for reliable and understandable software. Many techniques, with associated tools, have been developed to support software design. Some of the major ones will be described here.

It is necessary to examine the term 'good design'. A major visible difference between 'good' and 'bad' program structure is that the latter appears to be more complex. Good design entails a structure which both solves the problem in hand and is readily understood.

It is generally agreed that complexity, as perceived by the brain, can be reduced in three main ways:

1. *Partitioning*. Dividing the program into parts having identifiable and well-understood boundaries.
2. *Hierarchy*. The top-down approach described already in Chapter 7.
3. *Independence*. Minimizing the coupling between parts of the system.

The design techniques described here, most of which are supported by powerful tools, are largely based on these principles. They fall into two groups:

1. *Process-oriented*. This concentrates on analysing the problem in terms of processes, which themselves are decomposed to give the program structure. The program instructions and data are kept separate.
2. *Data-oriented*. This emphasizes the data design component of software and on the techniques for deriving the data types and structure.

9.2 PROCESS-ORIENTED TECHNIQUES

The following design approaches are commonly used and each has strengths in solving particular types of problem. They may be used separately or, sometimes, in combination.

9.2.1 Flow charting

This is probably the most familiar and popular technique and also the most readily understood. It is simply a method for graphical representation of the flow of the program and is primarily concerned with the flow of control. Flow charts were at one time the norm but have recently gone out of favour. However, for the majority of applications, where the function is some type of process control, then flow diagrams are still helpful, albeit informal, guides to communication and understanding. Safety-related systems tend to be of this type.

Figure 9.1 is an example of a flow chart. The reader may care to show

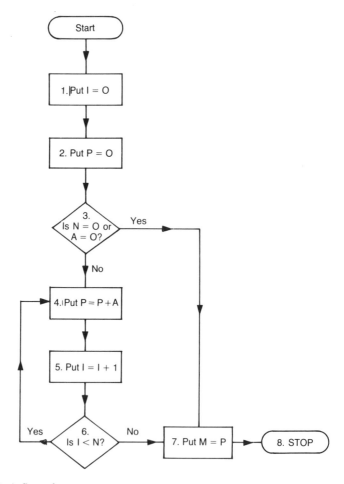

Fig. 9.1 A flow chart.

that this computes M as $N \times A$ and to consider if there is a potential endless loop at step 6.

9.2.2 Modular programming

The basic concepts of this early method are as follows:

- Each module implements a single and independent function.
- Each module has a single entry and exit point and the module size is as small as possible (compatible with the above concept).
- Each module can be designed and coded by different programmers in a team and can be separately tested.
- The whole system is synthesized from these modules.

This is basically good practice and is certainly not new. It lacks, however, the framework needed to make comparative assessments of alternative designs.

9.2.3 Functional decomposition

This method is essentially based on a 'divide and conquer' strategy. An important concept used in the method, and used elsewhere, is 'information hiding', in which strongly related functions that share some common data areas are wrapped up in a single module with multiple entry points. Since only these specific functions share this data, it is 'hidden away' inside the module. Only information genuinely needed by other modules appears in this module interface.

This technique was one of the first to employ 'stepwise requirement' which means refining the design at each stage of decomposition – an iterative process. The advantage of functional decomposition is in its applicability, whereas its disadvantage is a lack of uniqueness of solution which leads to variability.

9.2.4 Data flow

These methods use information flow as a driving force for the software design process. Various mapping functions are used to transform information flow into a software structure. The basic method, of which there are variants, is based on the following procedure:

1. Identify the flow of data in the problem and draw a data flow graph.
2. Identify the incoming, central and outgoing transform elements.
3. Factor the incoming, central and outgoing transform elements branches to form hierarchical program structure.
4. Refine and optimize the program formed in step (3).

Structured analysis design technique (SADT), which is a specific methodology, is an example of this and is described in the next section.

9.2.5 Data-structure design

The two main methods, from Jackson and from Warnier, enable the overall and the detailed design to proceed concurrently. The Jackson methodology is discussed in the next section.

9.3 DATA-ORIENTED TECHNIQUES

These techniques emphasize the data-design components of a software system. Two techniques (OODT and CCDM) are described in the next section. They both tie in with formal specification methods, thus enabling the correctness of the design to be tested.

9.4 SOME AVAILABLE METHODOLOGIES

Each of the various methods just described has strengths and weaknesses and a detailed discussion of these is beyond the scope of this book. In recent years there has been a trend to package these methods into so-called 'methodologies'. These packages typically comprise:

- a set of techniques/diagrams;
- a means for managing inter-relationships between these techniques;
- a step-by-step prescription for carrying out the design process with these techniques;
- accompanying procedures for configuration management, project control, etc.

An important point to note is that each methodology employs a range of techniques. Examples include data flow diagrams, entity–relationship diagrams, state-transition diagrams and process/function hierarchies. Each of these techniques presents a 'window' on the problem, the aim of the methodologies being to maximize visibility via the provision of multiple viewpoints.

9.4.1 Modular approach to software construction operation and test (MASCOT)

This is a method for the design and implementation of real-time systems. The method is widely used in the UK defence and avionics industries and originated from work done at RSRE. MASCOT is characterized by the use of a graphical data-flow network as the medium for expressing software structure. It is combined with a systematic development method which ensures that this structure is accurately reflected in the resultant software. Inter-process communication is handled by a special type of design element which encapsulates the shared data storage and the access mechanisms which implement the synchronizing actions necessary to preserve the integrity of the shared data. All the parallel processing knowledge of the system is thus isolated from the purely algorithmic concerns dealt with in the processes. A MASCOT application is tested and operated in a standard context which provides a set of run-time executive-level facilities for such purposes as process scheduling and synchronization.

Mascot was originally developed to assist in the design and development of Coral 66 based systems. Recently, however, the development of Mascot 3 has extended the capability of Mascot and also facilitates more readily the use of Mascot in an Ada-based environment.

9.4.2 SSADM

This grew out of work by the UK Government's Central Computer and Telecommunications Agency and Learmonth, Burchett Management Services, to devise a standard software design methodology applicable to the broad scope of work performed by various government departments.

SSADM is a well-defined step-by-step approach. It regards functions and data with equal importance. SSADM is divided into six stages:

1. *Analysis.* Construct a logical model of the system.
2. *Specification of requirements.* Document the problems of the current system and the requirements of the new system.
3. *Selection of system option.* Identify and document the operational requirements of the new system.
4. *Logical data design.* Complete a detailed logical data design.
5. *Logical process design.* Complete a set of detailed logical process designs.
6. *Physical design.* Translate the logical design into database or file descriptions and the logical process designs into program specifications.

The primary techniques used in the six stages, but not in all, are data-flow diagrams, entity models, entity life histories, data normalization, process outlines and physical design control. A standard set of forms to assist in developing systems also exists. CASE toolsets are now available.

9.4.3 Jackson system development (JSD)

In this method, emphasis is laid on defining models of the 'real world', including defining the terms used and abstractions. It claims that, by using the real world as a model to guide the implementation, the ultimate design will anticipate changes emanating from the users in the real world. The models are detailed in terms of entities, actions and order (i.e. sequential or alternative selection).

When complete, the real-world models are used as the basis for implementation, by adding functions, state vectors and system timing details. Neither verification nor validation are included in the method, nor is there any provision for feedback.

It can be summarized as:

1. Identify and draw the structure of the input and output data.
2. Draw a program structure by merging these data-structure diagrams.
3. Derive and allocate the discrete operations composing the program.
4. Convert the program structure to program text.

9.4.4 Structured analysis and design technique (SADT) – Ross

This has been in use since 1974 and is a general-purpose modelling technique which can be used to describe a range of problems not necessarily confined to computer systems. It is a graphical language involving top-down decomposition of complex problems into easily perceivable elements. SADT consists of three aspects:

1. the graphical language which communicates the requirement (**actigrams**);
2. methods which decompose the problem so that the graphical language can be used to describe it;
3. management and human factors rules which guide and control the above methods and diagrams.

The result is an ordered set of interrelated diagrams where each diagram must contain three to six boxes and occupy a single page. The number of diagrams will depend on the complexity of the problem and they will be connected by upwards and downwards referencing in a logical hierarchical structure. A top-down overview diagram will précis the total problem.

Diagrams consist only of boxes, arrows and text. Arrows represent relationships between boxes and should not be confused with data-flow or sequence arrows in other types of diagram. Figure 9.2 shows (a) an overview structure and (b) a single diagram (actigram).

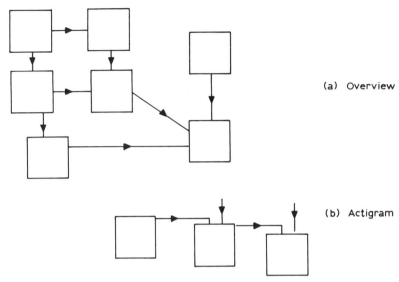

(a) Overview

(b) Actigram

Fig. 9.2 (a) Overview structure; (b) actigram.

9.4.5 Structured system analysis (SSA) – Yourdon, De Marco

This dates from the 1970s and is still very much in vogue. Top-down and graphical techniques make it fairly similar to SADT but it incorporates some additional data features. These are:

- data-flow diagrams;
- data dictionaries;
- process logic diagrams;
- data structures.

The Yourdon method has undergone significant development. For example, it has been enhanced with features to cope with real time.

A standard data dictionary is used to define the various data elements in the requirements. The diagrammatic logic for describing the problem includes decision trees and decision tables. SSA is, hence, applicable to data-processing systems and real-time problems with substantial data flow and manipulation.

9.4.6 Petri-nets

This technique has evolved over the last ten years as a method for describing real-time systems. The elements of the net are:

- token types which specify each type of information;
- places;

- transitions;
- arcs;
- initial marking.

The important feature is the translator which converts the Petri-net into a program structure such as Ada. Petri-nets are also mentioned in section 8.2.3.

9.4.7 Object-oriented design technique (OODT)

This is a data-oriented method which exploits the ideas of 'information hiding' and 'abstract data types'. It treats all the resources (i.e. data, modules, subsystems...) as objects. Each object encapsulates a data type inside the set of procedures which, in turn, knows how to manipulate the data type.

Using this methodology, a designer can create his own abstractions instead of mapping the problem domain into the predefined control and data structures of an implementation language. Various different kinds of abstract types can be created in a design process. In this way a designer can concentrate on the system design without worrying about the data objects used by the system. The feature of complete separation between specification and implementation in Ada is suitable for OODT. The method can be summarized as:

1. Define the problem.
2. Develop an informal strategy which is a sequence of steps to satisfy the system requirement.
3. Formalize the strategy by identifying the objects and their attributes, identifying operations on those objects, establishing interfaces and implementing the operations.

9.4.8 Conceptual database design methodology (CCDM)

This is another data-oriented method which guides a designer in the process of translating data and requirements into a database conceptual schema. This approach aims to establish a 'unified conceptual model' inheriting richer semantic meaning and using the data abstraction concept to facilitate software design. In fact it is a kind of knowledge representation which ranges from the real-world problem to machine-executable code.

9.5 TOOLS

Most of the established design methodologies are supported by computer-aided system engineering (CASE) just as the requirements languages in

Chapter 8 were seen to be similarly supported. These tools support the individual features of the methods (e.g. graphics and diagrams) and the interrelationships between features (e.g. data definitions relating to two different diagrams).

The functions of the CASE tool include aids to constructing the diagrams, checking consistency through the design, library and configuration control, outputs and reporting.

The tools come as packages for each of the methodologies in question. For example SSADM will have a supporting tool set which combines all the various elements.

10

Review and test

The design cycle emphasizes the feedback feature whereby each stage is reviewed (tested) for conformance with the previous stage. This chapter deals with the techniques for carrying out those checks.

Review and test are essentially similar in that they both 'test' for compliance with some higher-level requirement. The difference is that, whereas test involves executing the code, review is an intellectual comparison of functions with requirements.

10.1 REVIEWS

10.1.1 What are reviews?

There are two common misconceptions about design review which are:

1. that they are schedule progress meetings;
2. that they appraise the designer.

These are dangerous misunderstandings in that they deflect from the real purpose which is to measure (verify) the design, at specific milestones, against the requirements. This highlights the need for baselines, as described in section 7.4.

The features of a review should provide the feedback loop which judges the adequacy and completeness of the design and provides confidence to proceed to the next stage (Fig. 10.1). They should be geared to:

- making the design visible;
- providing a means of tracing the requirement through the design;
- measuring the functions against the requirement;
- identifying faults.

The process cannot be left to chance, or to the whim of the project, so there is a need for these design reviews to be a formal requirement. The procedures need to identify:

- *Review points.* What stages in the design will be subject to review? Some of these arise naturally because of the life-cycle model. For example:

DESIGN REVIEW

Viewpoints

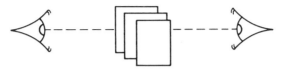

Management   User / Developer

Does the level of information   Does it contain the data to
meet the contractor requirements?   proceed to the next stage ?

Fig. 10.1 Design review.

—requirement specification;
—functional specification;
—test strategy/plan;
—preliminary design (conceptual design);
—detailed design;
—coded modules;
—integration tests;
—functional system test;
—acceptance test;
—major modifications.

- *Participants.* It is necessary to define interested and relevant parties and who will lead the review. They should be drawn from as many different aspects of the project as possible. Their responsibilities should be defined. With the exception of code reviews (which may be restricted to peers) the following must be involved:
  —chairman (calls and conducts review);
  —management;
  —designer (presents and justifies the design);
  —peers (provides objective views);
  —quality (ensures test requirements are realistic);
  —user/field (ensures operating and maintenance requirements can be met).
- *Procedure.* The author of the document will ensure that it is ready for review. It will be circulated, prior to the review, with adequate time for the participants to comment. The author will consider the comments prior to the review, thus ensuring that aspects which need to be reviewed are given adequate attention.
- *Records and follow-up.* There must be details of the written records to be kept and the follow-up actions which result. It is necessary to record who is involved, what faults were discovered and what actions were agreed.

- *Checklists.* These provide a useful *aide-memoire* and a means of recording lessons learnt from previous reviews. Appendix 1 provides a number of checklists for the different types of review.

  They provide a structure for reviews as well as a vehicle for recording results.

  They should, however, be regarded as catalysts rather than go/nogo checks. By their nature they tend to be extremely open-ended questions to which either yes or no answers provide little illumination. They should be used to prompt review of key teams and should not constrain the user.

10.1.2 Document reviews

Document reviews are rather different from code reviews because they involve mostly comparisons of text. They are thus the hardest to conduct thoroughly.

- *Requirements specification.* This is undoubtedly the most problematical review. The requirements specification, being at the top of the design cycle, has no higher document against which to be compared. Furthermore, being written in free language, it has the maximum opportunity for ambiguity, omission and error. The following checklist is thus valuable in attempting to formalize and direct the review:
  —*What not how.* The requirements specification should not prejudge the design and should, therefore, attempt to describe measurable requirements rather than functional solutions.
  —*Completeness.* Are all the items needed to describe the application/requirement included (e.g. reliability, maintainability, extendability, operability, weight, power)?
  —*Correctness.* Are the items stated correctly and are they credibly achievable?
  —*Precision/ambiguity.* Are the items exact (rather than vague) and are they stated in a way that has a single meaning? Are they easy to read?
  —*Consistency.* The items should not conflict with each other.
  —*Testability.* Are the requirements such as can be demonstrated, by test, during the design and implementation? (e.g. extremely high reliability cannot be demonstrated by test).
  —*Traceability.* The requirements need to be traceable to their origin in the application in question.
  —*Feasibility.* The items must be capable of being implemented with the technology and resources available.
  —*Manageability of items.* The items need to be capable of some change without undue impact on the other items.

- *Functional specification.* Most of the above checklist is also applicable to the functional specification. However, there is now a higher-level document against which to review, namely the requirements specification.

It is still early in the life cycle to fix the design. Concentration should be on stating how the requirements are to be achieved in functional terms rather than by specifying hardware or even software solutions.

—*Detailed design.* This includes the review of design documents such as are described in Chapter 9, including the textual aspects of the module specifications. As well as the items in the above checklist, the following issues should also be considered:

—*Design breakdown.* In Chapter 7, guidance was given as to the reasonable size for a design module. The review needs to question if the design has been sufficiently decomposed, as opposed to over-decomposed.

—*Module description.* Does the module execute a single well-defined function? Are the functions fully and clearly described? Do they include important secondary functions such as error handling, input range traps, arithmetic precision requirements, etc.?

—*Connections between modules.* Are interfaces between modules correct and compatible? Is the coupling between modules minimized?

10.1.3 Code review methods

This is an extension of the document review methodology to the lower level of coded instructions. It can involve a combination of three methods:

1. inspections and walk-throughs;
2. static analysis;
3. metrics.

The latter two are specific techniques which provide formalized information about the code. Static analysis is fully described in the next chapter and provides various quality measures as well as semantic descriptions of the code. Metrics, described in Chapter 15, provide higher-level generic measures which may assist in identifying key areas for review.

These two techniques provide inputs to the inspections and walk-throughs.

- *Peer review.* This is the practice whereby a peer checks a module against the design documents and then comments to the author. The author needs to provide the peer with the full documentation for the module including:

—code;

—module specification;

—change documentation;

—any test data.

- *Code inspection.* This is a more formal review with the primary intention of finding faults, not rectifying them. The technique was originally devised by Fagan, at IBM, and has proved to be an extremely effective method of review during design, code and test.

  Code inspection involves a group of people studying the code and attempting to find faults. Past histories, as well as the code documentation, are used to assist the process.

  For that reason the inspections should be carried out carefully, and data collected over a period of time, so that trend data is gathered to yield useful information as well as refining future reviews.

  The process is not trivial and staff need to be trained in order to carry out this type of review.

- *Code walkthrough.* There are several types of walk-through which include higher levels of design as well as code. A walk-through involves the author in describing the rationale (justification) for the code to a team who attempt to identify faults in the logic.

  Again, records are important both for reference later in the design cycle and for future walk-throughs.

10.1.4 Review of test

Test is described in later sections. Review of test, as distinct from test itself, is the review of the documented test results against the test specification. Without a full test specification, including a description of the satisfactory test results required, it is almost impossible to decide on the validity of test results. This highlights the need for detailed test documentation. 'Review status' is an important 'label' for a document and should therefore be part of the configuration parameters.

Particular review points pertinent to the test process are:

- production of the test plan/strategy;
- production of test specifications;
- module tests;
- integration tests;
- functional tests;
- acceptance tests;
- testing of changes/modifications.

10.2 TEST

10.2.1 Limitations of test

The main limitation in software testing is the inability to foresee the combinations of external conditions and program states which will lead to failure. We are easily disposed to specifying what a system **should** do. It is less easy to think of tests which prove that a system will not do what we do not want it to do.

Furthermore, the permutation of execution possibilities, together with possible input conditions, is usually many orders of magnitude beyond the time and resources available to even the most extended test programme. One academic exercise sought totally to prove a piece of software involving 1600 lines of source code – it required a three-year research project.

Hence, practical limitations, during test, include:

- The range of test conditions and loads which can actually be applied. It may only be possible to apply environmental conditions individually or in a limited number of combinations and this will depend on the test equipment (e.g. simulators, emulators) available.
- The range of operator actions which can be foreseen and planned for in the test procedure. These should include misuse test but will, of course, be limited by the imagination of the test writer.
- The extent of the operating instructions.
- The choice of the language and its compiler which will have an effect on the difficulties actually experienced during testing.
- The fact that timing-related problems/faults, usually the most common in real-time applications software, are the hardest to foresee. They are also the hardest to diagnose.
- Management constraints of time and cost. Since test is one of the last activities before despatch it is the one most likely to be truncated in favour of delivery.

Be suspicious of repeated slippage during a test programme. It is invariably a symptom that each test procedure is revealing a large number of faults (bugs) which require extensive rework (i.e. redesign). It is unlikely, therefore, that each test will have been repeated after each modification (i.e. fix) in which case additional unrevealed faults are almost certain to have been introduced by the modifications.

10.2.2 Types of test

Testing involves using real (live) inputs and data to exercise the performance of the code either in simulators or actual equipment. Types of testing include:

- *Symbolic evaluation.* A low-level parametric test whereby a path is followed through the code and the effect of various inputs on the corresponding outputs is determined. It validates performance only of specific variables rather than actual functions.
- *Functional tests.* This treats the software as a black box and tests the functions by observing outputs in response to input conditions and data.
- *Stress tests.* These are also black box tests and impose a range of extreme and illegal input conditions so as to stress the capabilities of the software. Input data volume and rate, processing time, utilization of data and memory are all tested beyond the design capability.
- *Environmental tests.* These include electromagnetic interference tests. Software systems are particularly prone to data corruption resulting from mains and airborne interference. Only real functional tests, utilizing the finished hardware, are valid since the effects are hardware-dependent although it is the software which is affected. Some would argue that electromagnetic interference is a hardware phenomenon but it is a system-wide issue and must be addressed.
- *Simulation tests.* These arise when only part of the system has been designed and it is necessary to substitute for data inputs or processing features of the system not yet available.

10.2.3 Levels of test

Module tests

These are stand-alone tests of individual modules not yet integrated into the system. Hardware will probably not be available at the stage when module tests are being carried out. Data inputs are therefore simulated manually or by means of test drivers with results and outputs being displayed on the VDU and printer.

Integration tests

This is a most important phase of testing. **Bottom-up** integration is the traditional approach whereby modules are tested together and a pyramid is built up. Only then is it possible to test the system as a complete set of functions. An alternative approach is the **top-down** method which involves building a set of simulation drivers, known as **stubs**, in order to provide a complete artificial system. This was also described in section 4.7. Modules, and groups of modules, can then be tested as they become available. This approach has several advantages:

- A single test specification can apply throughout.
- All possible interactions of a module to the remainder of the system are likely to be tested.
- Complex system timing faults are likely to be revealed at an earlier stage.

There are many problems which arise during the process of integrating a system.

Diagnosis of the causes of failure, during integration and test, can be complicated by the fact that faults can interact to give symptoms quite different from those which they would produce as individual bugs. As a result, the rework after a particular test may not be adequate although it might seem that the problem has been rectified.

Modules, or subsystems, may perform correctly when tested alone but fail in combination. Unless this is foreseen during the writing of the integration test procedures, hidden faults can remain.

The time required for development and production of the various test harnesses may be underestimated. In that case integration tests will commence with incomplete test facilities and the result will be harder diagnosis of faults and incomplete testing.

Failures may relate to loading, timing and speed features of the inputs, outputs and data.

If the interfaces between modules and between the system and the tester are not fully understood, tests will not be conclusive and diagnosis will be harder.

The ease of testability of software is clearly a function of the code itself and it would seem obvious that this must be designed in. The most powerful method of achieving this is to provide built-in self-test routines in the code. This is an area which may well provide an application for expert systems.

System tests

The purpose of system testing is to utilize known input stimuli and data to check that the outputs conform to the established specification. These performance tests include:

- *Functional tests.* To test the defined performance.
- *Environmental tests at stress limits.* It is often pointed out that software is not affected by temperature or humidity. This is true but, nevertheless, the changes in electrical characteristics which result can alter timing features and thereby cause faults.
- *Misuse tests.* Take account of the fact that products will be used outside their stipulated range of operating conditions.

- *Maintainability tests.* To demonstrate ease of diagnosis and repair under simulated fault conditions.

Various techniques and test tools are employed and these will be outlined in the next two sections.

Production tests

The above test levels constitute qualification tests because they 'qualify' the design against the specification. Production tests, on the other hand, are repetitive and merely confirm that the build of production items has not changed.

10.2.4 Test tools

- *Test drivers.* These are used to input data into a module under test and to receive the resulting data output for checking. They are simulators which can mimic unavailable items of hardware or software.
- *Test beds.* More sophisticated than the simple driver described above, they can display simultaneously the source code alongside the executing program. They show the values of variables and indicate those portions of code affected.
- *Emulators.* 'Intelligent' communications analysers having programmable stimulus and response facilities are used to emulate parts of the system (including their responses) not yet developed. In this way the software is tested as if it were surrounded by a real system.
- *Assertion checkers.* Insert code statements (probes) and flag the results.
- *Path testers.* Similar to the static testers but require the code to be executed.
- *Mutation analysers.* Seed intentional errors into the code to test the fault tolerance of the system.
- *Symbolic execution tools.* Execute the arithmetic and logic with symbolic variables following calculus rules. It could be argued that this is a static test since no execution is involved, the functions being tested symbolically.

The TESTBED tool (section 11.4) contains a module of static analysis. It is also a dynamic analysis tool. It produces **test effectiveness ratios** that define how well a program has been tested. Heavily used as well as unused statements are highlighted. The source code is compiled, linked and executed with appropriate sets of test data under control of a menu system. Upon termination of the user program an additional file is generated by the instrumentation. Dynamic analysis is invoked to interrogate this file to generate reports on the effectiveness of the data simulation.

This dynamic operation can be repeated, with selection of alternate sets of data, until a satisfactory test effectiveness is obtained.

Current packages are numerous and include:

- *ADATEST*, from IPL Information Processing Ltd. It is a CASE tool for supporting the unit and integration testing phases of the life cycle for software written in Ada. It provides both test coverage and static analysis.
- *Cantata*, from IPL Information Processing Ltd. It caters for both C and C++. It provides test coverage and static analysis.
- *FX* from Microplus Ltd. It sets up test files, provides macro facilities to decode files and provides access for amendments at the byte level.
- *Mans* from Compuleer. This provides forward and reverse engineering methods for Modula-2, Pascal, FORTRAN, PL/1 and dBaseIII. It provides test data through CASE analysis.
- *Orion ICE* from Orion Instruments. A self-contained emulation and analysis system for embedded microprocessor applications for most 8-, 16- and 32-bit devices.

10.2.5 Test management

Software testing is gradually undergoing a transition from being a 'black art' to becoming a science. In other words, test methods based on undocumented experience and subjective judgements are being replaced by formally designed tests.

One essential requirement is the existence of a test manager, who must be appointed at the beginning of the project. The whole structure and philosophy of the tests are dependent on the requirements specification and on the system configuration. The test plan and an outline of test methods must therefore begin to evolve, along with the hierarchy of documents, right from the beginning. Lead times for the procurement of simulators, test hardware, environmental facilities, etc., are long, and this adds greater emphasis to the need for test management at the earliest possible stage.

The first document, as regards testing, is the test strategy. This may be a separate document or may form part of the quality plan. It outlines the various levels of test (described in the remainder of this chapter) and how these will build up to a final functional system test. Broad details of the test hardware and software which will be needed to carry out the various integration, simulation, loading and other tests will also be given. This, and the subsequent test documents, should not be produced by the designers but by a separate test authority.

Other essential documents will follow as the design proceeds. These include:

- *Test specifications.* One for each separate test activity, of which there may be several dozen. It will describe the functions to be tested and the test method to be employed, including the range of values which will be covered. The test equipment required is also described here.
- *Test procedures.* The actual test instructions down to the details of connecting test equipment and the actual inputs to be applied and their sequence. A good test procedure should contain the anticipated result of each test and a record sheet on which to record the results.
- *Test records.* There should be a test record for every test and, as mentioned above, this may be a part of the test procedure document.
- *Test utilities specification.* Both the hardware and computer facilities needed for all the tests are specified here. Any test software (i.e. programs which provide test data so as to simulate modules or hardware items not yet designed) is also described here.
- *Test reports.* There should be a test report for each test or group of tests. The main benefit is that the report provides a medium for recording any actions which arise as a result of the faults revealed. The actions, having been formally recorded, can then be reviewed until they are discharged.

Perhaps the most important things to bear in mind are:

- All test documents, including results, should be kept and placed under configuration control.
- Testers should always be independent of the designer since the temptation to show that one's module works is strong.

Static analysis

11.1 WHAT IS STATIC ANALYSIS?

In section 10.1.3 it was explained that static analysis was one particular technique for the review and analysis of source code. Indeed some of the tools available are powerful and enable the technique to be integrated into the design process. A practical example is given in this chapter.

The principle of static analysis involves operating on the source code to reveal facts and features in order for it to be compared with its specification for correctness. It does not involve executing the code – that is dynamic test, which is covered in Chapter 10.

A program is thus validated algebraically rather than for specific values of variables, as is the case with dynamic test.

Consider the following piece of code:

```
BEGIN
INTEGER A, B, C, D, E
A := 0
NEXT: INPUT C:
IF C < 0 THEN GOTO EXIT:
B := B + C
D := B/A
GOTO NEXT:
PRINT B, D;
EXIT: END;
```

Static analysis will detect that:

- B is not initialized before use.
- E is never used.
- A is zero and is used as a divisor.
- The PRINT B, D; command is never used because of the preceding statement.

The following sections describe three currently available tools.

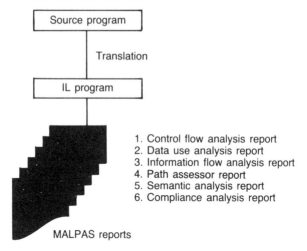

Fig. 11.1 Overview of MALPAS.

11.2 MALPAS

MALPAS was developed by Royal Signals and Radar Establishment (now DRA Malvern) and is currently supplied by TA Consultancy Services, Farnham, Surrey. Figure 11.1 gives an overview of the analysis process.

MALPAS is based on six analysis techniques, each of which investigates different aspects of a program. The analysis techniques may be applied separately but are often used sequentially with each successive technique revealing increasing detail about the program. The analysis techniques are:

1. *Control-flow analysis.* This analyser identifies the possible entry and exit points to the module, pieces of unreachable code and any infinitely looping dynamic halts. It gives an initial feel for the structure and quality of the program and is particularly useful when analysing assembly code lacking the high-level control structures.
2. *Data-use analysis.* This analyser identifies all the inputs and outputs of the module and checks that data is being correctly handled. For example, it checks that each variable is initialized before being used.
3. *Information-flow analysis.* Each procedure, within the code, is analysed to deduce the information on which each output depends. As well as discovering certain types of program errors, it is the first analysis technique to identify the functionality of the program.
4. *Path assessor.* This is used to provide a metric (see also Chapter 15) on the complexity of a procedure. The number of paths through the code

is reported for each procedure. This measure provides a direct relationship to the difficulty of testing the procedure, as well as indicating how difficult it will be to verify.

5. *Semantic analysis*. This identifies the actions taken on each feasible path through a procedure. In particular, it rewrites imperative, step-by-step procedures into a declarative, parallel assignment form. The analyst can use this to provide an alternative perspective on the function of the procedure. The result of the analyser is to tell the analyst the actual relationship of the variables to each other.

6. *Compliance analysis*. This attempts to prove that a procedure satisfies a specified condition. For example, compliance analysis could be used to check that the result of the procedure *sort* is a sequence of items where each item is bigger than the preceding one. The report from the compliance analysis identifies those input values for which the procedure will fail.

MALPAS is used on source code but, prior to carrying out the analysis, it is necessary to translate the source code into the MALPAS Intermediate Language (IL). This obviates the need for a different version of MALPAS to be written for each possible programming language. The translation of the source code into IL is possible for virtually any high-level language or assembly code and may be performed either by hand or by the use of an automatic translator. Several automatic translators are in existence for a variety of languages currently including Ada, C, Pascal, CORAL 66, PL/M-86, FORTRAN, ASM86 and 6809.

The following example, which is reproduced by kind permission of TA Consultancy Services, is more instructive than a theoretical description of each of the analysis techniques.

MALPAS example

This example consists of a short program intended to control the water-cooling system of a motor car fitted with a thermostat and an electric fan. The MALPAS reports are listed at the end of this chapter and are numbered MALPAS 1 to MALPAS 11. The specification for the program is as follows:

The thermostat aperture should be closed at a water temperature of 83°C (*tempclose*) and fully open at 96°C (*tempopen*) and should open linearly between the two temperatures. The fan should turn on at 95°C (*tempon*) and off at 86°C (*tempoff*). It is intended that the program should positively switch the fan on or off in order to prevent partial switching. Figure 11.2 illustrates these requirements.

The program has been implemented in Pascal and a listing of the

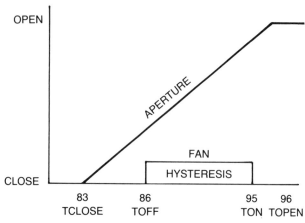

Fig. 11.2 MALPAS example.

source code is shown in MALPAS 1. Although the program is valid Pascal, it is not intended as an example of good coding practice. The basis for the implementation is the procedure *control* that satisfies the requirements outlined above. It is intended that this procedure is called repeatedly inside a control loop that also sets up the engine temperature variable *temp* and sets the aperture and fan from the variables *aperture* and *fan*. Note that the Pascal can be annotated with special comments ('@ DERIVES aperture ... etc....') which are used, later, by MALPAS.

Intermediate language translation

Pascal programs can be automatically translated into MALPAS Intermediate Language (IL) programs by using the Pascal translator and the IL program appears in MALPAS 2. This simple example could be manually translated but normally the automatic translator is needed.

The IL program consists of two sections, the first of these containing assorted declarations and the second being the procedure definitions (or PROC bodies). A clear similarity exists between the Pascal procedure definitions and the corresponding IL procedure definitions. This greatly helps in relating the analysis results back to the original Pascal program.

MALPAS analyses each procedure individually. This allows the analysis process to be broken down just as programs are broken into separate procedures. However, unlike the execution of a program, the analysis of the procedures can be performed concurrently. That is to say, there is no predefined order in which analysis must be done. In practice, the analysis is often performed 'bottom-up', where the analysis starts with those procedures which call no others, and continues with those procedures which only call analysed procedures. Using this approach, a picture of the behaviour of a program can be built up, although it must be emphasized that timing features cannot be addressed.

Note that each procedure has both a procedure definition and a separate procedure specification (or PROCSPEC). The procedure specification is used to define all the significant characteristics of the procedure, such as the inputs and outputs. The basic operation of MALPAS is to analyse the procedure definition and compare the results against its specification. In the case of Pascal, as with other high-level languages, the translator can suggest a procedure specification based on the Pascal procedure declaration. However, the specification can also record much more information, such as the relationship between the inputs and outputs. In our example, the Pascal annotations have been carried through to the IL, and indicate that the resulting values of the variables *aperture* and *fan* are dependent solely on the input value of the variable *temp*.

To aid in setting up the analysis sequence, one of the first things that MALPAS generates is a procedure call graph. Typically this is used to identify those procedures which call no others and so which will be analysed first.

Control-flow analysis

Control-flow analysis examines the structure of a procedure to identify all entry and exit points. It also identifies all loops with their entry and exit points. Ideally, in high integrity software, all procedures and all loops should be well structured with single entry and exit points. Control-flow analysis also reveals more serious errors within the program such as unreachable code and dynamic halts.

The report on the control-flow analysis is given in MALPAS 3. As with many of the analysis reports, it has two sections. The first is the analysis detail, and the second is a summary of any possible problems found. It is quite common for an analyst to look firstly at the summary section before going into the analysis detail. In our example, the summary reports a perfectly normal well structured control flow. In particular, there is no unreachable code and there are no dynamic halts. There is, therefore, no need to look further into the analysis detail.

This form of analysis is of most benefit when applied to assembly code because assembly code lacks the high-level language control constructs such as **if** and **while**. Also, it is common for assembly language programmers to minimize the space needed for their code, which can easily lead to poor structuring. MALPAS 3 also shows the graph which can be generated from the node structure.

Data-use analysis

Data-use analysis describes how data (i.e. variables and formal parameters) is used within the procedure and from this one can check, for example, that all outputs are written on each path through the procedure. This may be of particular benefit on a large procedure for checking the lists of specified inputs and outputs.

MALPAS 4 gives the report from the data-use analysis when applied to our example. The summary section has identified a possible error over the use of the parameter *aperture*. It tells us that, despite being classified as both an input and an output (INOUT), the initial value of the variable is never used. In fact, the error here is due to the classification of the parameter as INOUT (see MALPAS 2). This classification was suggested by the Pascal translator since in the original Pascal parameter *aperture* is a **var** parameter. If we wanted to, we could reclassify the parameter as an output only (OUT) and the error message would disappear.

The above example is highly typical of what happens during analysis. The summary reports a possible error, and the analyst can then focus attention on just that aspect of the program. MALPAS raises questions which prompt closer inspection of the code. It can be argued, therefore, that using MALPAS will make better use of the analyst's time by focusing the available effort on the areas of most importance. In this case, having addressed the issue, the analyst can move on to a more detailed study of the program.

The category R shows that *temp* is read every time the program runs (as one would hope). It can be seen from the category W that only *aperture* is updated every time the program runs. This is an early indication that all is not well since it was a requirement for the *fan* to be written (i.e. positively switched) every time. Notice that, in this example, there is nothing in the category A (written twice without an intervening read). This is nevertheless a useful category which could point to problems.

Information-flow analysis

Information-flow analysis identifies all the information upon which each output depends and provides an initial check that the procedure outputs are dependent upon the correct inputs. Also, if the dependencies are specified in a DERIVES list, it compares these against the calculated dependencies.

In the summary section of MALPAS 5 several possible errors are identified. The first of these is confirmation of the error reported earlier in the data-use analysis. In particular, the initial value of the parameter *aperture*, despite being classified as an input and output, has no effect on any of the procedure outputs. Again, if the parameter is reclassified as an output only this error message will be removed.

The second possible error relates to a discrepancy between the procedure definition and the procedure specification. The report indicates that the final value of the parameter *aperture* depends on more than just the parameter *temp* as specified in the derives. Examination of the analysis detail shows that all four additional dependencies are constants. MALPAS is correct in that the final value of *aperture* does (and should) depend upon these values, but it is common practice to simplify the procedure specification to identify only those variable dependencies. In this case there is no error, merely an acceptable simplifying of the procedure specification.

The third, and more important, possible error is concerned with the parameter *fan*. The list of discovered dependencies includes some constants that might be expected from the specification, such as *on*, *off*, *tempon* and *tempoff*. However, it is of interest that it *also* depends on the constants *tempopen* and *tempclose*, and on its own initial value (indicated by *fan* being in the list). The two constants are concerned with aperture opening and closing, and it is surprising to see that the fan is also affected by their value. The dependence of the parameter *fan* on its initial value might, at first sight, be surprising. However, if we consider that the fan must stay off until it gets hot, and then must remain on until the engine cools, then we can see fairly clearly that the fan is affected by its previous state.

Here we have started asking some in depth questions about the nature of the implementation. At this stage, the analyst can try to find answers to these questions, or simply hold them pending further analysis.

Finally, it is worth noticing that by identifying the parameters on which an output depends, this analysis can also help focus any dynamic testing that is being done. For example, since the parameter *aperture* depends only on the parameter *temp*, we can test the behaviour of the procedure with respect to the aperture output solely by varying the engine temperature. In this sense, MALPAS has identified the functionality of the procedure *control*.

Path assessor

MALPAS can count the number of paths through a procedure. This is a useful metric that indicates the procedure's complexity. For example, TA Consultancy Services has previously identified procedures with greater than 10^{10} paths through them. Now, it is impractical to test such procedures, and this sort of measure emphasizes that the procedure should be further decomposed. The report, in MALPAS 6, shows that there are six paths through our example program. This can be seen in the graph in MALPAS 3.

Semantic analysis

Semantic analysis is powerful as it describes the functional relationships between program inputs and outputs for each semantically possible path through the program. In other words, it describes the actions taken on each feasible path through the procedure body. Hence, for the whole range of procedure inputs, it will reveal exactly what the procedure outputs in all circumstances.

The analysis identifies each path through the procedure by a condition on the input values. For each path, the analysis reveals the actions taken when the path condition is met. The analyst should then compare this against the specification to decide if the procedure will behave correctly. To aid in this comparison, the results can be presented in several different formats, such as decision tables. This allows the analyst to choose an output format to suit the design documentation format.

MALPAS 7 shows one such report format for the semantic analysis of our example. In this format the IL is 'rewritten' as a multibranching IF conditional statement. Each branch of the conditional statement corresponds to a possible path through the procedure. Then, for each branch, the set of assignments that take place on that path are given.

In our example, semantic analysis has identified just five feasible paths through the procedure. Presumably #10#12#33#35 and #10#12#11#35 are logically the same (see MALPAS 3). MALPAS can identify the infeasible path, but it can also be found by inspection of the procedure. Referring back to the Pascal (MALPAS 1), after calculating the linear scaling for *aperture*, if the first following conditional (i.e. *temp > tempon*) is true, then the second following conditional (i.e. *temp > tempoff*) **AND** (*fan < > off*) will also be true. Therefore, the path through the code to take the first following branch, but not the second, is impossible.

A thing to note in the semantic analysis report is that whereas the specification defines what happens at 83°C, 96°C and in between, the program actually deals with what happens at strictly less than 83°C, strictly greater than 96°C and in between. Fortunately, substituting 83 and 96 for *temp* in the expression for *aperture* gives the correct values. Therefore, the code is correct, but could perhaps have been written to make this clearer.

The specification required that the value in aperture should be linearly dependent on *temp* between the two given temperatures. It is apparent that the expression given for *aperture* is indeed linear on *temp* and we have already established that it is correct at the two end points. Therefore, the first statement of the specification has been satisfied by the code.

Now consider the second statement of the specification relating to the output *fan*. The semantic analysis report tells us that the fan is turned on (i.e. *fan := on*) under any one of three conditions:

1. *temp* > 96} i.e. very hot
2. (*fan* = on) **and** (*temp* < 96) **and** (*temp* > 86) i.e. already on, but still fairly hot
3. *temp* = 96}

However, the specification requires that the fan is turned on at 95°C, which is not satisfied by any of these conditions. A similar assessment of when the fan is turned off (i.e. *fan* := *off*) reveals similar problems. Therefore, the procedure fails to satisfy the requirements of the second statement of the specification.

Other alternative report formats are shown in MALPAS 8 and MALPAS 9. In MALPAS 8 information is presented as a decision table. The conditions and assignments are all labelled, and the table at the bottom indicates the appropriate association for each path. MALPAS 9 is similar, but focuses on the conditions under which an assignment takes place.

The clear and precise description of the procedure provided by semantic analysis is invaluable for verifying the procedure code against its specification, either during code development or as part of a final assessment or certification exercise. This analysis is particularly useful for detecting subtle coding errors, either from the actions or from the predicates that determine those actions.

Another major benefit of this analysis is that it often reveals feasible paths through the procedure that the programmer was unaware of and may not have discovered despite extensive testing. In such cases it may be that the procedure will do something unexpected over a range of input conditions and, whilst such input values may be outside the design range for the system with only a very remote chance that the conditions will be encountered in practice, it is of great benefit for MALPAS to reveal the existence of such conditions and to identify what happens in those circumstances.

Compliance analysis

Compliance analysis is a further stage of detailed functional analysis. Whereas semantic analysis reveals what a procedure will do, compliance analysis compares what the procedure does against a specification. The specification needs to be encoded as a condition that relates the inputs and outputs after the procedure has executed.

An example is given in MALPAS 10, where a partial specification is defined for the procedure *control* in the POST clause of the procedure specification. The only aspect of the required behaviour that is defined is that 'The fan should be turned on at 95°C', and this is captured by the condition:

$$\text{POST ('temp} > = \text{tempon)} \rightarrow (\text{fan} = \text{on})$$

This may be read as 'if the temperature is greater than or equal to 95°C, then the fan should be on.'

Compliance analysis identifies the threat condition to the procedure. That is to say, the condition of the inputs under which the procedure will fail. If the procedure satisfies the specification, then the threat condition is *false* in that no inputs will cause the procedure to fail.

The report of the compliance analysis for this example is given in MALPAS 11. It has identified a threat to the procedure when the temperature reaches 95°C and the fan is not yet on. This confirms the assessment reached from the semantic analysis.

Conclusions

The example analysis given above gives an illustration of how MALPAS can be used in the verification of code. In this example, we have taken a small sample of Pascal and applied all the MALPAS analysis techniques to it. The analysis has found:

- good structured programming practice;
- errors introduced during the translation process (i.e. the classification of *aperture* as both input and output);
- good data handling;
- errors introduced when encoding the specification in IL (i.e. that the result in *fan* depends on the starting value of *fan*);
- correct behaviour of the implementation with respect to the aperture control;
- incorrect behaviour of the implementation with respect to the fan control.

Therefore, the procedure *control* fails to satisfy the specification. Whilst a small example is the best way to illustrate some of the possibilities of static analysis, large pieces of analysis have their own problems. Most of these are similar to the problems of writing large programs. For example, there can be problems associated with configuration control and the interfaces between separately analysed procedures. To date, MALPAS has been applied successfully to programs of up to 100 000 lines of source code, and this is not seen as an upper limit.

It is fair to say that the above example did not include any of the things which make analysis difficult nor provide the scope for a full presentation of MALPAS's capabilities.

Static analysis of programs containing interrupts is difficult since things can be happening 'behind one's back' and the technique cannot handle timing-related features of the software. It has been suggested, however, that to write programs that are easy to analyse, one only needs to apply all the good structured programming practices that should be applied for high-integrity software.

The best way forward is to build the use of static analysis into the software design cycle. The results can be fed into other parts of the development process, such as dynamic testing.

Static analysis can be as much a part of the development process as any other development tool.

MALPAS 1. Pascal Source Program

```pascal
program cool;
const
  tempclose   = 83;
  tempopen    = 96;
  tempon      = 95;
  tempoff     = 86;
  opened      = 100;
  closed      = 0;
type
  status      = (off, on);

procedure control    (temp : integer;
                      var aperture : integer;
                      var fan : status0 {@
DERIVES    aperture FROM temp,
           fan       FROM temp
};
  begin
    if temp < tempclose then begin
      aperture   := closed;
      fan        := off
    end
    else if temp > tempopen then begin
      aperture   := opened;
      fan        := on
    end
    else begin
      aperture   := opened  * (temp – tempclose)
                         div (tempopen – tempclose);
      if temp > tempon then
        fan:= on;
      if (temp > tempoff    and (fan < > off) then
        fan:= on
    end
  end
begin
end.
```

MALPAS 2. Intermediate Language Program

```
TITLE cool;
[Pascal to Malpas IL Translator – Release 3.0]

_INCLUDE/NOLIST "PASCALTX$DIR:FIXED.PREAMBLE"

TYPE status = (off,on);

CONST tempclose : integer = +83;
CONST tempopen : integer = +96;
CONST tempon : integer = +95;
CONST tempoff : integer = +86;
CONST opened : integer = +100;
CONST closed : integer = +0;

PROCSPEC control ( IN      temp : integer,
                   INOUT aperture : integer,
                   INOUT fan : status)
[*> BEGIN User IL]

DERIVES   aperture FROM temp,
          fan       FROM temp
[* > END User IL]
;

PROC control;
  IF temp < tempclose THEN
    aperture := closed;
    fan := off
  ELSE
    IF temp > tempopen THEN
      aperture := opened;
      fan := on
    ELSE
      aperture := opened * (temp – tempclose)
              DIV (tempopen – tempclose);
      IF temp > tempon THEN
        fan := on
      ENDIF;
      IF (temp > tempoff) AND (fan < > off) THEN
        fan := on
      ENDIF
    ENDIF
  ENDIF
ENDPROC [*control*]

FINISH
```

MALPAS 3. Control Flow Analysis Report

After ONE-ONE, 16 nodes removed. No nodes with self-loops removed.

Node id	No of predecessors	Successor nodes	
---------	--------------------	-----------------	
#START	0	#1	
#33	2	#35	
#35	2	#2	
#1	1	#2	#4
#2	3	#END	
#4	1	#2	#7
#7	1	#33	#10
#10	1	#11	#12
#11	2	#35	
#12	1	#33	#11
#END	1		

After KASAI (from One-ONE), No nodes removed. After HECHT (from ONE-ONE-, NO nodes removed. After HK (from HECHT), No nodes removed. After TOTAL (from HK), NO nodes removed.

Control Flow Summary
The procedure is well structured
The procedure has no unreachable code and no dynamic halts.
The graph was fully reduced after the following stages:
   ONE-ONE, KASAI, HECHT, HK, TOTAL
The graph was not fully reduced after the following stages:
   None

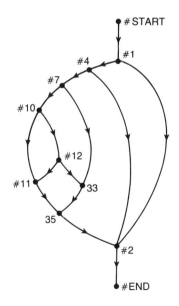

MALPAS 4. Data Use Analysis Report

Key

= = =

H = Data read and not subsequently written on some path between the nodes

I = Data read and not previously written on some path between the nodes

A = Data written twice with no intervening read on some path between the nodes

U = Data written and not subsequently read on some path between the nodes

V = Data written and not previously read on some path between the nodes

R = Data read on all paths between the nodes

W = Data written on all paths between the nodes

E = Data read on some path between the nodes

L = Data written on some path between the nodes

After ONE-ONE

From node	To node	Data Use Expression
#START	#END	H : fan temp
		I : fan temp
		U : aperture fan
		V : aperture fan
		R : temp
		W : aperture
		E : fan temp
		L : aperture fan

Summary of Possible Errors

= = = = = = = = = = = = =

INOUTs always written but whose initial values are never read: aperture

MALPAS 5. Information Flow Analysis Report

Information Flow
= = = = = = = =

After ONE-ONE

  From node #START to node #END

                Identifier   may depend on identifier(s)

                aperture   INs/OUTs   : temp
                              CONSTANTs   : closed opened
                                              tempclose tempopen

                fan   INs/OUTs   : fan temp
                              CONSTANTs   : off on tempclose
                                              tempoff tempon
                                              tempopen

Summary of Possible Errors
= = = = = = = = = = = = = =

The set of INOUTs not affecting INOUTs or OUTs
is as follows   : aperture

Information Flow dependencies not in DERIVES
aperture   : closed opened tempclose tempopen
fan   : fan off on tempclose tempoff tempon
                 tempopen

MALPAS 6. Path Assessor Report

Path Assessor Output
= = = = = = = = = =

After ONE-ONE
  From   To
  Node   Node   Number of paths
#START   #END   6

MALPAS 7. Semantic Analysis Report

After ONE-ONE

From node : #START
To node   :   #END

IF temp < 83
THEN MAP

  aperture := 0;
  fan := off;

ENDMAP
[————————————————————————————————————]
ELSIF temp > 96
THEN MAP

  aperture := 100;
  fan := on;

ENDMAP
[————————————————————————————————————]
ELSIF (temp > 82) AND (temp < 87) OR (fan = off) AND
      (temp > 82) AND (temp < 96)
THEN MAP

  aperture := (100 * temp – 8300) DIV 13;

ENDMAP
[————————————————————————————————————]
ELSIF (fan = on) AND (temp < 96) AND (temp > 86)
THEN MAP

  aperture := (100 * temp – 8300) DIV 13;
  fan := on;

ENDMAP
[————————————————————————————————————]
ELSIF temp = 96
THEN MAP

  aperture := (100 * temp – 8300) DIV 13;
  fan := on;

ENDMAP ENDIF

MALPAS 8. Semantic Analysis Decision Tables Report

After ONE-ONE

From node : #START
TO node : #END

Conditions
==========

C1: temp > 82
C2: temp > 96
C3: temp > 86
C4: fan = off
C5: temp > 95
C6: fan = on
C7: temp = 96

Actions
=======

Assignments to aperture
  A11: 0
  A12: 100
  A13: (100 * temp − 8300) DIV 13

Assignments to fan
  A21: off
  A22 on

Paths Table
===========

Conditions	Paths					
	1	2	3/1	3/2	4	5
C1	F		T	T		
C2		T				
C3			F		T	
C4				T		
C5				F	F	
C6					T	
C7						T
aperture	A11	A12	A13	A13	A13	A13
fan	A21	A22			A22	A22

[————————————————————————————————————]

MALPAS 9. Semantic Analysis Transformations Report

After ONE-ONE

From node : #START
To node   :   #END

Conditions
= = = = =

    C1:   temp > 82
    C2:   temp > 96
    C3:   temp > 86
    C4:   fan = off
    C5:   temp > 95
    C6:   fan = on
    C7:   temp = 96

Actions
= = = =

Assignments to aperture
    A11: 0
    A12: 100
    A13: (100 * temp – 8300) DIV 13

Assignments to fan
    A21: off
    A22: on

Transforms Table
= = = = = = = = = = = = = = = =

	C1	C2	C3	C4	C5	C6	C7	Action
aperture	F							A11
		T						A12
							T	A13
OR	T		F					A13
OR	T			T	F			A13
OR			T		F	T		A13
fan	F							A21
		T						A22
OR							T	A22
OR			T		F	T		A22
	T		F					NA
OR	T			T	F			NA

[———————————————————   ————————————————————————————————]

MALPAS 10. Augmented Intermediate Language Program

TITLE cool;

[Pascal to Malpas IL Translator – Release 3.0]

–INCLUDE/NOLIST "PASCALTX$DIR:FIXED.PREAMBLE"

REPLACE (a, b : boolean) a ⟶ **b**
BY NOT a OR b;

TYPE status = (off,on);

CONST tempclose : integer = +83;
CONST tempopen : integer = +96;
CONST tempon : integer = +95;
CONST tempoff : integer = +86;
CONST opened : integer = +100;
CONST closed : integer = +0;

PROCSPEC control (IN   temp : integer
             INOUT aperture : integer,
             INOUT fan : status)
[*> BEGIN User IL]

DERIVES   aperture FROM temp,
            fan   FROM temp
[*> END User IL]
POST ('temp >= tempon) ⟶ (fan = on)
;

PROC control;
  IF temp < tempclose THEN
    aperture := closed;
    fan := off
  ELSE
    If temp > tempopen THEN
      aperture := opened;
      fan := on
    ELSE
      aperture := opened * (temp – tempclose)
                  DIV (tempopen – tempclose);
      IF temp > tempon THEN
        fan := on
      ENDIF;
      IF (temp > tempoff) AND (fan <> off) THEN
        fan := on
      ENDIF
    ENDIF
  ENDIF
ENDPROC [*control*]

FINISH

MALPAS 11. Compliance Analysis Report

After ONE-ONE

From node : #START
To node   : #END

_threat := (temp = 95) AND (fan = off)

11.3 SPADE

SPADE was developed at Southampton University and is now available from Program Validation Ltd, Southampton, UK. It also involves an intermediate language known as Functional Description Language (FDL). An FDL model of a program can be constructed automatically, using a translator, or by hand. FDL is not a programming language but a method of describing a program in terms of states and transitions. Figure 11.3 represents the structure of SPADE.

This automatic translation is available for Pascal, INTEL 8080 and a Modula 2 version. An Ada subset, called SPARK, is also available. This is a limited subset of Ada intended for the implementation of safety-critical software. SPADE can currently be run on DEC VAX machines (including Micro Vax II and 11/730) under the VMS (Virtual Memory System) operating system.

SPADE consists of a number of 'flow analysers' and 'semantic analysers' as follows:

- *Control-flow analyser*. This addresses the control flow and loop structure of the program and reports on unused code, multiple entry and similar faults.
- *Data-flow analyser*. This seeks undefined data variables and unused definitions.
- *Information-flow analyser*. This constructs the relationships between inputs and outputs and checks their consistency with the specification. It will, as a result, indicate ineffective statements and variables.
- *Partial-program extractor*. Taking a specified variable, the partial program extractor identifies just those statements which affect that value. These are then assembled as a 'partial program'.
- *Verification-condition generator*. This describes the path functions and the conditions under which they are executed. Verification can thus be carried out if a specification is provided.
- *Symbolic interpreter*. The text is executed and paths are identified. Data-flow errors, check statements and run time tests are included.
- *Theorem checker*. This proofchecker (written in PROLOG) permits verification at an arithmetic/logical level.

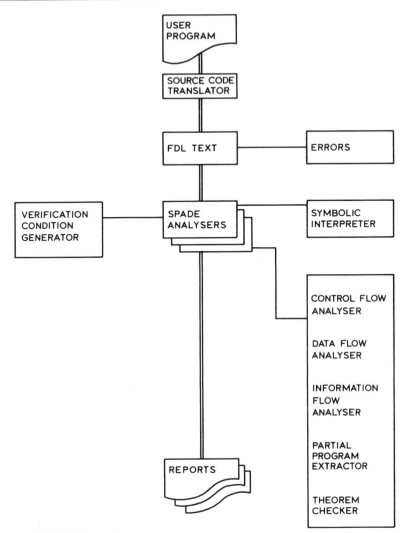

Fig. 11.3 SPADE overview.

11.4 TESTBED (LDRA)

Formally known as LDRA, TESTBED was developed by Liverpool Data
Research Associates and is now marked by Program Analysers Ltd of
Newbury, Berkshire, UK.

TESTBED involves dynamic as well as static analysis and is therefore
also included in section 10.2. It is available for CORAL 66, Pascal,

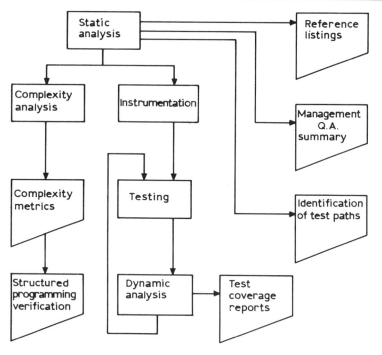

Fig. 11.4 TESTBED overview.

FORTRAN, COBOL, PL/1, C, PL/M86 and Ada and will run on UNIX, IBM, VAX, SUN and GOULD systems.

TESTBED identifies program paths as a number of path fragments during static analysis of control flow. It generates reference listings and management quality assurance summaries. The user may then subject the software to complexity analysis which will produce complexity metrics and structured programming verification reports. Figure 11.4 gives an outline of the TESTBED structure. The dynamic testing aspects are described in section 10.2.

Languages and processors | 12

12.1 PROGRAMMING LANGUAGE – THE COMMUNICATION MEDIUM

The process of translating a design into some particular programming language is known as programming. Traditionally the coding phase has always been emphasized at the expense of the rest of the life cycle. This is understandable since the programmer enjoys communicating with the computer and the means of doing this is by coding instructions via a mutually understood language.

Strictly speaking this is not true since the original source code, created by the programmer, has to be translated into a form that the computer can understand. Nevertheless it remains that the programming language is perceived as the medium through which the programmer expresses an interpretation of the design. This can be in a recognized code or in a formal methodology such as has been described in Chapters 8 and 9.

The number of programming languages is large. Even a specific language may have numerous variations. Languages fall into three main groups:

1. procedural;
2. declarative;
3. object-oriented.

The type of language with which most programmers are familiar is known as **procedural** (sometimes called **imperative**). Included in this group are FORTRAN, Pascal and Ada.

Programming in a procedural language involves 'prescribing' the manner in which the computer is to go about solving the problem. That is to say, one explicitly specifies the control flow and algorithms necessary to carry out a given computation.

Another group consists of languages known as **declarative** (sometimes called **applicative**). These specify the form of the problem (i.e. 'what'), but do not prescribe the algorithm.

These two language categories tend to be used in different problem areas. There is now considerable interest in declarative languages such as LISP and PROLOG for use over a wide range of problems.

As a further illustration of the difference between procedural and declarative languages, consider a program for taking the last two elements of a list and swapping them if $k-1$ is bigger than k. It then decrements k and keeps going back through the list until $k-1$ is smaller than k. The outer loop ensures that this is repeated for the whole list (i.e. a bubble sort).

The procedural language, C, might define the means of computing the solution by, for example:

```
sort (v,n)
int v[ ], n;
{
  int j, k, temp;
  for (j=0; j<n, j++)
    for (k=n; j<k; k- -)
      if (v[k-1] > v[k])
        {temp = v[k-1];
         v[k-1] = v[k];
         v[k] = temp
        }
}
```

A declarative language, however, would proceed differently. This PROLOG sort program uses recursion to deconstruct the list and then put the elements back together in order. If $X < Y$ then they are put in the right order in the reconstructed list Z. If $X < Y$ then it recursively deconstructs Z until the right place is found. The second clause for sort unifies the input list Xs with the beginning of the, to be constructed, output list Ys.

```
sort ([X | Xs], Ys) :- sort (Xs,Zs), insert (X,Ys,Zs).
sort ([ ],[ ]).
insert (X, [ ], [X]).
insert (X, [Y | Ys], [Y | Zs]) :- X > Y, insert (X,Ys,Zs).
insert (X, [Y | Ys], [X,Y | Ys]) :- X < = Y.
```

Apart from a large variety of languages there are also programming differences which arise from the type of application involved. The term 'real-time' is used for any processing system which must respond to external events, or stimuli, within some period of time. For example an automatic teller machine, outside a bank, is a real-time system since it must respond immediately to customer demands for information and money and must interface with data in the bank. Most real-time systems involve physical outputs which are used to operate electrical and mechanical equipment. Safety and control systems are nearly always real-time since they involve responding to plant and operator commands and provide actual commands to operate plant and safety equipment.

On the other hand, a piece of software which performs payroll calculations is not a real-time system since it has only to produce information and causes no actual outputs (other than a printer) to be actuated.

Because of the need for a response with real-time systems, the computer language must have certain attributes over and above those used for non real-time applications. FORTRAN and COBOL are not real-time languages in that they do not have the necessary constructs which allow one to respond to those external stimuli.

Some manufacturers of compilers do, however, provide add-on facilities to allow the language to cope with real-time applications. Those languages were not designed with real-time applications in mind and will not, therefore, be efficient with add-on facilities.

More recently, languages have been designed specifically for real-time applications, the best known being Ada and Modula 2.

The choice of a language for a particular application is not easy and is often made as a result of factors other than the programming problem. For example, it may have been decided that, because of a harsh environment, only one type of computer hardware is suitable. If that machine can only be programmed in, say, FORTRAN, then the choice is narrowed to one. Then the system and software designers have to adapt their design such that the use of FORTRAN can achieve the design aims.

With the recent adoption, by various government agencies, of 'standard' languages with validated compilers (e.g. Pascal and Ada) the problem has now been reversed. Often the situation is that a language is specified and the task is to select a system which is compatible.

Figure 12.1 provides a summary of the language types. First-generation languages are in fact machine code which was, in the 1960s, what was used to program computers. Second-generation languages are the assembler codes which allow binary commands to be replaced with relatively low-level alphanumeric commands. Third-generation languages permit far higher levels of sophistication within each command and include both the procedural and declarative languages already mentioned. They also include the 'object-oriented' languages which are also addressed in this chapter. Fourth-generation languages are normally associated with the commercial world, typically database applications. They enable data to be processed and sorted with high-level commands and are also described in this chapter.

It sometimes occurs that specific (bit level) functions are required for which the high-level language cannot cope. In this case it is possible to include segments of assembler code within the high-level code. This carries

1st Generation	**MACHINE CODE**
	10101110 10010001

2nd Generation	**ASSEMBLER**
	8085, Z80, 6800 etc.

3rd Generation   **HIGH LEVEL LANGUAGE**

Procedural (line by line instructions)

Pascal	CORAL 66
BASIC	etc.

Declarative (state the problem)

LISP	Hope
PROLOG	(FORTH)

Object Oriented (models)

SMALLTALK

4th Generation   **DATA BASED (not real time)**

MANTIS
CICS
SQL

Fig. 12.1 Language types.

a far higher possibility of making errors and is therefore discouraged by many standard and guidance documents.

12.2 COMPILERS AND ASSEMBLERS

Figure 12.2 introduces a number of terms relating to computer languages and places them in context. Machine code is the binary logic (1s and 0s) which can be handled by the central processing unit (CPU) of the computer. This is far removed from the 'source code' commands which are written by the programmer. These can be in high-level language (Pascal, FORTRAN, BASIC, etc.) or in an assembler code. Procedural high-level languages are very similar to each other and consist of statements as shown in the example in Chapter 11. They include complex commands, each of which requires many sequential actions at the machine-code level. An example is the command GOSUB, which requires the control flow to be routed to a different address in the program memory whilst storing the information necessary to return at the appropriate command. The **compiler**, which is the program which converts the

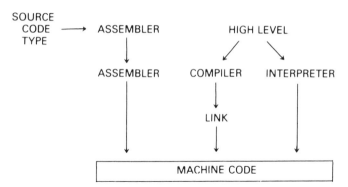

Fig. 12.2 Some important terms.

high-level instructions into machine code, must convert all the statements into sufficiently detailed binary code for the computer to carry out the functions defined. A compiler also requires a **linker** to integrate compiled modules of code.

Since the instructions of a declarative language are of a higher level than those in procedural languages their compilers are therefore more complex.

Assembler code is not dramatically different from high-level code. It is a procedural language but does not contain the rich 'packaged' commands available in a high-level language. Assembler programming, therefore, entails more lines of instructions than are necessary in a high-level language. For example, the square root command would have to be programmed by use of simpler arithmetic commands. The 'compiler' equivalent for converting assembler code into machine code is known as an **assembler**.

Figure 12.2 also makes reference to an **interpreter**. The most commonly used interpreter is the BASIC interpreter. It differs from the compiler in that as each source command is entered it is subject to a syntactical check and then executed, thus enabling the program to be 'tested' as it is entered. The compiler, on the other hand, takes the complete source code and converts it in one action.

The great emphasis on the use of high-level languages, together with efforts to standardize them, has led to the production of language-validation suites. The use of high-level language confers many benefits (e.g. high-level functions in a single instruction) but has an associated drawback. Thus, the programmer is dependent on the skill of the compiler writer to generate machine code which accurately models his use of the language commands. Also, the difficulties of portability (dealt with later) impact on this feature.

Compiler-validation suites have therefore been developed in order to exercise compilers against a standard and to provide deviance checks. Some suites extend to checking quality and performance factors such as speed of compilation. The development of these suites is expensive and difficult. Furthermore they need to be kept under constant review in order to be effective and to meet the needs of users.

Because Ada is, itself, a standard, an Ada compiler can take that name only if it passes the validation tests. The US government now requires that all Pascal development done on government projects uses a validated Pascal compiler. The UK MOD Defence Standard 00-55 imposes similar requirements.

For the above reasons the use of languages for which there are no formal standards or no validated compilers is becoming rarer. Nevertheless, they will continue to be useful for some time and it is essential that such compilers and languages are carefully reviewed, especially in the context of safety-related systems.

12.3 PROGRAM FEATURES

12.3.1 Program structures

At the higher levels, instructions are usually written in modules in order to facilitate readability and testing. Some general rules for defining and sizing modules were discussed in Chapter 7.

At the basic level languages have a syntax with control structures which utilize three types of construct:

1. *Sequence commands*, which involve forwards flow through the program. Arithmetic commands, print commands, input commands all imply that the next function to be executed will be the next in the sequence of instructions.
2. *Selection commands*, which involve a jump to another part of the sequence of instructions or a choice followed by a jump. Examples are GOTO, GOSUB, IF > THEN > ELSE.
3. *Iteration* which involves looping back to repeat a specific sequence of instructions until some condition is satisfied. In the example of code, earlier in this chapter, the IF command involves a DO WHILST concept.

Some of these constructs (e.g. IF > THEN > ELSE) enable block structuring of the code, and hence support the concept of structured programming. Others (e.g. GOTO) do not and can adversely affect a program's readability. Most modern third-generation procedural languages are block structured.

12.3.2 Simplicity

Perhaps the overriding requirement for a language is for it to be inherently simple. Achieving this leads to a number of advantages with respect to training, maintainability and portability. PLC languages are generally simpler than conventional high-level languages. They represent such a large group of languages and have their own specific advantages and drawbacks that a separate section of this chapter is devoted to them.

The OCCAM language, developed for the INMOS transputer, is another example of a language designed for a specific need but with simplicity as the uppermost requirement.

12.3.3 Security

A secure language is one which is able to deal with errors made during programming or which occur during running. Because software needs to be reliable it is necessary that the language intrinsically allows one to create reliable programs.

The first stage in this is for programming errors to be easily identified and detected. This is partly a feature of the compiler (or translator) which would be expected to recognize all syntactical errors. The cost of correction at this stage is small compared with the costs of error correction during testing or field use.

Strong data typing is one of the most important features of security. This involves being forced to declare variables and to state the type (e.g. alphanumeric, logic statement, binary number, integer). For example, volume and length could be derived from a mass variable but a length value could not be assigned to a volume variable. Also Js and Ks, assigned to loop counters, must initially be declared as integer types. All this helps to prevent erroneous use of variables in expressions and forces the programmer to think more clearly about the way in which data is to be handled and transformed.

Another feature is the detection of run-time errors which are faults not detected during compilation. Thus, if an error condition occurs which is outside the predicted scope of the program, facilities are provided to deal with it before it leads to a failure.

12.3.4 Adaptability

With real-time systems the language must allow the programmer sufficient flexibility to deal with the outside environment. In other words commands to the real-time outputs need to be able to deal with many types of exotic peripheral. The alternative, which involves resorting to blocks of assembler code, greatly jeopardizes the integrity of the system. The practice is strongly discouraged by some standards (see Chapter 5) and the language should be able to cope with the real-time operations needed.

12.3.5 Readability

An easy-to-read, and thus more easily understood, program is particularly important in terms of:

- review;
- test;
- modification.

Modification particularly requires good readability since the modifier may well not be the same person, nor have access to the original person, who wrote the code.

FORTRAN does little to enforce readability, whereas Pascal and Ada lend themselves to good structure, and hence readability, by virtue of their block structure.

12.3.6 Portability

The idea of language portability has been around for some time but its realization in an actual language has taken many years to effect. This is the requirement to be able to move code between different machines. Inevitably there has to be compromise because often the design of a compiler takes account of the architecture of the underlying hardware, thus reducing or even preventing machine portability.

An example of portability is the ISO definition of Pascal which allows developers to be confident of the portability of programs between systems/machines which support the standard.

12.3.7 Efficiency

Efficiency in a language has a number of distinct and often conflicting aspects. Until the recent fall in the cost of hardware, one of the most important considerations was the efficient use of available memory. It was often necessary to go to extreme lengths to squeeze a program into the available memory, often to the detriment of some of the other requirements described in this section.

As well as memory, speed of execution is another aspect of efficiency. In real-time systems the response to external stimuli is usually important.

With the relative decrease in hardware cost, speed and memory are much less the constraining factors than they once were. Thus the onus of obtaining efficient programs falls more on the language designer and compiler writer than the applications programmer.

12.3.8 Concurrency

One of the most important facilities of a real-time language is its apparent ability to execute several actions simultaneously. This is related to the concept of multitasking, which is the ability to appear to execute more than one task simultaneously. This can be achieved in one of two ways:

1. dividing up the processor (CPU) time between the tasks and relying upon the fact that the processing speed is so fast compared with the real-time events that processing appears to be simultaneous;
2. providing a multiple processing architecture (more than one CPU) and an appropriate synchronizing mechanism.

An obvious difficulty of achieving concurrency is that some or all of the concurrent tasks may be dependent on each other. Arrangements therefore have to be made to ensure that some tasks are completed before others are allowed to begin.

In the Ada language this is achieved by a facility known as the 'rendezvous' which allows two tasks to communicate.

Another technique is to use a message-passing arrangement in which all task interaction is via the transmission of messages.

A common approach in high-level languages is to use a construct known as the buffer.

A necessary facility, for real-time systems, is a clock for delaying tasks or for waiting until a specific time.

12.4 PLCs AND THEIR LANGUAGES

There is an important difference between conventional high-level languages, used on mainframe, mini and PC architectures, and PLCs (programmable logic controllers). This is that any high-level language can be applied to any machine given that a compiler is available. For PLCs, however, there is usually only a single compiler per machine, so the choice of a proprietary PLC fixes the language to be used. Processor and language issues cannot therefore be split.

Safety issues arise here because choice of a PLC imposes the disadvantages of any specific PLC instruction set. Some PLC languages are known to contain 'unhygienic' features which can readily lead to errors.

The earlier comments concerning compiler validation apply equally here. It is advisable to seek formal certification or, if that is not available, evidence of satisfactory extensive field use.

PLCs tend to use simpler language sets, many of which closely resemble the ladder notation based on hardware relay logic diagrams. Different manufacturers use different notations. They vary in complexity from simple ladder logic to branching and multitasking languages similar to the procedural high-level languages.

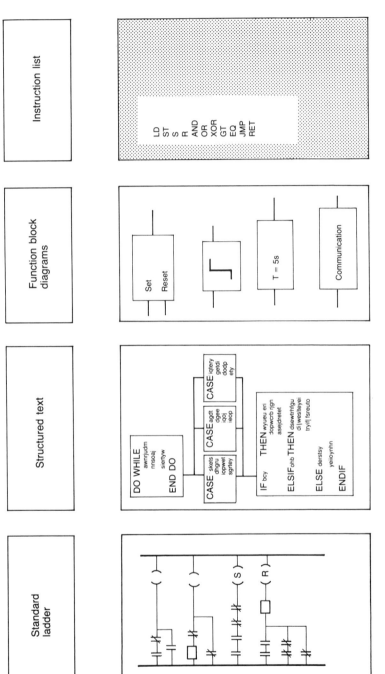

Fig. 12.3 Programmable logic controllers: languages in IEC 1131-3.

Some proposals for standardization have been outlined by the IEC standard 1131, which describes four types of PLC languages (Fig. 12.3).

1. *The standard ladder* is a graphical representation of the logic.
2. *Structured text* is a form of block-structured high-level language.
3. *Functional block diagrams* are also graphical. The identities of the blocks take on specific functions as, for example, timers and re-sets.
4. *Instruction list* is somewhat like assembler code, being a low-level language. Currently it is not widely used.

12.5 SOME RECOMMENDATIONS

When choosing and using languages there are a number of guidelines which should be taken into account.

The validated compilers, referred to earlier, often apply to specific subsets (hygienic subsets) of a language. It is advisable to make use of one of these hygienic subsets. These are available for Pascal and Ada but **not** for PLCs.

Static analysis, described in Chapter 11, should be applied wherever a translator is available. Unfortunately, one of the major disadvantages of PLCs at present is that static analysis translators do not exist.

If neither validated compiler nor static analysis is a possibility, then

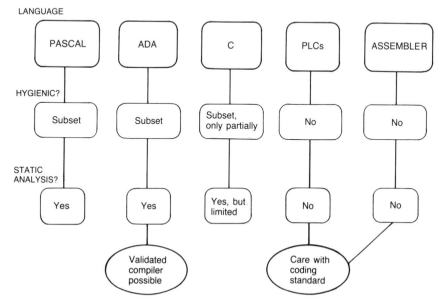

Fig. 12.4 Desirable language features for safety.

PROGRAMMERS

DESIGN AIDS

CODING PROGRAMS

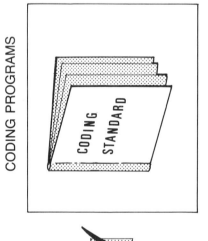

(a)

(b)

develop a coding standard which describes preferred constructs and forbids specific practices.

Always use a structured (top-down) analysis and apply block structuring to the source code (including with PLCs).

Restrict the size of modules as described in Chapter 7 and control entry and exit points.

Use standard versions of languages. Use the IEC 1131 standard with PLCs.

Ensure that programmers are experienced in both the language itself and the particular area of application.

Make use of CASE tools and other design aids wherever they are available.

Where safety is a particular criterion then the recommendations become more important. Figure 12.4 compares some language options often considered in safety-related systems and Fig. 12.5 summarizes these thoughts in general.

12.6 CURRENT LANGUAGES

It is worth while considering the languages currently available and their areas of application.

12.6.1 Procedural languages

Ada

Ada grew out of the realization that, in defence software development in the United States, many different languages were in use. No standard existed for defence work, particularly for embedded real-time systems. The language was selected in 1979 and a draft ANSI standard produced in 1980. The 1983 version is proposed as an ISO standard and compilers are available for a number of host machines, including the DEC VAX, although many more are in preparation. Problems have been revealed and overcome but it is likely that Ada compilers will always consume more computing power than others. Nevertheless this will be far offset by gains in programmer productivity and program reliability.

In particular, Ada addresses the needs of real-time systems, especially from the point of view of security. Ada is a strongly typed language with facilities for 'information hiding' and is strongly biased towards top-down design. Some critics have viewed it as highly complex, which makes it harder to verify. The verification problem has, to some extent, been addressed by the production of Ada subsets.

Ada is supported by a development environment which includes a context-sensitive editor and configuration management tools.

Pascal

Developed from ALGOL in the 1960s and 1970s, and originally intended as a language for teaching purposes, Pascal has grown in recent years to become a full development language. It was designed to encourage a top-down approach to system design and programming, whereby nested sub-routines reflect a successive decomposition of the design into subsystems and modules. The language constructs are 'block-structured' and thus Pascal supports structured programming.

The introduction of an ISO/BSI standard in 1983 and the development of a Pascal compiler validation suite provided a further boost to the language. Processors for the ISO standard are available for most systems and Pascal is now one of the most popular languages.

Modula 2

Modula 2 grew out of the work done by N. Wirth on Pascal and is intended to correct some of the problems identified in Pascal, and also to achieve the same goals as Ada within a simpler framework. All Modula 2 programs are made up of separately compilable modules, each of which contains details of the external and internal objects. It is highly readable. A draft standard for the language is being prepared.

C

This is a controversial language since many would say that it cannot be made hygienic. One reason for this is the use of pointers which themselves are treated as variables. Thus, addresses can be changed by various programming features. Such features confound predictability and, for example, can preclude the use of static analysis. Nevertheless C is powerful and continues to gain in popularity.

UNIX is closely related to C and thus C is seen, by many, as the language to use for UNIX-based systems.

It is a high-level language which allows access to features normally only visible in assembler.

FORTRAN

FORTRAN now dates back over 30 years and yet it is still in widespread use. Originally it was completely unstructured, whereas more recent versions introduce some structured concepts. It has been widely used for scientific and engineering applications.

CORAL 66

This was the preferred language of the UK MOD for real-time embedded systems, for many years. It has also been widely used for industrial and commercial control systems. It has largely been replaced by Ada, Pascal and C.

COBOL

This still dominates the commercial applications field. It was originated by the US DOD. Attention was paid to good data management and fast I/O.

BASIC

Stands for Beginners All-purpose Symbolic Instruction Code. It is available on all small computers and has become the universal language for engineers and other do-it-yourself programmers. Many versions exist, most of which permit instructions to be input, via an interpreter, for immediate response. There are also BASIC compilers available.

Its disadvantage is that it is not a structured language but nevertheless continues to be very popular although, as more engineers learn formal software engineering techniques during their education, the trend to use other, more hygienic, languages has begun.

ALGOL 60

This was the first truly structured language and was developed to provide all the now accepted language structures necessary for the design of good programs. CORAL 66 was heavily based on ALGOL.

APL

This stands for a programming language. It is an IBM-developed language which uses special symbols and keyboards to provide a very powerful and succinct language for modelling.

PL/1

Another IBM language which is somewhat like ALGOL. PL/M is the microprocessor version.

12.6.2 Declarative languages

These languages are problem-oriented rather than procedure-oriented as has been described earlier. They manipulate functions rather than data and combine the primitive functions (e.g. $+$, $*$, $\sqrt{}$) to form a final function, namely the program. The program is then applied to the input data.

They are likely to lead to the solution of a much larger class of problem in the future.

PROLOG

This is probably the best known of the declarative languages. The appearance of PROLOG was mainly connected with the growth of interest in expert systems. It is seen as a good vehicle for developing those systems although its applications are not confined to that purpose. As higher-performance computers become available PROLOG is likely to see even wider use.

LISP

This was developed by John McCarthy at MIT in the late 1950s and is a highly specialized language for the area of artificial intelligence. Since declarative languages are concerned with difficult ill-defined problems, the task of the programmer is no longer simply to code a procedural solution (see earlier example) but rather to explore the problem for possible solutions.

LISP was designed as an interactive language so that a program interacts with the programmer to support experimentation with new ideas. Any LISP implementation is supplied with aids for program development, such as editors.

HOPE

This is a functional programming language in which each function is represented by a set of equations that, together, provide a result for the whole range of functional arguments. A program is a hierarchy of these functions with an invocation of the highest-level function. HOPE allows the programmer to define specific (polymorphic) data types that are checked by the compiler. These types allow for the creation of functions that can be applied to more than one type of data, for example a routine that can set numbers, characters, strings or records.

As an example one can define *max* in the following way. The function definition comes in two parts. First is the declaration and then one or more recursion equations.

First declare the argument and result types:

dec max:num#num→num

dec is a reserved word meaning 'a declaration'. In this example the two numbers are arguments which return a single number as a result of the function.

The next step is to give the types of the arguments:

where:

num means 'an integer';
means 'and a';
→ means 'yields'.

Now, only one recursion equation is needed to define the function *max*:

—max (x,y) < = **if** x > y **then** x **else** y

where:

— means 'the value of'
< = means 'is defined as'.

Now, a program using *max* might read:

max(10,20) + max(1,max(2,3))

This would yield the answer 23.

As a further example we will use this *max* function to define a new function '*max* of 3':

— max of 3 (x,y.z) < = max(x,max(y,z))

FORTH

This was designed by Charles Moore in the 1960s. FORTH is difficult to classify into these chapter sections. It is a little like LISP but also contains some assembler functions. One of the disadvantages of high-level languages is the relative inefficiency of the compilers which need to take account of a large number of hardware architectures.

Assemblers, on the other hand, are specific to a processor and can be made more efficient. FORTH steers a middle course between these two extremes.

A key feature of FORTH is the stack which, unlike most high-level applications, is controlled directly by the programmer. It has a high degree of programmer interaction and fast execution speeds.

12.6.3 Object-oriented languages

The conventional approach is based on the ideas of program and data. Programs manipulate data which is, both conceptually and in terms of storage, separate from the program logic. Therefore, when a change occurs to a process the logic will change and perhaps the data. If the data structure is changed then, probably, other programs that access that data will have to be changed as well.

The problem could be diminished by this third-generation object-oriented approach in which software is designed as a number of **objects**, independent of their environment. The idea is that an object consists of some data and a set of operations to be performed on that data. The particular object behaviour is initialized by some other object which requires that particular function/service.

An object's state is defined by the values, at any time, of its attributes which can only be changed by the receipt of messages. Objects will also have pre- and postconditions which have to be satisfied before an incoming message can be acted on. Once an object has been defined other objects can make use of those functions by a form of inheritance. Data within an object is not, as such, available to other objects – only the functions of the object can be accessed since data, divorced from the logic which manipulates it, is not necessarily usable.

Object-oriented software is thus more maintainable and lends itself well to reuse.

SMALLTALK

SMALLTALK 80 is one such object-oriented language. Objects can include integers (a familiar concept from the foregoing languages) but also any other group (e.g. lists, dictionaries, fire detectors).

A further breakdown of classification introduces **class**. Thus, a set of objects which are of the same type can be classified. Each object in a class is known as an instance so 'classes' and 'instances' are not dissimilar to 'types' and 'variables' in Pascal.

They emulate by means of setting up models and the first step in programming is to define the classes and objects.

Others

C++ and Objective C are derivatives of C and support object-orientation.

12.6.4 Fourth-generation languages

These are evolving through a need for commercial programming environments which achieve greater productivity. They are normally associated with specific databases and are not used for process-control applications.

Examples of fourth-generation languages include FOCUS, CICS and MANTIS.

13 | Achieving fault tolerance in design

A frequent misconception is that the elimination of errors during design is the sole factor in achieving quality software. This is too simplistic an assumption. In practice all software is likely to contain residual faults, albeit at very low levels, after extensive debug and quality activities. Compare, therefore, two safety systems, one of which has some low level of unknown residual faults and another which has double the number. Assume that the code having the greater number of faults has been carefully structured and limited in its ability to access variables and code in such a way as to restrict the propagation of errors. Assume, also, that there are a number of error check routines in the code which enable the program to reinitialize at known acceptable values when an error is detected. If, in addition to these features, the safety system and its software are designed in such a way that individual failures do not cause total loss of function, then it will at least continue to offer a degraded level of protection. An example of the latter is a fire protection system which measures more than one parameter (i.e. UV light, smoke, rate of temperature rise). The interpretation of each type of input and the generation of the executive output action could be dealt with by separate parts of the hardware and software. This fault-tolerant type of design offers a far higher level of integrity than the system which, despite containing fewer faults, implies worse consequences in the event of failure.

There are many hardware design and system configuration features which have a direct influence on software reliability. The available strategies for achieving fault tolerance are described in the following sections, which are summarized in Fig. 13.1.

13.1 REDUNDANCY AND DIVERSITY

The reason for considering a system's configuration is that, of all the aspects that affect failures, configuration (in the sense of redundancy and diversity) is the major factor.

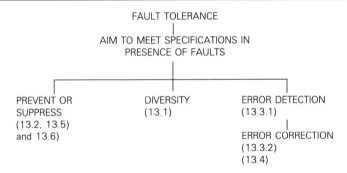

Fig. 13.1 Fault tolerance strategies.

Random hardware failures can be protected against by various forms of redundancy in that it provides a configuration whereby coincident failures are needed to lead to a system level failure. When assessing the effects of redundancy, each segment of the system needs to be considered separately to ensure that there is no unnecessary hardware and/or complexity which would cause additional maintenance, and hence increase system errors due to the additional human activities.

When the redundancy takes the form of duplicated or triplicated units the redundant elements are usually the central processing units (CPUs) since they handle all input/outputs (I/O). The input modules are usually an order more reliable than the input field devices (i.e. sensors and instrumentation). Therefore, field devices can easily dominate the failure rate of a real-time safety system and their inputs are frequently voted in order to achieve overall system reliability.

As was illustrated in Fig. 5.1 there are three basic configurations of system:

(a) a simplex PES acting alone;
(b) one or more PESs acting in combination with one or more non-programmable systems (including safety monitors);
(c) a number of PESs acting in combination (with or without diversity).

Simplex PES

Simplex software-based systems (with no other form of protection) are often used where previously a simplex non-programmable system has been used. This is sometimes considered adequate, after appropriate risk assessment, for the protection required.

In these cases particular attention needs to be given to self-test in order to reveal dormant failures. The system should also be designed to fail to a safe state.

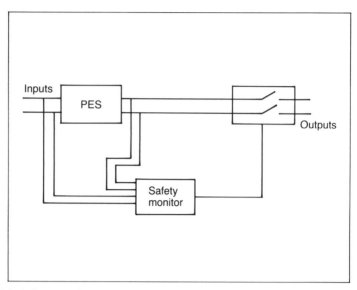

Fig. 13.2 Safety monitor.

One or more PESs acting in combination with one or more non-programmable features (including safety monitors)

This configuration potentially offers a high level of protection because some, or all, of the functions are duplicated by alternative levels of protection, such as electrical, pneumatic or other means.

A typical example, for emergency shutdown systems (ESD), is to have a duplex PES with mechanical protection devices plus manual push buttons connected directly to remove power from all output circuits.

One application of this override principle is known as the **safety monitor**. It consists of a device which interrogates the safety-related parameters (e.g. inputs and outputs) and overrides the action of the PES when the parameters fail to conform to predetermined rules. Figure 13.2 illustrates this arrangement. It is important that the safety monitor itself is designed so that failures within itself lead to a safe condition.

It should not be assumed, however, that safety monitors always fail to a safe condition. Therefore failure mode and effect analysis (FMEA) during the design, followed by suitable testing, should be undertaken. Safety monitors can be hardware devices but are also implemented by means of look-up tables in read-only memory (ROM). In that sense there is an element of software in the safety monitor but there is no execution of programmed instructions since no CPU is involved. Typical examples are emergency shutdown (ESD) and fire/gas detection and control equipment.

A number of PESs acting in combination (with or without diversity)

This arrangement is often used where it is necessary to increase reliability, in respect of hardware failures, and where previously two conventional systems would have been used. This configuration is rarely used in this simple form without additional levels of protection. Manual pushbuttons, connected directly to the output circuits, and other overrides are usually implemented.

If the replicated systems are identical, or even similar, then the problem of common mode failures, in respect of both hardware and software, can dominate the assessment. This is where a failure, due to some common cause, effects all channels of the redundancy. Typical root causes are:

- *design*: common supplies, elements common to all channels, poor tolerancing;
- *manufacturing*: batch-related component or process problems;
- *operations*: maintenance and other human induced failures;
- *environment*: electromagnetic interference, lightning, etc.

Duplication of hardware, containing identical software, is no defence against the software failures. Redundancy only protects against random hardware failures.

The use of diversity, as a form of software 'redundancy', is a controversial technique. Firstly, it is inadequate to implement diversity using merely separate designers producing separate source code. The commonality of techniques, training and software engineering culture, together with the fact that errors may be created high in the design cycle, means that failures will be propagated throughout both sets of code.

As a minimum requirement, different processors should be used in each element of the redundancy and the separation of effort should occur far higher than the coding stage. Although this would enhance the safety integrity of the design it is never a total defence since ambiguities and errors at the requirements stage would still propagate through both of the diverse designs. Minimum requirements for diversity are:

- separate module specifications;
- separate source code;
- different types of CPU;
- separate power sources.

Other, desirable requirements would add:

- CPUs with different clock rates;
- different languages;
- different memory types;
- different supply voltages.

Software diversity is also referred to as *N*-version programming, dissimilar software and multiversion software.

13.2 ERROR PREVENTION

A number of design features involving both hardware circuitry and software techniques can contribute substantially to the system reliability. Some of these features prevent faults from occurring in the first place and others improve the fault tolerance of the system so as to render them non-critical.

13.2.1 Electromagnetic interference (EMI)

Electromagnetic interference is a significant problem with programmable systems. Screening and buffering techniques are useful and varied tests should be carried out. These should include passing interrupted current through loops close to the equipment and electrostatic discharge on to equipment surfaces.

Power supplies should be designed to resist mains-borne interference and transient spikes. In addition, the program should cater for power-fail recovery routines in order that the processing can recover from short-duration losses of power. The use of separate, preferably diverse, power supplies for each channel is essential, otherwise the power supply failure rate will swamp any improvement which may have been gained from redundancy.

Tests for resistance to EMI include:

- variation of supply frequency;
- variation of supply voltage;
- supply interruption (up to 500 ms);
- spikes on supply (in kV orders);
- electrostatic discharge on to surfaces (*c* 20 kV);
- electromagnetic radiation (VHF to UHF up to 10 V/m);
- ionizing radiation;
- electromagnetic radiation from high-voltage spikes in close-proximity cable.

13.2.2 Hardware design and architecture

Faults in one programmable device should not be capable of affecting another. Protection by means of buffers at inputs and outputs is desirable since it prevents faulty ports from pulling other devices into an incorrect state and helps to contain the error, thus minimizing its effect and aiding diagnosis.

The input and output ports of solid-state devices usually fail to a permanent high or low condition. Circuit design can achieve better reliability, from a hazard point of view, by ensuring that failures are to a fail-safe condition. For example, a comparator circuit should be designed to fail to a 'no comparison' state which is then detected as an error.

Memory should have adequate spare capacity to cater for expansion and overload eventualities. In the same way processor speeds and bus sizes should take account of future requirements.

Experience indicates that a large proportion of failures, from system integration and test onwards, result from timing problems of interaction between the software and the hardware equipment which it is controlling. Generous timing tolerances can be consciously specified during both hardware design and software writing so as to minimize this problem. It is not possible, of course, to foresee all the possible combinations of real-time inputs and software states and it will still be necessary to uncover many of these faults by extensive and imaginative test procedures.

Also, graphics and human interfaces will have a significant influence on system reliability since they will influence the responses made by operators to various system states.

The previous paragraphs address some main features of design tolerance but the checklists at the end of this chapter suggest some additional areas for review.

13.3 ERROR IDENTIFICATION AND CORRECTION

Whereas the previous section dealt with design features which prevent the generation or propagation of errors, this section deals with their timely identification and correction.

The timely display of fault and error codes is a powerful aid to both reliability and maintainability because it helps the operator to recover from situations which, although not total system failures, might otherwise propagate in such a way.

13.3.1 Error detection

This is achieved by a number of techniques.

Watchdog timer techniques involve using the processor clock to monitor outputs to verify that they are not stuck in one state. Unless it receives a reset within a predetermined period it will halt the processing. Many watchdog timers only require resetting within a loosely defined time and the result is rarely fail-safe. The technique will pick up a significant number of faults providing that the design of the watchdog is adequate, which implies an adequate understanding of the likely failure modes in the first place. The timer itself can be periodically reset, thereby adding an element of sequence checking to its capability. It can also cater for endless loops by ensuring that defined points can only occur between two watchdog signals.

A large proportion of the hardware in a programmable system consists of memory. It is possible to check the state of a memory by writing a known bit into each location and then checking that it can be re-read. This walking-bit technique minimizes software corruption faults by flagging up failed memory. In the case of ROMs checksum techniques are needed which will verify the contents (which should not change) against predetermined checksum values.

The relay runner technique involves the setting up of a control variable which is incremented by known amounts at defined stages in the program. Its value, at any stage of execution, is thus predictable and if the value is incorrect there is evidence that an incorrect path has been implemented since the last satisfactory check of the variable.

Another technique is the use of code which effectively carries out the function of built-in test equipment. More sophisticated than the above-mentioned watchdog, it examines the state of the program and makes diagnostic judgements (designed in by the programmer) which enable instructions either in the form of codes or English language to be output to the user.

13.3.2 Error correction

An extension of this philosophy is to provide code which can, having diagnosed that an error has been generated, correct the value or values in store so as to effect a recovery. The simplest example of error-detection software is the parity digit, whereby an additional digit is included with some value. The binary value of the parity digit is set according to the value of the sum of the digits comprising the variable in question. If additional redundant information is provided it is also possible to deduce the bits which are in error and an algorithm can be designed which corrects them. More sophisticated checksum techniques have been developed from this idea.

Error detection and correction is thus a form of redundancy, not through hardware replication but by the use of additional code. The recovery philosophy is based on checking the acceptability of specific results (variables, data, outputs) and, if one of the tests fails, moving to an alternative path which will enable the program to recover. It is clearly not realistic to check the result of every step (instruction) in a program. However, the modular nature of the design will enable a realistic apportionment of the checks across the program functions. Each check determines (by using an ELSE command) the next instruction. In this way the

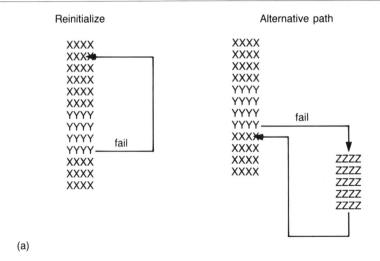

(a)

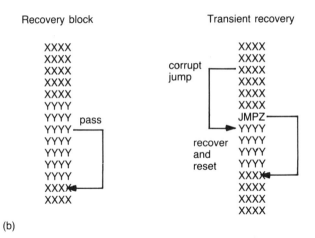

(b)

Fig. 13.3 Recovery techniques.

program is steered either to a recovery routine or to the 'no fault' sequence. The recovery sequence must contain some form of acceptance test to verify if the program has regained a satisfactory state. There are seven main approaches to such error recovery:

1. *Reinitialization* (Fig. 13.3(a)). This involves resetting the system to a known acceptable state and reinitializing the processing. Variables are reset to predetermined or known good values. The difficulty is deriving sufficient information to recreate the state immediately prior to the error. Clearly, remembering the state of all relevant variables prior to

entering each block is far too inefficient. The program must jump to a predetermined position where known values and states apply.

2. *Alternative path* (Fig. 13.3(a)). In the case of mathematical routines a second path, or try, can be provided. If the result of a particular calculation is not satisfactory then an alternative calculation can be performed.

3. *Recovery blocks* (Fig. 13.3(b)). These consist of blocks consisting of an acceptance test for the calculation with one or more alternative routines which are used if the test fails.

4. *Exception handling*. This consists of identifying conditions which are defined as exceptional and which require additional code to carry out the processing.

5. *Memorizing executed cases*. Here a record is made during certification of code of the allowed paths for program execution. This information is stored in some way and when the program is executed in its real environment the actual execution is compared with this allowed set. If an uncertified path is executed then safety action is taken.

6. *Error-correcting codes*. Here we try to detect and correct errors in sensitive information by using different types of code, e.g. Hamming codes (section 13.4).

7. *Manual recovery*. In the event of failure, control of the system is returned to an operator who attempts to control the system rather than leaving it to automatic means.

8. *Transient recovery*. Unlike the foregoing, this technique operates at machine code level. It is known that spurious jumps in processors, due to corruption of the program counter, are not random. Study of particular processors has revealed a statistical pattern of more and less likely spurious jump addresses. The technique (illustrated in Fig. 13.3(b)) is to seed the preceding address to those more likely addresses with a jump instruction which takes the normal execution of the code to a later address. The intervening memory is then used to contain recovery software for the occasions when the offending spurious jump occurs. The greater the number of these seeds, the greater the improvement in error rate.

13.4 DATA COMMUNICATION

The data communications medium between parts of the system or between systems in different locations is a source of bit error. Parity and checksum techniques are used to detect and correct these. A data bit error rate of 10^{-6} means that one binary bit in 1 000 000 will be corrupted. By sending checksum codes far fewer than 1 in 1 000 000 messages will be corrupted.

For example, a 112-bit message may contain 96 bits of data and 16 bits of coded information derived from the other 96. A comparison of those 96 bits with the 16, after their receipt at the other end of a communications link, permits error correction to take place. The simplest method is for the software at the receiving end to request a retransmission of the message until the checksum computes correctly. In this way only 1 in 2 to the power 16 (65 536) of corrupted messages will propagate undetected.

13.5 GRACEFUL DEGRADATION AND RECOVERY

The whole design philosophy should take account of the need to operate in degraded modes. This can only be achieved at the requirements level where functional diversity can be specified, levels of system function can be defined and the operating requirements grouped into categories.

The software design decomposition should attempt to minimize the routes of communication between groups of modules so that errors are discouraged from propagating through the system. In this way errors are more likely to be confined to single functions or, at most, groups of functions. The system may then be able to provide service, albeit at a degraded level, by means of other functions. This is of particular importance in software systems controlling hazardous processes.

The incidence of mains-borne interference has already been mentioned. It is not uncommon for mains power to disappear for short intervals. Power fail recovery routines are part of the software and can enable a system to resume normal operation without failing. These must be designed in and thoroughly proved during system test.

13.6 ELECTROMAGNETIC COMPATIBILITY (EMC)

For safety-related equipment, and in particular those based on software systems, the issue of EMC is important. The emergence of Electromagnetic Compatibility Regulations (1992), in response to EC directive (89/336/EEC) and its amendment (92/31/EEC), has drawn further attention to the area.

Indeed there have been safety-related incidents pointed out to the HSE, attributed to electromagnetic interference (EMI), involving programmable equipment.

Programmable architectures, where data and program flow can be corrupted, tend to be more susceptible to EMI than their hardwired counterparts. The higher the required safety integrity (see Chapter 2) of the protection system the more important are the defence measures against EMI. This will also depend upon the electrical disturbances anticipated from a particular environment. There is an IEC guidance document (CD 77B(sec)122) being drafted that describes and classifies the levels likely to be expected from different types of location. This will assist in specifying immunity levels.

Some important design considerations are:

- Power sources where high-frequency mains borne interference is possible. Consideration should be given to independent power supply. Selection of power supplies requires care since some features can cause interference.
- Cables and connections where screening performance may be critical. Parallel cable runs are undesirable and consideration should be given to mechanical protection, impedance matching and length of cables.
- Earthing, bonding and screening require attention to items such as braiding, aperture screening and single earth terminals.
- Relying on means of suppression carries the danger that subsequent removal of the suppression device provides a possible source of failure.
- Optical isolation is beneficial so long as the over-voltage characteristics are taken account of.
- Fibre optics provide a very high degree of protection.
- Environmental considerations are important, in particular lightning. Amplitudes of 2–6 kV are not infrequent and suitable protection of programmable devices should be considered.

The European standards being prepared under the directives are classified as basic, generic, product family and product standards respectively. Although it is likely to be some time before a compatible set of standards is fully established under the directive, current guidance is as follows:

- *Basic standards.* Basic standards are informative documents only; compliance with a basic standard is not sufficient to satisfy legal requirements. The basic standard IEC 1000 will eventually be the definitive standard, but is still under development.
- *Generic standards.* Generic standards specify test and test limits for all types of equipment in specific environments. Compliance with a relevant generic standard is, in the absence of a relevant product standard (see below), sufficient to satisfy the legal requirements. The generic standards EN 50081-1 and EN 50082-1 (Part 1) cover emission and immunity respectively for domestic, commercial and industrial applications. Part 2 is aimed at heavier industrial environments.
- *Product and product family standards.* These standards specify tests and test limits for specific groups of products. Where relevant product standards exist, they should be used in preference to the generic standards and will ensure that legal requirements are satisfied. In general the new standards applicable to the directive have not yet been

prepared but there are many existing standards for most product categories which are satisfactory for present purposes. The Manufacturing Technology Division, Department of Trade and Industry, or BSI Standards Technical Services, Milton Keynes should be consulted for further guidance.

13.7 HIGH-INTEGRITY SYSTEMS

The achievement of high integrity in systems is of particular interest in the military field where hardware together with its embedded software is required to survive extremely harsh environments and still exhibit high levels of reliability. In the early 1980s the UK Ministry of Defence began a research programme at the Royal Signals and Radar Research Establishment (RSRE) into developing microprocessors for such applications. The result has been the verifiable integrated processor for enhanced reliability (VIPER) chip.

The root causes of failure in commercial microprocessors are:

- imprecise specification of what is required;
- inadequate verification of the gate-level design against that specification.

To overcome these problems the designers of VIPER have used formal mathematical techniques both to specify and subsequently to verify their microprocessor. By doing this, RSRE have produced a microprocessor of proven capability. As has already been pointed out, however, hardware is only as reliable as the software which drives it. In order to achieve the combining of high-integrity hardware with high-integrity software a new computer language called Newspeak is being developed which has, as its goal, the production of safe and reliable programs.

The chip has been designed to form the main component of a self-checking computer module. Such a module would incorporate two VIPER chips, one operating as the active processor, able to read and write to the data bus, and another (monitor) processor which would only be permitted to read from the data bus. It incorporates a bank of comparison logic so that if illegal operations are attempted the processor stops and remains in that state until RESET is asserted. Also any discrepancy between the two processors can be quickly detected and execution halted. Details of the cause of any halt in execution are recorded in an on-chip diagnostic register and, provided that the detected error is non-critical to the module's performance, the processors can be restarted.

At present, programs for VIPER are written in a language called VISTA, which is a structured assembler. Programs written in VISTA can be translated into the intermediate languages MALPAS and SPADE (see Chapter 11) and thus subjected to static analysis. The commercial production of VIPER and the Newspeak compiler will herald a new era in high-integrity system design and production.

PART FOUR

Management Issues

These final two chapters cover project management issues as well as various methods which attempt to measure software.

Software management issues

During development, a number of management aspects need to be considered, such as estimating methods, security issues, subcontracted software and integrity assessments as well as specific initiatives.

14.1 ESTIMATING METHODS

14.1.1 Seeking metrics for estimation

The process of developing software is not just about coding – it involves documentation, design, programming, file building, testing, training, quality assurance and, above all, management. The development of software has been characterized by cost overruns and schedule slippage. Since the level of investment in software is increasing all the time, managers need the answers to key questions such as 'How much will it cost to develop?', 'How long will it take and with how many staff?', 'What levels of productivity can be expected?' All of these questions, in principle, can be answered with a single quantity. The question is – can we provide such a number, or **metric**, for software?

A reasonable approach might be to study the many software projects in the past, gather data and thus set up models which, in theory, should permit the prediction of the parameters required and thus answer the above question with some degree of accuracy. The costs, manpower levels, durations and so on could thus be predicted.

A starting point might be, for example, the number of source code statements generated per man–month. Every manager knows, however, that just because an average programmer generates ten lines per day, ten programmers will not necessarily generate 45 000 lines in two years. These are, of course, statistical averages and it must not be assumed that one particular programmer will perform in that way. The single productivity figure does not take into account the complexity of the given task, the spread of abilities in the team, interface problems and so on. Also, as has been said, software is not simply the generation of code. Clearly the amount of data and the number of parameters in these models must be very large in order even to approximate realistic values. How do the actual techniques already generated cope?

14.1.2 Actual methods

The major current software packages which attempt this scheduling model are:

- SLIM;
- GECOMO;
- PRICE S;
- ARTEMIS.

The attraction of better control of projects via support tools is clear. Several attempts at providing them have been made.

Software Life-Cycle Management (SLIM) provides cost, time, personnel and machine estimates for developing computer software. Its accuracy has been validated using over a thousand different projects, in both the USA and Europe and covering a wide range of applications. The basis of SLIM is the work of Laurance Putnam of Quantitative Software Management Inc. It can be used from the beginning a project and provides information on productivity, minimum cost and time forecasts, risk profiles and manpower estimates. The question arises, 'How accurate are the values provided by such models?'

A number of useful studies and user surveys have revealed quite a variation in response. Whilst some projects have certainly benefited from the use of these tools, some users have reported as much as a 50% discrepancy in the values produced. It seems that in spite of quite large databases and complicated parametric models it is still possible to produce projects which defy these models.

Perhaps the best point made about these tools is that, used carefully throughout a project, they provide guidance on how various project parameters are behaving. Certainly on larger projects (i.e. over 100 000 source code statements) some benefit is likely from the tools and from the disciplines needed to collect and input the necessary data.

14.2 SECURITY

A 1993 survey by NCC, ICL and the DTI indicated that 80% of companies had experienced at least one breach of IT security in the previous two years. A similar survey in 1991 suggested only 50%.

Formal security policies and procedures are now a must to cover such items as backup, storage, access controls, formal legal obligations on staff.

Such measures may not eradicate the security breaches but will certainly mitigate the effects.

A code of practice for IT security management is available on order from BSI Publications, Milton Keynes MK14 6LE.

14.2.1 Security against data theft

There are two ways of preventing unauthorized people from reading confidential or sensitive information:

- by denying them access;
- by making the files unreadable to them.

As a first line of defence, one can lock floppy discs away in a safe at the end of each day, but with large files, or a large number of smaller files, this can be very inconvenient. Then again there are programs where repeated disc access would make this very slow. There are devices such as keyboard locks or post-fitted locks which may be used to deter most attempts at prying but these do not equal the ultimate security of locking data in a safe.

The second method is to make files unreadable to unauthorized people by the use of specialized security packages which encrypt files before writing to disc, and decode them after reading from disc, and before passing them to the user program. These tools may be purely software or include add-in hardware cards for the PC. To use one's files a password may be required which is then used in a hashing algorithm to code or decode the files. Alternatively a dongle, or electronic key, is plugged into the card and supplies the necessary encription code.

It is important to remember that security measures are only as good as one's commitment to use them properly. Passwords are not popular and a very short list includes the majority in use. Common names and dates continue to dominate that list.

Essential factors are:

- commitment from management and staff;
- a hierarchy of responsibility to ensure that appropriate and adequate measures are taken;
- a training programme for all staff.

14.2.2 Security against data loss

There are various ways of protecting against losing data. The main defence is to take copies of all files on a regular basis. Programs are not usually copy protected and many software houses recommend that backup working copies are made. It is important to:

- follow their instructions;
- label discs carefully;
- store backup and master discs carefully in different locations;
- record the serial number of the machine on which each copy of the programs is loaded. Do not make unauthorized copies. In the United States some of the larger software houses have started to take large corporations to court for breach of copyright, primarily to deter others.

Personal data files are harder to protect since they will change and will need constant copying to keep them current. One must make a cost judgement as to the value of data against the value of time taken in protecting it, and take into account the probability of data loss. The most common loss of data occurs when working on a spreadsheet and loading another without saving the first.

There are programs which will overcome this – one called BOOKMARK regularly saves files to disc either after an elapse of time, or after a preset number of keystrikes. This will also protect against unexpected power loss. After losing a large spreadsheet, with several hours work, most people will soon get into the habit of regularly saving their work, and in most packages it is harder to lose work without making a definite decision to exit without saving and, fortunately, power failures are relatively infrequent.

If a hard disc is corrupted, or files become erased, or a machine fails, then one wishes one had backed up the hard disc. There are tape streamer systems which will back up an entire 40M byte hard disc in a single operation. There are programs specifically for backing up files. The best-known and widely used is probably FASTBACK, which saves the files to floppy disc, and can either copy an entire disc or selective directories. It is fast and efficient and at the end of the operation states how long it spent copying files, and how long one took changing discs. Usually one spends more time than it does.

'XTREE' is another popular package which includes back-up routines as well as its more widely known file handling. One feature is its control of file attributes which means an archive bit can be set off after copying each file, but this will be reset when the file is next written to. By using this, one can do a selective backup on just those files previously written to. The time spent in saving files to disc can become tedious, so it is important not to copy more files than necessary. If work files and program files are lumped together, life becomes much more difficult.

14.2.3 CRAMM assessments

Computer Risk Analysis and Management Methodology (CRAMM) is a package developed by CCTA (The UK Government Centre for Information Systems) and BIS Information Systems Ltd. It became approved as the UK government preferred method for identifying and justifying security measures for protecting IT systems carrying government unclassified but sensitive data.

The method is currently available from ACT Business Systems Ltd of Wimbledon.

The CRAMM methodology essentially:

- defines assets, threats and vulnerabilities;
- evaluates risks;
- justifies security measures.

- *Assets* can be physical (hardware, documentation, buildings), software (operating system, applications packages) or data.
- *Threats* can be accidental (flood, fire, human error) or deliberate (staff, outsiders). They include fire, water, staff shortage, wilful damage, theft, infiltration, misuse, hardware failure, power and environmental failure, etc.
- *Vulnerabilities* are the weaknesses of a system such as access to a dialled network, building access, shared premises, etc.
- *Risks* are the impacts of the threats (as a result of the vulnerabilities) on disclosure, modification, availability and loss of data.

The three stages of the method are:

- *Stage 1*, which involves identifying the assets and the boundary of the system. The impact of loss of each asset, in terms of unavailability, is determined as are dependencies between assets. A review is important, at the end of this stage, to establish management commitment and to confirm that there is an awareness of the problems involved.
- *Stage 2*, which involves identifying the threats and vulnerabilities. Threats are mapped to specific assets and then, having regard to the vulnerabilities, the risks are assessed. There is a form of quantification whereby the risks are scored according to their seriousness. Again, there is a management review at the end of this stage.
- *Stage 3* is concerned with prioritizing and managing the identified risks. A security policy is developed and defences outlined.

Figure 14.1 provides a pictorial view of the CRAMM approach. The main concepts are:

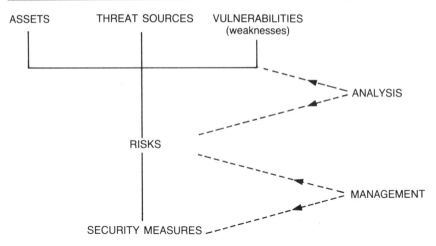

Fig. 14.1 The CRAMM approach.

- a common metric approach to assist reviewers to obtain an objective valuation;
- levels of risk are matched to specific defences.

14.3 VIRUSES

It is a myth to assume that viruses are only imported as a result of illegal software or bulletin boards. There are many cases of viruses appearing on reputable supplies of unformatted discs or in products from major software suppliers. No one is immune.

Much has been written in the press about computer viruses. Many articles have been rather too alarmist but there is nevertheless cause for caution and a need for awareness rather than panic on the subject. So called 'viruses' are rogue programs designed to do some form of damage to a computer or communications system. One known type of PC virus consists of extra code embedded in the COMMAND.COM file which writes itself into every copy of this file that it comes across. If a floppy disc is 'infected' in this way and a program from it run on hard disc the virus embeds itself into the COMMAND.COM on that hard disc. Putting another floppy disc in the PC causes its COMMAND.COM to become 'infected'. One such virus waits until it has replicated itself a number of times before doing any damage. It then starts a malevolent process, such as destroying all the files on the disc.

Viruses can be embedded in any program, such as a popular utility. They can do anything intended from the sort of malicious destruction of data described above to something totally innocuous such as putting a random dot on the screen. As soon as a particular virus is discovered, someone will write a program to detect and 'kill' it. Virus programmers are therefore continually looking for newer ways to avoid detection.

There is no cure for viruses but sensitive defences include:

- be careful where you get software from – some 'shareware' and software downloaded from bulletin boards have been known to be infected;
- not using illegal copies of copyright software;
- backing up hard disc data and keeping several copies.

Viruses are, however, rare and there is a hundred times better chance of losing data through one's own mistakes.

14.4 SAFETY-RELATED INTEGRITY ASSESSMENTS

14.4.1 Carrying out assessments

In view of the widespread use of the HSE guidelines, together with the impending EC umbrella documentation, formal safety integrity assessments are more and more frequently required. These inevitably involve some assessment of the software quality.

Assessments should be undertaken wherever software is used in a safety-related application. The perception that a programmable system is supplemented by some additional level of safety protection does not relax the need to make a formal demonstration of safety integrity and, as support to a safety report in the case of CIMAH top tier sites, such studies are essential. The assessment should follow from, and, where appropriate, use the results of, a formal hazard and operability (HAZOP) study. If modifications to a plant, or its control system, are subsequently carried out, then a further assessment should be undertaken.

In order to encourage consistency in the approach to assessing programmable systems it would be beneficial to follow a number of defined steps.

Defining the safety system (Step 1)

The first step in a programmable system safety integrity study is to define the boundary of the 'safety system' and the safety functions that it performs.

This boundary should not be limited by the terminology which describes the system. The emergency shutdown (ESD) system for a plant is almost certain to constitute a safety system by virtue of the function it performs rather than because of its name. However, any PES can also constitute a safety system if it can exhibit hazardous failure modes. It is the possibility of a hazardous failure mode which determines a safety system – not its description.

In many cases a system carries out both control and safety functions, in which case there is still the need for a study.

Identifying the hazardous failure modes and establishing safety criteria (Step 2)

A safety system could have a number of possible failure modes, each resulting in different consequences. It is important to define which failure modes are to be assessed since the results of a study are not necessarily the same for each mode.

The safety life cycle shows the need to establish risk criteria at an early stage. The alternative approaches of quantified risk assessment and safety-integrity levels are available. Where possible a quantified risk assessment approach provides an objective evaluation.

Two contrasting failure modes are often observed with safety systems. One of these is **spurious action** – as for example unwarranted shutdown (in the case of ESD), or unwarranted executive action, in the case of fire detection. The other is, **loss of function** – such as to lead to failure of either shutdown or executive actions.

A spurious failure mode (e.g. false alarm) is sometimes wrongly referred to as a fail-safe condition. In some circumstances this is not a correct statement since a spurious plant shut down or unwanted fire suppression action can constitute a hazard.

Assessing the system configuration (Step 3)

The main feature of a system which determines its reliability and safety integrity is its configuration. In other words, the degree of redundancy and diversity in the configuring or voting of both hardwired and programmable elements is the major factor in determining the safety integrity. Possibilities include:

1. *Total hardwired override.* In many applications the system is specifically designed so that no single failure can cause a hazardous failure mode.

Early in the study it is important to examine those elements (circuits) of the system which are controlled by the programmable part of the architecture. The idea is to establish that, for all states of each programmable output, the functions are achieved by non-programmable overrides.

This is simply illustrated in Fig. 14.2. The input causes a relay (R1) to open a contact (R1/1) which, in addition to the PES output, causes the solenoid (R2) to release. Thus, the multiple failure of the PES and a

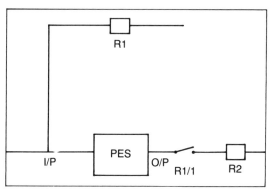

Fig. 14.2 Hardwired override.

hardware component would be required in order for the safety solenoid (R2) not to release.

If it can be established that this 'total hardwired override' configuration applies then, in general terms, the software safety integrity is less critical. The remaining steps of the assessment will be carried out but with reasonable balance between cost and detail.

2. *Single software failure.* If it is established that any one software failure mode can cause a hazardous failure, then usually the system does not have adequate safety integrity.

The remaining steps of the assessment would be carried out but the recommendations and executive summary would emphasize that early redesign is required. A reassessment would then follow the modifications.

In some cases where the hazardous failure leads to a low consequence this configuration is acceptable but the remaining steps of the assessment would require extra vigour.

3. *Multiple software failures.* Another possibility includes the use of redundancy whereby two or more software-controlled circuit elements (e.g. outputs) need to fail simultaneously in order for a hazardous failure mode to occur. In such cases it is very likely that the use of common software in each redundant channel will permit a single fault to cause the hazardous failure mode.

The use of diverse software would therefore provide an effective but not total defence. Diversity often implies both software and hardware diversity within the redundancy. This was addressed in greater detail in Chapter 13.

Assessing the hardware reliability (Step 4)

Although the assessment is primarily aimed at the fact that programmable elements are involved, it is nevertheless necessary to carry out traditional hardware reliability predictions for the failure modes defined in Step 2.

This could involve failure-mode analysis, fault-tree analysis, system modelling or other reliability prediction techniques.

The hardware reliability assessment should be compared with any predictions or empirical data for similar systems.

Assessing the software quality (Step 5)

This should include a number of areas of qualitative assessment:

- fault tolerance (Chapter 13);
- software quality review. This should involve a detailed review of:
  —document structure;
  —document and media control;
  —design standards;
  —coding methods;
  —languages and compilers;
  —design review records and methods;
  —validation methods;
  —test strategy;
  —test records;
  —records of remedial action.
- Formal methods (Chapters 8 and 9).

Making recommendations

In order that necessary improvements are implemented a safety integrity study should, wherever possible, make recommendations. These should cover:

- configuration of the design;
- operating methods;
- maintenance philosophy;
- test;
- documentation;
- fault tolerance;
- coding and language.

14.4.2 Benefits and drawbacks

Assessments of software quality carry a number of benefits:

- *Confidence.* By identifying and removing specific faults, and by noting the good design features, confidence is established in the system.

- *Feedback*. Design faults are fed back and corrected at earlier stages in the design cycle, thus saving cost. Histories of design faults will lead to better future design.
- *Liability*. As discussed in Chapter 4, the trend is towards absolute liability for fatality and injury irrespective of negligence. This trend will doubtless extend to environmentally related failures. Although best endeavours do not provide a total defence the existence of well-documented assessments, with remedial actions as appropriate, will provide some mitigation.

On the other hand:

- *Lack of metrics*. Since there is still not yet a totally satisfactory way to quantify the quality of software, assessments remain qualitative.
- *False confidence*. Lack of precision in describing the assessed quality of software has already been explained. Nevertheless there is a danger that the knowledge that an assessment has been carried out can lead to false confidence.
- *Relevance of parameters*. Although software quality activities contribute to lowering error rates they are not a guarantee of fault-free design. There will inevitably remain unknown parameters which therefore will not be addressed.
- *Error rate versus fault tolerance*. It is important that assessments do not concentrate on error prevention alone because the benefits of fault tolerance may often outweigh excessive efforts to prevent faults.

14.5 SUBCONTRACTED SOFTWARE

14.5.1 Shelf versus custom software

In terms of evaluation, and of confidence in the final product, the quality problem is much the same. The circumstances of a proprietary (off-the-shelf) product are that the visibility to the purchaser is greatly reduced. Custom software, however, is usually produced on a project basis such that the various activities of specification, design, test, review and commissioning are visible to the customer.

In the case of 'off-the-shelf' software the evaluation is usually restricted to:

- evidence of field experience (if any);
- data from other users;
- a vendor appraisal.

14.5.2 Vendor appraisal

The requirement for a vendor appraisal is stated in most of the quality systems and this is necessary for both of the above types of purchase. Clearly, in the 'off-the-shelf' case, it is even more critical due to its being the main point of assessment.

The features which should be investigated are, broadly, those which have been outlined in this chapter. In Chapter 5 the systems and procedures which should be looked for are outlined.

A small vendor may well exercise adequate control by the use of simple, perhaps informal, documents. It should therefore always be the aim to establish that genuine control is being applied rather than efforts being directed to the production of impressive manuals and standards which are not actually being used.

14.5.3 Field experience and history

This will apply to proprietary software packages rather than to custom packages. The following questions should be addressed:

- Who has purchased and used the package?
- Is there evidence of documented defects and subsequent corrective action?
- How long has the package been in active use by consumers?

If it proves possible to contact users they might be asked:

- Do you keep a detailed log of the results obtained in using the package?
- What is your experience with the vendor in following up and resolving problems?
- Is the documentation adequate to permit easy modification of the package?

14.6 INITIATIVES

These include:

14.6.1 Institution of Electrical Engineers Safety Critical Systems Committee

Formed in 1989 this IEE committee, which works through its Public Affairs Board, seeks to advise on matters related to safety critical systems including aspects of software quality such as formal methods, competence and accreditation, training requirements and academic syllabi.

14.6.2 Inter-Institutional Group on Safety Critical Systems

Formed in 1990, this group provides a forum through which chartered engineers of different disciplines, engaged in research, development, design and operation of safety-critical systems, can be informed of recent developments in technology and their use in the solution of specific problems. Its members represents a number of the chartered institutions together with the British Computer Society and the Safety and Reliability Society.

14.6.3 Institution of Gas Engineers POPES Panel

This committee, which works through its safety committee, advises on safety of programmable equipment in the gas (and process) industry. It drafts the SR15 publication described in Chapter 5.

14.6.4 British Computer Society

Similar in intent to the IEE Safety Critical Systems committee, the BCS also has a Safety Critical Systems Group. At any time the group has working task forces addressing specific issues such as training and accreditation.

14.6.5 Safety Critical Systems Club

This was sponsored, in 1991, by the DTI, which encouraged and funded the Club for the first three years. The purpose is to encourage the dissemination of information and techniques. There is a steering group made up of representatives from the IEE, BCS, NPL, DTI, consultancies and industry.

The Club organizes technical meetings for presentations and discussions and publishes a newsletter.

14.6.6 Hazards Forum

Although not specifically addressing software, the Hazards Forum, which is a consortium of engineering and other institutions, is concerned with safety in all types of engineering. It is currently contactable via the Institution of Civil Engineers.

Given that there is a strong desire to measure the quality of software, it is not surprising that there have been considerable efforts to find models whereby this can be achieved. There is no absolute standard for quality, and claims are based relative to some perceived norm or level against which features are compared.

An obvious measure of quality is the number and rate of occurrence of failures related to the software and this has led to methods aimed at predicting error rates either from identifiable features of the code or from extrapolations of observed failures.

This chapter deals with two areas of activity which are both aimed at quantifying error rates and other measurable features of software.

15.1 METRICS

15.1.1 What are metrics?

Traditionally the quality of software has been evaluated by qualitative features. The features, described in Chapters 7 to 13, give rise to subjective judgements of code quality.

On the other hand, it has been a theme of this book that the path towards better software involves a more formal and structured approach to design. It would seem that such a trend would encourage the development of more measurable features of the code.

Such quantified measures are known as **metrics**. Measures of size, complexity, structure and programming resources are identified and attempts are made to relate them, by means of models, to the quality, cost and implementation time of the code. The obvious example is the relationship, if any, of branching complexity of the code to its error rate.

Despite increasing interest over the last 20 years, this science of software metrication is not particularly well formulated. For one thing, characteristics of software projects greatly affect the results obtained by applying them. Thus, comparisons between projects are not easy to achieve in view of the variation between their features.

There are two main applications of metrics:

1. *project control*, whereby metrics are used to predict coding and test times, productivity and machine usage;
2. *quality*, whereby metrics are related to reliability and safety as, for example, by attempting to predict code error rates.

The actual metrics fall into four broad groups:

1. *Code metrics*. These record the more easily quantified aspects of the code. They are, therefore, not available until well into the design cycle and hence do not provide the total picture. Examples are lines of code and cyclometric complexity (a measure of path and execution complexity).
2. *Structure metrics*. These address the higher levels of design and include information complexity (which concerns data flow) review complexity, invocation complexity and stability.
3. *Hybrid metrics*. These are modified structure metrics weighted to take account of various code features. Examples are weighted information flow, weighted review complexity and weighted stability.
4. *Programmer metrics*. These include the number of changes, number of documents, number of years of programmer experience and the mix of experience.

The following section describes the more common metrics.

15.1.2 Some practical metrics

The following abbreviations are used in describing 13 metrics.

- LOC = number of executable lines of code;
- v = number of referenced variables;
- c = number of different commands;
- n = number of modules (Note: 1 rung = 1 module in ladder logic);
- z = 1 (not complicated) to 5 (complicated);
- cp = number of control path crossings;
- E = number of edges in the flow diagram;
- N = number of vertices;
- P = number of connected components (usually 1);
- ds = number of design statements (e.g. line of pseudo code, control flow box, text sentence);
- fi = number of other modules which call that module;
- fo = number of other modules called by that module;
- F = number of faults found;
- w = weeks since start of test;
- wrd = words in document;
- sen = sentences in document;

- *hrd*   = number of words > two syllables;
- *Q*   = number of comment lines;
- *MM*   = staff months for code development.

The first ten are code metrics and the remaining three are project-related.

1. *Lines of code.* Somewhat oversimple and, as a minimum, requires assumptions to be stated. Examples are the inclusion or otherwise of comment in the total, the inclusion or otherwise of blank lines, begins, ends, etc.

$$= LOC$$

2. *Percentage comment.* A reasonable measure of visibility within the code.

$$= Q \times 100/(Q + LOC)$$

3. *Module complexity.* This is a straightforward measure which is best applied at module level. Applied to an entire suite of software the value will be an average of all modules and will therefore be of less value. Applied to a number of modules in the same language a range can be established for purposes of comparison.

$$= LOC \times \log_{10}(v + c)$$

4. *Subjective complexity.* Since this is subjective it relies on consistency between assessors and, unlike module complexity above, cannot be applied without experience.

$$= \Sigma_{(all\ modules)}\ [\text{a subjective rating of } z \text{ from 1 to 5}]/n$$

5. *Control path cross.* This is simply *cp*, the number of times that the control paths cross and is a further measure of complexity.

$$= cp$$

6. *Design complexity.* This uses McCabe's formula and, again, should be applied at module level for comparisons of complexity.

$$= E - N + 2P$$

(*Note*: Choose the highest 10% complexity (average).)

7. *Design to code expansion rate.* This relates the code to the statements in the higher levels of documentation. The measure will be language specific and comparisons can only be made within a given language. For consistency it will be important to define lines of code (does this include comment?) and design statements (does this mean line of pseudo code?).

$$= LOC/ds$$

8. *Fan-in, fan-out.* Another measure of module complexity which is calculated from the number of calls in and out of the module. It is important not to confused 'CALL' with 'READ' and 'WRITE'.

$$= (fi \times fo)^2$$

9. *Fault detection rate.* A simple measure of fault rate.

$$= F \times 1000/(LOC \times w)$$

10. *Gunning's fog index.* This applies to natural language text and hence to the specification documents.

$$= 0.4(wrd/sen + 100hrd/wrd)$$

11. *COCOMO.* This stands for construction cost model and is a predictor metric which purports to assess the staff months of effort.

$$MM = 5.2 \times (LOC/1000)^{0.91}$$

12. *Number of changes by type.* This involves counting the number of changes by purpose. The categories are fault correction, planned enhancement, requirements change, improve clarity, improve maintainability, improve documentation, insert debug code, remove debug code, optimize time, optimize space, optimize accuracy, correct design deficiency, adapt to environmental change.

13. *Staff quality.* This involves counting the years of experience of a developer in the following areas: software engineering, the application area, the specific role (e.g. programmer, tester), the programming environment, the language.

15.1.3 Applying metrics

It is important to take several measurements since no single measure (metric) will provide a meaningful description of a module or project.

It is important to collect data over a number of modules and of projects so that ranges of values of each metric, often classified by coding language, can be established. Only in this way can meaningful judgements be made since there are no absolute values which can be quoted.

The literature does however suggest a number of target minima for a module. These are:

- design complexity < 11;
- *LOC* (executable) < 200;
- comment > 60%.

Aggregating metrics by attempting to combine them into a single 'measure' or 'rating' for the code is not thought to be desirable. This will lose the discrimination available from a number of measures. It is analogous to attempting to combine a number of measurable features of a consumer item (price, reliability, ease of use, power consumption, size, etc.) into a single number.

A key area of interest is the validation of the metrics against actual working systems. Preferably, historical project data should be used to provide objective evidence of the relationships.

Comparison of metrics within a project is likely to be more meaningful than comparisons between projects. This is because there are likely to be factors which differ between projects which will affect the metrics but which themselves are not necessarily identified or measured.

15.1.4 Applying metrics to PLCs

Although not language specific, metrics generally rely on source code being written in conventional (non-graphical) high-level branching languages. PLCs (programmable logic controllers), however, usually require the use of proprietary language sets which involve ladder logic and/or graphical techniques as has been described in Chapter 12.

Terms used in section 15.1.2 above such as 'lines of code', 'number of modules' and 'fan in/fan out' do not have the same meaning in a ladder language. An equivalent entity is therefore needed in order to apply the metrics.

The main items requiring an equivalent are:

- *module*: equivalent to a rung in the ladder;
- *line of code*: equivalent to conditions of the rung;
- *fan in*: equivalent to the number of entities in the input conditions of the rung;
- *fan out*: equivalent to the number of entities in the output conditions of the rung.

Figure 15.1 illustrates this equivalence.

15.1.5 Limitations of metrics

Major limitations arise from:

- *The use of only single dependent variables.* A simple model might address the relationship between, say, error rate and a particular complexity measure. This approach fails to recognize the interrelationships between parameters. One designer might achieve error-free code by patient documentation and review of his/her code whereas another might code faster and expend effort on debug and test. The resulting error rate for the two developers might be the same whereas the metrics would not.

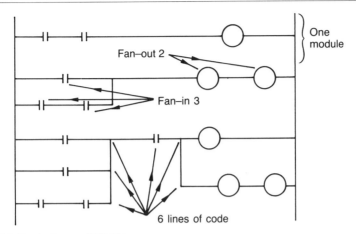

Fig. 15.1 Equivalence of PLC terms.

- *The use of only a single independent variable.* In other words, only one metric is chosen to model the software performance. This is similarly limiting to the practice of aggregating metrics as mentioned earlier.
- *The assumption of linearity.* This assumption has often led to the rejection of a metric as a valid indicator of software quality. An example would be the assumption that doubling the lines of code will double error rate, cost, programming time, etc. More sophisticated models would probably be needed.
- *Misuse.* Each metric describes a particular feature of the software. Judging performance on the number of lines of code alone would lead to the erroneous conclusion that the use of assembly language is more productive than that of high-level language.

Given that correlations can be established between the variables of interest and the metrics, the problem lies in the repeatability of the model. It is tempting to assume that, having observed a historical connection between error rate and coding time, a repeatable model has been established. This is potentially dangerous, as has long been demonstrated in hardware reliability technology where failure rates are wrongly assumed to be predictable from component sizes, stress levels and so on. The COCOMO metric (11) above may well suffer from this limitation.

One benefit of even imprecise models is that those modules more likely to contain errors can be identified and additional review effort directed to them rather than applied at random. In other words despite the lack of absolute accuracy, metrics provide useful measures of comparison.

This work is still subject to development and many are optimistic of the eventual outcome. Nevertheless only the continued collection and analysis

Title of assessment/module/system _____

Date _____Assessor _____

_____	LOC	= number of executable lines of code
_____	v	= number of referenced variables
_____	c	= number of different commands
_____	n	= number of modules (*Note*: 1 rung = 1 module in ladder logic)
_____	z	= 1 not complicated................5 complicated
_____	cp	= number of control path crossings
_____	E	= number of edges in the flow diagram
_____	N	= number of vertices
_____	P	= number of connected components (usually 1)
_____	ds	= number of design statements (e.g. line of pseudo code, control flow box, text sentence)
_____	fi	= number of other modules which call that module
_____	fo	= number of other modules called by that module
_____	F	= number of faults found
_____	w	= weeks since start of test
_____	wrd	= words in document
_____	sen	= sentences in document
_____	hrd	= number of words > two syllables
_____	Q	= number of comment lines

_____	Number of changes for	Fault correction
_____		Planned enhancement
_____		Requirements change
_____		Improved clarity
_____		Improved maintainability
_____		Improved documentation
_____		Inserting debug code
_____		Removing debug code
_____		Optimizing time
_____		Optimizing space
_____		Optimizing accuracy
_____		Correcting design deficiency
_____		Adapting to environmental change
_____	Number of years developer	• software engineering
_____		• the application area
_____		• the specific role
_____		• the programming environment
_____		• the language

Fig. 15.2 Assessment sheet.

of empirical data will enable these models to be established and validated. Figure 15.2 shows an assessment sheet suitable for the metrics described in this chapter. This can be adapted for other metrics or to suit the user's requirements.

15.1.6 Failure data acquisition

In order to optimize the accuracy of metrics it is important to have sufficient failure data to enable the models firstly to be derived and secondly to be validated. The following minimum data are required:

- a description of the running conditions;
- date and time of start of run;
- date and time of the incident/failure;
- date and time of restart;
- date and time of normal termination had there been no failure;
- effect of failure on system;
- data and I/O load and any environmental factors;
- detailed narrative of the incident.

In many cases it is only possible to count the number of failures which have occurred in a given time or during a given number of tests. Under those circumstances the construction of metrics is highly unlikely. There still remains the problem that some metrics are 'hung up' on the concept of time. We need to think in terms of the number of new patterns and routes used in a system rather than the number of hours of running.

15.2 FAILURE DISTRIBUTION MODELLING

Several statistical models have been developed for the purpose of estimating software reliability. The models described here are unstructured models in that they treat the code as a black box and attempt to model the reliability against time. General opinion seems to be that no one model is better than the others at predicting the extrapolated reliability. Their basis is the assumption that the failures are distributed at random. This may not necessarily be true since they will occur only as a result of executing a specific path in the code and, perhaps, with specific inputs and interface conditions.

The problem, lightheartedly illustrated in Fig. 15.3, is that the data (Monday to Wednesday) may contain the information to predict a few days ahead but not necessarily to the time when the very low failure rates of interest are eventually achieved. In the same way, the Normal distribution models human height sufficiently well to enable statements to be made of how many people are between 6 ft and 6 ft 1 in. The ability of the

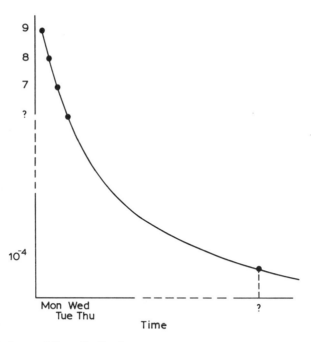

Fig. 15.3 Software failure distribution.

model to forecast accurately how many people exceed 7 ft is far less certain.

Since software failure rates are dependent on many human factors, as well as a number of project-related parameters (compilers, configuration control, hardware architectures, etc.), data obtained from one software program are unlikely to be applicable to other, ostensibly similar, programs.

The models are, nevertheless, useful as management tools in monitoring the effectiveness and progress of test. They are not predictive during design but only by extrapolating empirical data. No attempt to compare them is made here but a brief description is given.

15.2.1 The Poisson model

This is based on the assumption that faults are distributed at random throughout the software and that their occurrence is directly related to program run time. It is also assumed that the occurrence of a failure is not dependent on any previous errors.

Thus, the number of errors, $N(t)$, after a time, t, will be:

$$N(t) = A\, e^{-bt},$$

where A is the number of errors at the beginning and b is a constant rate.

15.2.2 The Musa models

(a) John Musa's basic execution time model is based on program execution time and assumes that:

- Failures are mutually independent and occur at a constant rate (i.e. at random).
- There is a representative mix of instructions and functions.
- The mean time between failures (MTBF) is greater than the execution times.
- Errors are removed when revealed.
- The failure rate is proportional to the number of faults remaining.

The failure rate, after n failures, is thus given as:

$$\lambda_n = \lambda_0(1 - n/V)$$

where:

λ_n is the failure rate after n failures;
λ_0 is the initial failure rate;
n is the number of failures experienced;
V is the number of failures remaining.

If, for example, the failure rate has declined to 0.25/CPU h, from 0.5/CPU h, after 50 failures, then:

$$0.25 = 0.5(1 - 50/V),$$

So $V = 100$.

(b) John Musa also proposes a logarithmic model for where it is assumed that faults in frequently executed code will be found earlier and result in larger decrements than later failures.

This is expressed as:

$$\lambda_n = \lambda_0 \exp(-\theta n)$$

where θ is the failure rate decay factor.

So, if an initial failure rate of 10/CPU h declines to 4/CPU h after 50 failures then:

$$4 = 10 \exp(-\theta \times 50)$$

Thus $= 0.018$.

The number of failures needed to be revealed to reduce the failure rate to a stated level can now be predicted by the model.

15.2.3 The Jelinski–Moranda model

This model, based on the analysis of NASA and US Navy data, assumes that failure rate is proportional to the current error content of a program, that the remaining faults are equally likely to become failures and that additional faults are not introduced.

This, like the Schick–Wolverton model, is exponentially based.

15.2.4 The Littlewood–Veral models

This is a Bayesian approach which estimates the time to the next failure by inference from the previous failures. An exponential distribution is assumed such that reliability increases with time as each failure is revealed and corrected.

Littlewood attempts to allow for different faults having different probabilities of propagating to become failures. In the model, the failure rate for each error type is allowed to fall each time that it is revealed.

15.2.5 The Shooman model

In this case empirical data from previous, similar, projects is used to provide the values of the constant (e.g. errors per instruction) for a reliability model. Again, a fixed number of faults, which decreases as the failures occur, is assumed. The model includes an error-correction rate parameter which, in practice, varies with the manpower levels available to the project.

15.2.6 The Schneidewind model

Another empirically based model which involves collecting data, identifying the distributions of failure and applying those distributions to the parameters of the project in question. Exponential and Weibull models are utilized as appropriate according to the way in which the failure rate changes.

15.2.7 The Brown and Lipow model

This involves defining the possible combinations of inputs to a program in order to model the reliability based on test results on a known number of input combinations. Since the complexity of software programs implies very large numbers of combinations, it is necessary to define subsets to which the model can be applied.

15.2.8 The Laplace, point process, model

A software program can be viewed as a 'black box' continuous repair process, in the time continuum, with failures being detected and corrected. Thus, the Laplace method can be used to indicate the trend in the process failure rate.

If a system exhibits a number of failures, n, after time zero at times t_1, t_2, t_3, t_4, ..., t_n, then the test statistic is:

$$U = \frac{[\Sigma t_i / n] - [t_0 / 2]}{t_0 \sqrt{[1/12n]}}$$

where t_0 is the time at which the test is truncated.

If $U = 0$ then there is no trend and the failure rate is constant.

If $U < 0$ then the failure rate is decreasing and if $U > 0$ it is increasing.

15.2.9 Seeding and tagging

A number of researchers have applied seeding and tagging techniques to the problem of estimating failure populations. The method involves the injection of known faults into the code. The success rate of debugging the known faults is used to predict the total population of failures by applying the ratio of successful diagnoses to the revealed non-seeded failures.

Thus if S faults are seeded and give rise to s failures then if, in the same time, f unseeded failures occur it is assumed that the total real faults is:

$$F = fS/s.$$

For this method to be successful one has to assume that the seeded failures are of the same type as the unknown failures and are thus equally likely to occur. In practice it is not so easy to be imaginative in creating test errors and the real faults are likely to be more subtle.

A disadvantage of seeding is that it may adversely affect the reliability as a result of the changes made around the seeded faults.

15.2.10 Dual-test team model

This involves the same concept as seeding but avoids the disadvantage of having to inject additional faults. Two independent test teams are used and the assumption is:

If team A finds say 30% of the faults found by team B then it will find 30% of all the faults.

Let Team A find A faults and let Team B find B faults.
Let the faults found by both teams be Y.
Let there be N total faults.

The effectiveness of Team A is:

$$E_A = A/N = X/B$$

The effectiveness of Team B is:

$$E_B = B/N = X/A$$

So, $E_A = X/(NE_B)$

Therefore $N = X/(E_A E_B)$

15.3 THE PROCESS CAPABILITY MATURITY MODEL

The Software Engineering Institute (SEI) have developed a five-level
process capability model. This is a type of metric, in that it involves
scoring criteria which enable a project or organization to assess its
maturity level in terms of software engineering practice. The philosophy is
that carrying out the assessment is a step to determining the appropriate
improvement goals.

The scoring questions are in seven sections:

1. organization;
2. resources, personnel and training;
3. technology management;
4. documented standards and procedures;
5. process metrics;
6. data management and analysis;
7. process control.

The questions are all yes/no and are each assigned to one of the five
levels. Questions marked with a # symbol are deemed to have greater
importance. It is assumed that everyone starts at level 1 and to reach level
2 80% of the level 2 questions and 90% of the # level 2 questions must
attract a yes.

Similarly, to reach level 3, 80% of the level 3 questions and 90% of the
level 3 questions must attract a yes. The same principle is applied for
reaching level 4 or 5.

There are 85 questions, of which the following is a sample.

Organization
L2   For each project, is there a designated software manager?
L2#   Is there a software configuration control function for each project?

Resources, personnel and training
L2   Does each developer have a private workstation/terminal?
L3# Is there a formal training programme required for design and code review leaders?

Technology management
L2   Is a mechanism used for maintaining awareness of the state of the art in software technology?
L5# Is a mechanism used for identifying and replacing obsolete technologies?

Documented standards and procedures
L3   Is a mechanism used for assessing existing designs and code for re-use in new applications?
L3# Does the organization use a standardized documented development process on each project?

Process metrics
L2   Are target computer memory utilization estimates and actuals tracked?
L4# Are design errors projected and compared with actuals?

Data management and analysis
L4   Is software productivity analysed for major process steps?
L5# Is a mechanism used for error cause analysis?

Process control
L2   Is a mechanism used for regular technical interchanges with the customer?
L4# Is a mechanism used for periodically assessing the software engineering process and implementing improvements?

PART FIVE

Case Study

This case study provides a hierarchy of documents representing the requirements and the design of a detection system. It is seeded with errors (mostly deliberate) and some guidance is given to the reader in identifying them. Substantial contributions were made to this exercise by Dr Paul Banks and Mr John Dixon.

Software system design exercise – addressable detection system

16

This exercise is in the form of a set of documents covering the design cycle of a simple system for the detection and annunciation of fire in an enclosed building. The design contains deliberate errors, omissions and ambiguities, some of which are obvious and others which will require more careful study to reveal them. The problem should be treated as a whole rather than as individual elements since the errors will often only be revealed by comparing requirements between documents. The documents include:

- a requirements specification;
- a functional specification;
- a software specification;
- module and submodule specifications;
- a quality plan;
- a test specification.

In Chapter 7, the need for a traceable document hierarchy was emphasized. Figure 16.1 is an outline of the document structure for this design. Some of the document numbers and titles have been deliberately omitted. An initial scan of the documents in this section will provide the information needed to complete the chart. It is strongly recommended that this is attempted before proceeding with the exercise.

The requirements and design documents which follow should be studied and compared with each other. The tutor's discussion notes near the end of this chapter describe some of the omissions, ambiguities and errors in order to guide the reader. The remaining errors, including the not so deliberate, we leave to you.

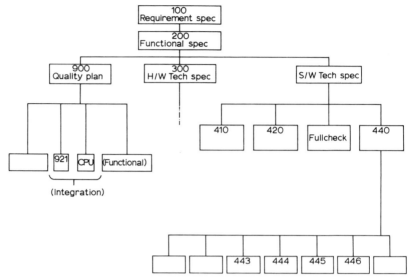

Fig. 16.1 Document hierarchy.

At the end of this section a revised functional specification (Issue 2.0) is given. Although by no means a model solution, it takes into account some of the errors in Issue 1.0.

PD352/100
Issue 1.0
1.1.88

REQUIREMENTS SPECIFICATION – ADDRESSABLE DETECTION SYSTEM

This document in no way represents an example document for use. Warning! Contains deliberate errors. For training purposes only.

PD352/100
Issue 1.0
1.1.88

1.0   Overview

A programmable detection system is required to provide both automatic executive actions and annunciation to the user. It is used to control fire water sprinklers and plant shutdown equipment. The equipment is required for use in enclosed spaces.

2.0   Objectives

2.1   The system is protecting a hazardous plant and thus must provide continuous monitoring of inputs and must always fail safe.

2.2   To provide visual and audible annunciation of detectors.

2.3   To provide automatic initiation of executive outputs.

3.0   Operating requirements

3.1   Switch on and switch off must not cause spurious actions.

3.2   Hardware failures of the equipment must automatically be detected, diagnosed and displayed to the operator.

3.3   The system must be capable of tolerating up to 24 h mains failure and respond to mains recovery without loss of function.

3.4   The system must be capable of periodic automatic self-test whereby the effect of simulated input signals is verified without loss of function.

3.5   The equipment is to operate on 220/240 V mains 50 Hz.

4.0   Functional requirements

4.1   Inputs must respond to digital and analogue transducers.

4.2   Inputs must be uniquely identifiable to the system.

PD352/100
Issue 1.0
1.1.88

4.3 Outputs must consist of:
   (a) signals to sprinkler systems;
   (b) volt-free output loops;
   (c) data to a display panel giving input status.

4.4 Maximum I/O capacities are:

   (a) 80 digital inputs;
   (b) 80 analogue inputs;
   (c) 50, volt free outputs;
   (d) 50, 24 V outputs;
   (e) provision for hardwired and RS232 interface to a graphics or mimic facility.

4.5 Ability to group inputs into definable zones.

4.6 A duplicated logic unit with the ability to initiate outputs on the basis of combinations and comparisons of the inputs of each zone.

4.7 Ability to respond to the following stimuli:

   (a) ultra-violet light (25 ms duration);
   (b) smoke (hydrocarbon fires);
   (c) infra-red light;
   (d) temperature;
   (e) rate of temperature rise.

4.8 All applications software shall be implemented using a block-structured language having an ISO standard version.

5.0 Environment

5.1 Ground-fixed enclosed buildings.

5.2 Ambient temperature range –10°C to 35°C.

5.3 Humidity to 95%.

5.4 Near proximity of hydrocarbon process plant.

PD352/100
Issue 1.0
1.1.88

6.0   Other requirements

6.1   The equipment must be repairable on line without total loss of function. A repair time object of 1 h is required.

6.2   The system must be able to accommodate future extensions either by an increase of I/O capacity or by interworking duplicate or higher numbers of equipments.

6.3   The probability of failure to respond to a valid input, on demand, shall not exceed 10^{-6}.

6.4   The incidence of spurious action shall not exceed one incident per annum.

6.5   A facility for logging events.

6.6   The following standards and guidelines will be applied during design and manufacture:

   (a) BS 5760;
   (b) BS 5750 (Part 1) 1987;
   (c) STARTS Purchasers Handbook;
   (d) HSE Document – Programmable Electronic Systems in Safety Related Applications 1987.

6.7   The equipment shall fit into an area $7\,m \times 3.5\,m$ with a ceiling height of $2\,m$.

6.8   The weight of the equipment including power supplies shall not exceed $500\,kg$.

PD352/200
Issue 1.0
1.1.88

FUNCTIONAL SPECIFICATION – ADDRESSABLE DETECTION SYSTEM

PD352/200
Issue 1.0
1.1.88

1.0 Introduction

1.1 The proposed system will perform the following functions on 220/240 V 50 Hz mains:

(a) Monitor the fire detectors to interrogate their status at one second intervals each.
(b) Initiate built-in test mode at system start-up and at operator request.
(c) Display status of each detector on a colour graphics screen.
(d) Trigger audible alarm in the event of fire detection.
(e) Trigger fire sprinkler systems and outputs to other control systems.
(f) Self-diagnose the computer system at start-up to detect faults.
(g) Print out system events.

1.2 The hardware configuration is as shown in Fig. 1.2.

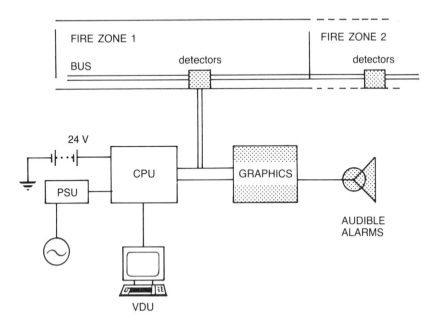

Fig. A1.2 Hardware schematic.

PD352/200
Issue 1.0
1.1.88

2.0   Facilities and functions

2.1   The system will allow connection of up to 127 detectors each of which is separately addressable.

2.2   A graphical display will provide a visual mimic of the status of each detector with a 'picture' of its location.

2.3   The audible alarm must be sounded when any event occurs.

2.4   A VDU will duplicate the information displayed by the mimic.

2.5   In the event of failure of the CPU the computer system will revert to the use of hardwired circuitry.

2.6   The system will provide a start-up mode of operation which will perform system checks and then go into normal operation. A system shutdown mode will also be provided.

2.7   During normal operation all events and operator commands will be logged on a disc.

3.0   System operation

3.1   Operator inputs
The system will be operated via the computer system keyboard. Commands may be entered, singly, at the keyboard. The set of commands is:

DIAG   Performs autodiagnosis on the computer system.
DEST($\langle n \rangle$)   Initiates detector self test where n denotes the detector.
STAT($\langle n \rangle$)   Forces a report of all detectors' status or, if n is specified, a particular detector.
CANC   Shuts down audible alarm.
LOG   Prints all status changes since last system restart.
MIMC   VDU reverts to zone mimic (see 3.3).

It will not be necessary for the operator to input data except where required by a command. This will enhance the security and integrity of the system.

PD352/200
Issue 1.0
1.1.88

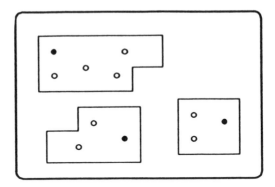

Fig. A3.2 The effect of MIMC.

At switch-on, the system will require the entry of a password known only to the operator. Password validation will be allowed only three times within a minute and then an enforced 20 minute delay will begin.

3.2   VDU format
The detectors will be polled sequentially and the VDU will normally display information in the form:

Time	*Detector*	*Status*
xx:xx:xx	*n*	OK

Upon the command MIMC (see 3.1) this will be replaced with a zonal mimic (see Fig. 3.2).
Activated detectors will be indicated by a change of colour and intermittent flashing.

3.3   MIMIC
The graphics panel will consist of groups of LED displays representing the fire zones and their individual detectors.

3.4   Log file layout
The log file, held on disc, will contain all command and response information and also the result of system start-up. Each message and response will be stored sequentially in the form:

⟨TIME, COMMAND, RESPONSE⟩ ⟨TIME, STATUS CHANGE⟩.

PD352/200
Issue 1.0
1.1.88

3.5   Detection logic

There are two levels of detection logic.

(a) A non-executive level which actuates the audible alarm and updates the VDU and mimic. This is normally triggered by the activation of a single detector.

However, the detection level shall be programmable by the user according to his requirements.

(b) An executive level which is normally used for the activation of outputs associated with the fire suppression systems. A typical arrangement would be the voting of two inputs out of *n*.

3.6   Executive outputs

These are triggered in response to the appropriate detection or manual inputs as preprogrammed during installation by the user. The executive outputs will consist of volt-free loops capable of switching 24 V solenoids and of carrying 50 mA. Both make and break conditions shall be available as the outputs.

4.0   Design, development and test

4.1   Hardware

(a) A standard 16-bit microcomputer will be chosen for this system implementation using the MS-DOS operating system. Hardware peripherals will be as specified in PD352/300.

(b) Suitable I/O units will be used to interface each detector with the binary bus to enable individual detector addressing.

(c) Eurorack equipment practice will be used.

4.2   Software

(a) The Pascal language will be used for the coding of all software except where it is necessary to interface to hardware, where assembly code will be used.

(b) A validated compiler will be used.

(c) A standard real-time operating system will be employed which has disc file facilities embedded. No special tailoring of the package is expected.

(d) The software developed for this system will be validated when the system is completely coded. In this way the testing will be more

PD352/200
Issue 1.0
1.1.88

efficient and the problems more quickly resolved. For this reason configuration control will not be applied until this stage is completed.

4.3 Test

Since this is a small system only a minimal project plan will be produced.

5.0 Operation and maintenance

5.1 The system will be attended by an operator who will be conversant with the output facilities. He or she will be capable of using the input commands.

5.2 Printed board changes will involve system re-start.

5.3 Detector changes will be possible without disenabling the system.

5.4 Removal of a detector shall not result in any alarm state but must be indicated at the operator station.

PD352/300
Issue 1.0
1.1.88

HARDWARE TECHNICAL SPECIFICATION – ADDRESSABLE DETECTION SYSTEM

This document in no way represents an example document for use. Warning! Contains deliberate errors. For training purposes only.

PD352/300
Issue 1.0
1.1.88

This document is not used in the case study

PD352/400
Issue 1.0
1.1.88

SOFTWARE TECHNICAL SPECIFICATION – ADDRESSABLE DETECTION SYSTEM

This document in no way represents an example document for use. Warning! Contains deliberate errors. For training purposes only.

PD352/400
Issue 1.0
1.1.88

1.0   Overall software design

1.1   Strategy
The software shall be designed using top-down techniques and coding using structured programming. The major programming language will be ANSI Pascal except where assembler code shall be used for the purpose of speed requirements.

Documentation will include use of an in-house pseudocode to describe the top levels of the design, with successive levels decomposed into pseudo-code. The functional specification is described in document PD352/200 (Functional Specification).

1.2   Design and development factors
A standard real-time operating system will be employed which has disc file facilities embedded. No special tailoring of the package is expected to be necessary.

2.0   Detailed software description

2.1   Top level
The software will be structured so that after initialization of the system the main body of the program will run continuously until shut down.

The modules defined within this document will each be the subject of a module design document. Test and QA are described elsewhere.

2.2   Data flow (logical design)
The data flow within the system is described by Fig. 1.

2.3   Software systems structure
The overall systems structure is shown as Fig. 2.

2.4   Control flow

2.4.1   The overall systems flow chart (flow control)
This is shown in Fig. 3.

2.4.2   The top level of design (pseudocode)
The top level of design is shown, expressed in pseudocode, covering the overall top-level systems flow chart.

PD352/400
Issue 1.0
1.1.88

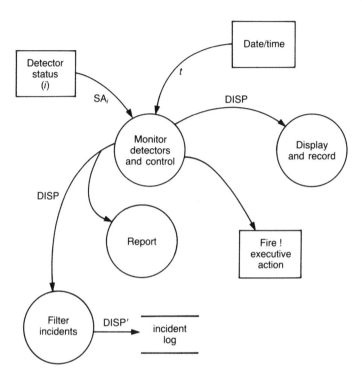

Fig. A1 Data flow.

The overall top level pseudocode will have the following structure:

```
supervisory module;
  begin
    initialize system;
    perform diagnostic checks;
    do forever;
    for i = 1 to n (where n is the maximum number of detectors)
      begin
        check status (i);
        check detector (i);
        set report;
      end for
    end do
  end supervisory module;
```

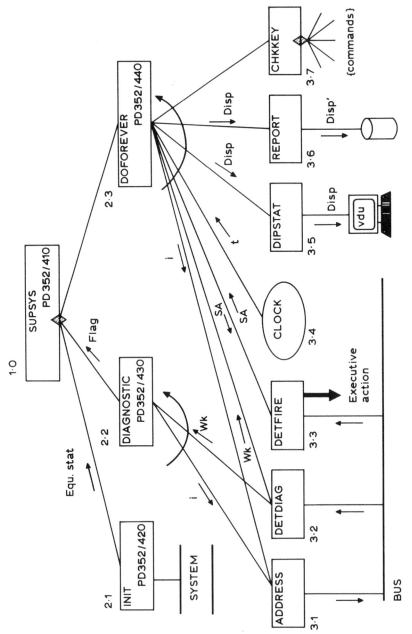

Fig. A2 Overall system structure chart. Note information in data dictionary (2.5).

PD352/400
Issue 1.0
1.1.88

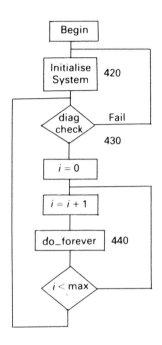

Fig. A3 Flow control.

Table 2.5 Data dictionary

Item	Type	Dimension	Description
i	Integer scalar	–	Control counter for detector sampling $1 \leqslant i \leqslant$ DMAX
Flag	Boolean scalar	–	True if detectors working, else false
WK	Boolean scalar	–	True if detector $[i]$ in working order, else false
EQU-	(Text arrays	(to be decided)	Message about outcome of initialization.
STAT	Boolean arrays)	(to be decided)	Logical flags for outcome of various activities of initialization.
t	Text array	12	Date and time, i.e. DDMMYYhhmmss
SA	Boolean array	$\geqslant$[DMAX]	Status array for detector fire status. For $[i] \leqslant$ [DMAX] then SA_i = TRUE = > Fire detected else SA_i = False
DISP	Data construct		$[SAi, t, i]$

PD352/400
Issue 1.0
1.1.88

3.0 Software system description
The overall software shall be modular in construction, each module will be testable and address one particular subsystem of the complete software description. The major subsystems are given below with their corresponding documentation number.

3.1 Supervisory system (PD352/410)
The purpose of this module is to amalgamate all lower levels of software within a cohesive whole.

3.2 Initialize (PD352/420)
The purpose of this module is to perform various checks at system start-up:
These functions are:

—Run diagnostics on main computer.
—Set up VDU and Graphics.
—Inform the operator of system state.

3.3 Diagnostic check (PD352/430)
The purpose of the diagnostic check module is to check the initial status of the detectors (a) before full operation and (b) at periodic intervals during operation.

3.4 Do forever module (PD352/440)
This loop is the principal mode of operation, it polls the detectors in sequence and reports on their status. Each pass will do the following.

- address detector;
- check detector operation;
- acquire status on fire detection;
- display status;
- report;
- check keyboard status;
- execute command.

PD352/400
Issue 1.0
1.1.88

The commands are:

DIAG   Performs autodiagnosis on the computer system.

DEST$\langle n \rangle$ Initiates detector self-test where n denotes the detector.

STAT$\langle n \rangle$ Forces a report of all detectors' status or if specified, that of a particular detector.

CANC   Shuts down audible alarm.

LOG   Prints all status changes since last system restart.

PD352/440
Issue 1.0
1.1.88

SOFTWARE TECHNICAL SPECIFICATION – ADDRESSABLE DETECTION SYSTEM

DO FOREVER MODULE – VERSION 001

PD352/440
Issue 1.0
1.1.88

1.0 Module definition

This loop is the principal mode of operation since it polls the detectors in sequence and reports on their condition. Each diversion through the loop will address the following submodules, each submodule shown below is the subject of a software design document (written in pseudocode for ease of understanding).

1.1 Address the detector (PD352/441)

Unless otherwise directed each detector will be addressed sequentially starting at detector 1 and progressing to detector n.

1.2 Check detector (PD352/442)

Module will perform a basic diagnostic check on the addressed detector.

1.3 Acquire status on fire detection (PD352/443)

Fire status will be reported on a fire is detected basis. Polling will take place between detectors in the same zone as will voting.

1.4 Display status (PD352/444)

This software module will indicate the presence of the detector and its status will be reported on the VDU.

1.5 Report (PD352/445)

This software module will record all status changes onto the disc drive.

1.6 Check keyboard (PD352/446)

This module will check the keyboard for admissible input.

1.7 Execute command (PD352/447)

This module will, on receipt of a significant input from the keyboard, execute a given command.
The commands are:

DIAG	Performs autodiagnosis on the computer system.
DEST$\langle n \rangle$	Initiates detector self-test where n denotes the detector.
STAT$\langle n \rangle$	Forces a report of all detectors status or, if specified, a particular detector.
CANC	Shut down audible alarm.
LOG	Prints all status changes since last system restart.

PD352/440
Issue 1.0
1.1.88

2.0   Control strategy

2.1   System flowchart for do forever loop

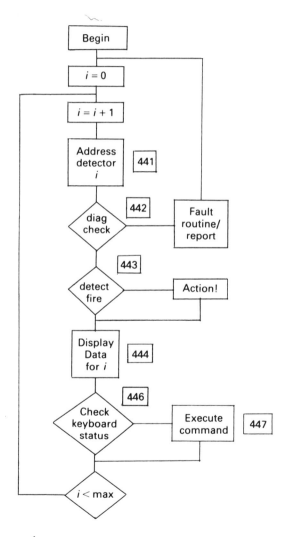

Fig. B1 Do forever loop.

PD352/440
Issue 1.0
1.1.88

2.2 Do forever module code

```
Begin {Main loop}
    Begin
        Address Detector (i);
        Begin
            Set address detector;
            Check detector;
            Begin
                Get detector data;
                if detector data ? OK then;
                Set fault (i);
            End (Check detector);

            Detector status;
            Begin
                Get detector status;
                if detector status ?OK then;
                Set alarm (i);
                Begin;
                    Set status (i) = T,
                End (Set alarm);
            End (Detector status);

            Display data (i);
            Begin
                Set Graphics region (i, status, fault);
            End (Display data (i))

            Report data (i);
            Begin
                Send output data to log;
                Send output to log;
                Send output to printer;
            End (Report data (i))

            Check Keyboard entry;
            Begin
                If command type then;
                Begin
                    Do case of command;
        DIAG:       Perform diagnostics;
                    Report results;
        DEST:       Perform detector self test;
                    Report results;
        STAT:       Report all detector status;
        CANC:       Cancel audible alarm;
        LOG:        Print all status changes;
        MIMC:       Perform route to mimic;
                End (If)
            End (Check Keyboard entry)
    End {Main loop}
```

PD352/443
Issue 1.0
1.1.88

SOFTWARE TECHNICAL SPECIFICATION – ADDRESSABLE DETECTION SYSTEM

DO FOREVER MODULE VERSION 001

DETFIRE SUBMODULE VERSION 001

PD352/443
Issue 1.0
1.1.88

SUBMODULE DEFINITIONS

1.0   Purpose

The module interrogates the detector status line returning status:

{FIRE / NO FIRE}

for the given detector, and by a voting system involving detectors in the same zone, signals the detection of a systems status of fire.

(a) Any one detector; status = Fire, will provoke an audible alarm.

(b) Any two or more detectors; status = Fire, in same zone will provide systems status equivalent to Fire, and provoke Fire execution action and will provide an audible siren. Fire executive action is the subject of another document and not addressed here.

2.0   Pseudocode detection status

```
Definition of Terms
Poll Detector (i)  =  Detector Status (i)
                   =  TRUE         FIRE
                      FALSE        OK

Begin
  Poll Detector (i)
  If detector Status (i) = TRUE then
    Set Audible Alarm;
    Do for all Other Detectors in same Zone
      If Detector Status (i) = True, for i = 1, then
        Set Executive Action;
      End If
    End Do
  End If
End (    )
```

Normally at this point in the documentation the module would be implemented in programming language.

PD352/900
Issue 1.0
1.1.88

QUALITY PLAN – ADDRESSABLE DETECTION SYSTEM

PD352/900
Issue 1.0
1.1.88

CONTENTS

PD352/900
Issue 1.0
1.1.88

(For the purpose of this exercise, only section 3 of the document is presented.)

.
.
.
.
.
.
.

3.0   Test strategy

3.1   Strategy
The development testing is based on a bottom-up strategy. Printed board assemblies (PBAs) will initially be tested alone. This will be followed by integration tests involving groups of PBAs. Functional tests will then be carried out on the complete system. These will include I/O load tests and misuse tests. Finally an environmental test will be applied.

3.2   PBA module tests
Each PBA will be subject to a stand-alone functional test on the programmable GENRAD XXXXX tester with simulated inputs programmed as appropriate. The PBA test specs are:

PD352/911	MOTHER BOARD
PD352/912	CPU BOARD
PD352/913	5 CCT I/O BOARD
PD352/914	COMMUNICATIONS BOARD
PD352/915	PSU

3.3   Integration tests
The purpose of these tests is to establish that boards can communicate and function together. The integration test specs are:

PD352/921	I/O–CPU INTEGRATION
PD352/922	COMMS–CPU INTEGRATION

PD352/900
Issue 1.0
1.1.88

3.4 Functional tests

The functional test specs are:

PD352/931	SYSTEM FUNCTIONAL TEST
PD352/932	I/O LOAD TEST
PD352/933	SYSTEM MARGINAL TESTS
PD352/934	MISUSE TESTS
PD352/935	ENVIRONMENTAL TEST

PD352/921
Issue 1.0
1.1.88

I/O–CPU INTEGRATION TEST SPECIFICATION – ADDRESSABLE DETECTION SYSTEM

PD352/921
Issue 1.0
1.1.88

1.0 Objective

To establish that input stimuli give rise to correct outputs whilst controlled by the CPU board.

2.0 Test hardware and software

2.1 I/O PBA with simulated inputs for three fire detectors and one manual call point (MCP).

2.2 I/O PBA with simulated alarm and executive outputs.

2.3 CPU PBA with application software including cause and effect logic for the simulated fire area.

2.4 Test PBA (PD352/921/001) to simulate the communications PBA responses and thus prevent communications failure errors which would otherwise shut down the system.

2.5 Communications analyser (XXXXXXXXXX) with connections to the CPU data bus.

3.0 Test procedure

3.1 Start-up
Connect power and switch on.
Observe that no outputs are activated.

3.2 Detector sampling
Set up and connect the communications analyser to the CPU address data bus.
Observe that the three detectors and MCP addresses are polled at no less than 1 s intervals.

3.3 Detector 1 out of 3 alarm
Simulate one detector input.
Observe simulated audible alarm output.

PD352/921
Issue 1.0
1.1.88

Repeat the test for No. 2 detector.
Repeat the test for No. 3 detector.

3.4 Manual call point executive action
Simulate the MCP input.
Observe simulated executive action output.

3.5 Detector 2 out of 3 executive action
Simulate Detectors 1 and 2 input.
Observe simulated executive output.
Repeat for Detectors 1 and 3.
Repeat for Detectors 2 and 3.
Repeat for all three detectors.
Repeat for MCP and all three detectors.

Tutor's discussion

Requirements specification PD352/100

1. There are a number of important items missing from this specification. The following are a few examples:

- Extendability (6.2) should be quantified.
- Maintenance scenario (e.g. frequency, type of on-line repair).
- Is equipment stand-alone or connected to other control systems?
- Several terms are not defined.

Attempt to list additional omissions.

2. There are many ambiguities, for example:

- Fail safe (2.1). Spurious action (6.4) is not necessarily safe.
- Simulated (3.4) can involve a number of methods.
- What sort of auto-test?

Attempt to list additional ambiguities.

3. Specifying a programmable electronic system (PES) in (1.0) is a design implementation – not a requirement. There are at least two other design decisions which should not be specified at this level. Attempt to identify them.

Functional specification PD352/200 (issue 1.0)

1. There are a number of items missing from this specification. The following are a few examples:

- The test functions (1.1b) are not defined.
- The heat, smoke, UV requirements are not brought forward from the requirements specification.
- Mains failure recovery is not addressed.
- Fig. 1.2 shows no output ports on the processor.

Attempt to list additional omissions.

2. There are many ambiguities, for example:

- 'Mimic' and 'Graphics' are not defined.
- 'Self-diagnosis' (1.1f) is not clear.
- (2.1) should include the word sequentially.

Attempt to list additional omissions.

3. The requirements specification calls for auto-test (RS 3.4) but the FS calls for operator-initiated test.

4. The functional specification is still too early in the hierarchy to specify design details such as PES and disc.

4. MS-DOS is not a real-time operating system.

Attempt to identify other errors.

Hardware technical specification PD352/300

In order to keep the exercise within reasonable bounds, a hardware specification is not given. It is where the details of PES type (erroneously mentioned above) should be found.

Software technical specification PD352/400

1. There are a number of items missing from this document. The following are a few examples:

- No arrows in Fig. 3.
- No watchdog facility.
- No power down sequence provision.
- MIMC missing in 3.4.

Attempt to list additional omissions.

2. There are ambiguities, for example:

- There is a mixture of graphical methods. THIS IS DELIBERATE IN ORDER TO ILLUSTRATE SOME OF THE POSSIBLE DESIGN METHODOLOGIES.
- The meanings of 'various' (3.2), 'cohesive' (3.1), etc.

3. The DO FOREVER does not return to the diagnostic in 2.4.

4. Assembler is called for in (1.1) for speed whereas the functional specification (4.2) justifies it on the basis of interfaces.

Attempt to identify other errors.

Do forever module PD352/440

1. Examples of items omitted are:

    - MIMC command on page 1.
    - No arrows on Fig. 1.

2. There is no voting carried out in the module.

3. If the nth detector is faulty (Fig. 1) then the $(n + 1)$th is never reached.

4. The seven modules in 1.0 do not map those in PD352/400.

Attempt to identify other errors.

DETFIRE sub module PD352/443

1. There is no export of status to the voting module in the 443 sub-system.

2. Detector status implies 'fire' or 'no fire'. Other states such as 'under maintenance' and 'failed auto-test' need to be considered.

Quality plan PD352/900

1. Only dynamic testing is specified. Reviews and static analysis are not addressed.

2. Test strategy only maps the hardware configuration.

Attempt to identify other shortcomings.

Test procedure PD352/921

1. The tests do not specify the expected result. Thus, there can be no objective pass/fail criteria.

2. Tests do not specify what should not happen.

Attempt to find other shortcomings.

PD352/200
Issue 2.0
2.1.88

FUNCTIONAL SPECIFICATION – ADDRESSABLE DETECTION SYSTEM

PD352/200
Issue 2.0
2.1.88

1.0   Introduction

1.1   The proposed system will perform the following functions on 220/ 240 V 50 Hz mains:

(a) Monitor each of the fire detectors at one second intervals to interrogate their output status.
(b) Initiate built-in test mode at system start-up during normal operation and at operator request. This involves auto test of detector and output loops and incorporates a diagnostic check of the equipment.
(c) Display status of each detector on a colour graphics screen.
(d) Trigger audible alarm in the event of fire detection.
(e) Trigger fire sprinkler systems and outputs to a shut-down system.
(f) Self-diagnose the computer system at start-up to detect faults (see 3.7).
(g) Print out alarms.

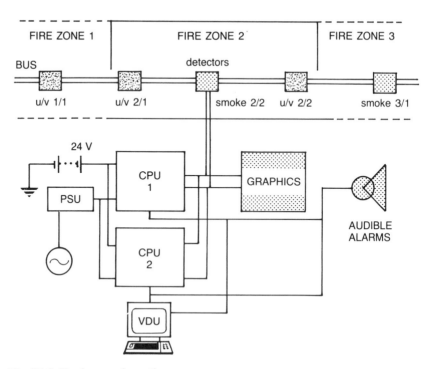

Fig. B1.2 Hardware schematic.

PD532/200
Issue 2.0
2.1.88

1.2   The hardware configuration is as shown in Fig. 1.2.

2.0   Facilities and functions

2.1   The system will allow connection of up to 160 detectors each of which is separately addressable. There may be UV, smoke (hydrocarbon fires), infra-red, temperature and rate-of-rise detectors.

2.2   A graphical display will provide a visual mimic of the status of each detector with a picture of its location. (See Fig. 3.2.)

2.3   The audible alarm must be sounded when one or more detectors activates.
   Alarms must differentiate between one detector or a zonal state of two or more.

2.4   A VDU will duplicate the information displayed by the mimic.

2.5   In the event of failure of the computer control, the system will revert to the use of hardwired circuitry.

2.6   The system will provide a start-up mode of operation which will perform system checks and then go into normal operation. A system shut-down mode will also be provided.

2.7   All events and operator commands will be logged on a permanent medium.

2.8   There shall be two alarm states:

   (a) level indicating a single detector only;
   (b) multiple alarm determined by preset zonal voting arrangements, resulting in alarm and executive action.

3.0   System operation

3.1   Operator commands
The system will be operated via the computer system keyboard. Commands may be entered, singly, at the keyboard. The set of

PD352/200
Issue 2.0
2.1.88

commands is:

DIAG	Performs autodiagnosis on the computer system.
DEST($\langle n \rangle$)	Initiates detector self-test where n denotes the detector.
STAT($\langle n \rangle$)	Forces a report of all detectors' status or, if n is specified, that of a particular detector.
CANC	Shuts down audible alarm (protected by a key switch).
LOG	Prints all status changes since last system restart.
MIMC	VDU reverts to zone mimic (see 3.2).
TIME	Time and date change input.

No other data input will be accepted by the system.

Use of these commands will require the entry of a password known only to the operator. Password validation will be allowed only three times within a minute and then an enforced 20 minute delay will begin. A separate password will be required to enable the use of the CANC command.

3.2 VDU format

The detectors will be polled sequentially and the VDU will normally display information in the form of Fig. 3.2.

Activated detectors will be indicated by a change of colour and flashing at 1 s intervals. Upon the command STAT this will be replaced with a list

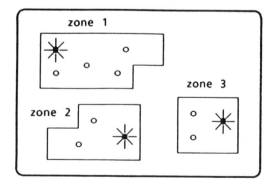

Fig. B3.2 VDU display.

PD352/200
Issue 2.0
2.1.88

of the states of the first 20 detectors in the form:

Time	Detector	Status
xx:xx:xx	No: Type:	OK
xx:xx:xx	No: Type:	ALARM

Subsequent commands will display blocks of 20 detectors.

3.3   MIMIC
The graphics panel will consist of groups of LED displays representing the fire zones and their individual detectors.

3.4   Log file layout
The log file will contain:

(i)   all commands;
(ii) response to commands;
(iii) detector response;
(iv) result of system start-up

in the form:

⟨TIME, COMMAND, RESPONSE⟩ ⟨TIME, STATUS CHANGE⟩.

3.5   Detection logic
There are two levels of detection logic, corresponding with states in 2.8(a) and 2.8(b).

(a) A non-executive level which actuates the audible alarm and updates the VDU and mimic. This is normally triggered by the activation of a single detector. However, the detection level shall be programmable by the user according to his requirements.

(b) An executive level which is normally used to activate outputs of the fire-suppression systems (e.g. halon, fire pumps). A typical arrangement would be the voting of two inputs out of n.

3.6   Executive outputs

These are triggered in response to the appropriate detector input or manual input as has been preprogrammed during installation by the user.

PD352/200
Issue 2.0
2.1.88

The executive outputs will consist of volt-free loops capable of switching 24 V solenoids and of carrying 50 mA. Non-executive outputs comprise the VDU and graphics. Both make and break conditions shall be available as the output state.

3.7 Diagnostic details

The autotest facility will perform the following checks.

(a) simulated detector inputs whilst outputs disenabled;
(b) simulated output signals whilst output function is disenabled;
(c) cause and effect logic functional checks;
(d) memory read/write checks.

4.0 Design, development

4.1 Hardware

(a) A microcomputer will be chosen for this system implementation using an appropriate real-time operating system. Hardware peripherals will be as specified in PD352/300.
(b) Suitable I/O units will be used to interface each detector with the binary bus to enable individual detector addressing.
(c) Eurorack equipment practice will be used.
(d) The PSU will consist of a battery float arrangement with capacity to provide a 24 h back-up in the events of mains failure.

4.2 Software

(a) A high-level language will be used for the coding of all software except where it is necessary to interface to hardware, where assembly code will be used.
(b) A validated compiler will be used.
(c) A standard real-time operating system will be employed which has disc-file facilities embedded. No special tailoring of the package is expected.

PD352/200
Issue 2.0
2.1.88

5.0   Operation and maintenance

5.1   The system will be attended by an operator who will be conversant with the output facilities. He or she will be capable of using the input commands.

5.2   Printed board changes will involve re-start-up of the system.

5.3   Detector changes will be possible without disenabling the system. Removal of a detector shall not result in any alarm state but must be indicated at the operator station.

Appendix 1

Checklists

The advantages and disadvantages of using checklists were reviewed in section 7.6. The following is a number of sample checklists which may be built on and developed by the user.

A1.1 QUALITY MANAGEMENT

1. Is there a senior person responsible for software quality who has adequate competence and authority to address all relevant issues?
2. Is there evidence of regular reviews of software standards?
3. Is there a written company requirement for planning software development?
4. Is there evidence of software training?
5. Is there good housekeeping of listings, specifications and computer hardware?
6. Is there a formal release procedure for deliverable software?
7. Is there a quality plan for each development, including:
   - organization of the team;
   - milestones;
   - codes of practice;
   - QC procedures including release;
   - purchased software;
   - documentation management;
   - support utilities;
   - installation;
   - test strategy?
8. Is there evidence of documented design reviews?
9. Is there evidence of defect reporting and corrective action?
10. Is there a fireproof media and file store or are media duplicated and stored in separate locations?

11. Are vendors' quality activities carried out by people not involved in the design of the product?
12. Is account taken of media shelf life?
13. Are there audits of documentation discrepancy?
14. Are the quality activities actually planned through the project?

A1.2 DOCUMENTATION STRUCTURE

A1.2.1 Requirements specification

1. Does the requirements specification include the following structure?:
   - an overview showing the system in relation to other plant;
   - objectives in terms of major functions (including consoles, panels, input/output devices, switches, timing, safety);
   - interfaces to plant, equipment, humans;
   - environment (temperature, humidity, vibration, radiation, etc.);
   - attributes (reliability, availability, maintainability, self-diagnostics);
   - documentation (specifications, manuals, drawings);
   - test and review (specific requirements for types of design review and test strategies).

A1.2.2 Other documents

1. Is there an adequate structure of documentation?
2. Are all issued documents issued and available?
3. Do specifications address system response under failure and unexpected conditions?
4. Is the format of the documents consistent?
5. Is change control in operation?
6. Are development notebooks in use (if so audit a sample for completeness)?
7. Are the requirements of the higher-level specifications accurately reflected down through the other documents to module level?
8. Is there a significant number of parameters left 'to be determined'?
9. Do actual documents and firmware (PROMs) correspond to the build state records? (do sample checks).
10. Are maintenance manuals:
    - adequately detailed and illustrated;
    - prepared during design;
    - objectively tested?
11. Are operating instructions adequately detailed and illustrated?
12. Is there a standard or guide for flow charts, diagrams, or pseudocode in the design of modules?

13. Are there written conventions for file naming and module labelling?
14. Is issue control correctly applied?
15. Is it easy to cross-reference to other documents?

A1.3 CONFIGURATION AND CHANGE CONTROL

1. Is there a documentation plan (e.g. list of all documents)?
2. Is there a procedure for the holding of originals?
3. Is there a procedure for the release of both media and documents?
4. Is there a change-control procedure?
5. Is there a procedure for the identification of the current version of all documents?

A1.4 PROGRAMMING STANDARDS

1. Is there a document defining programming standards?
2. Is each of the following covered:
   - use of globals;
   - hygienic language subsets;
   - error-correction software;
   - automatic fault diagnosis;
   - coding formats and layout;
   - comments;
   - rules for module identification;
   - size of codable units (i.e. module size);
   - file security;
   - operator error security;
   - unauthorized use security;
   - data organization and structures;
   - memory organization and backup;
   - use of PROM, EPROM, RAM, etc.;
   - treatment of variables (e.g. access);
   - block lengths;
   - recovery conventions;
   - range-checking arrays?
3. Is there a need for structured programming?
4. Is there a library of common program modules (subject to change control)?
5. Is a modular approach to software design in evidence?

A1.5 DESIGN REVIEW

A1.5.1 Requirements and design

1. Does the requirements specification adequately meet the following:
   - completeness in that all items necessary to define the problem have been specified;
   - correctness in that items are free from error;
   - preciseness, clarity and lack of ambiguity;
   - consistency in that items do not conflict;
   - relevance in that items pertain to the requirement;
   - testability in that it is possible to demonstrate each requirement;
   - traceability in that each element has a recognizable origin;
   - freedom from unwarranted design detail in that the requirements specification does not preempt design solutions (e.g. use of a PES)?
2. Are the operating cases and environments which the system will meet defined?
3. Are all safety constraints identified?
4. Is the system identifiable as modules and are these listed?
5. Has a failure-mode analysis been conducted?
6. Are all relevant documents available for the review?
7. Is the software specification complete, consistent, unambiguous and perceivable?
8. Is there traceability of the requirements through the specifications?
9. Are software quality auditing procedures included in the quality plan?
10. Have internal and external system interfaces been defined?
11. Are there specific design areas (e.g. processor speed, security) which create new difficulties?
12. Does safety integrity depend upon diversity, in which case how is this implemented?
13. Have adequate budgets for CPU, memory, I/O, timing, etc. been established in the light of the requirements?
14. Is the design expressed in terms of functional, operational and data diagrams?
15. Have all approved changes been included in the design?
16. Does the test and integration specification fully address the requirements?
17. Have changes been followed by adequate testing?

A1.5.2 Code

This checklist can be applied to each module of code inspected. It should be noted that, with some high-level languages, these checks are performed by the compiler. With weakly typed languages (e.g. C) the list should be extended. Alternatively, evidence of vendor code inspection to similar criteria will be sought.

1. Are all constants defined?
2. Are all unique values explicitly tested?
3. Are values stored after they have been calculated?
4. Are parameters restored on exits from interrupts?
5. Are incremental counts properly initialized (e.g. 0 or 1)?
6. Are internal variable names unique and meaningful?
7. Is there adequate COMMENT in the listings?
8. Are there time or cycle limits placed on infinite loops?
9. Are data structures protected or can they be accessed from many points?
10. Is the zero case taken into account in calculations?

A1.6   TEST

1. Are there written requirements for testing software?
2. Are the test plans/schedules/specifications which have been written in parallel with the design?
3. Is there a build-up of integration and testing (e.g. module test followed by subsystem and then system test)?
4. Is there evidence of test reporting and of remedial action?
5. Is a simulation planned (in the case of larger configurations)?
6. Are software prototypes envisaged for demonstrating system concepts to the user? If so at what stage will they be produced and what will they cover?
7. Is the test software under build state control?
8. Can the test facility demonstrate all operational modes including behaviour under degradation conditions?
9. Do tests address what the system will not do as well as what it will do?
10. Are power-up and power-fail tests included?

A1.7   DESIGN FEATURES

A1.7.1   Overall software design

1. Were estimates of size and timing carried out?
2. Is the system secure?
3. Is it testable as a whole and as subsystems or modules?
4. Are there standard interfaces for:
   - data transfer;
   - peripheral interconnections;
   - man/machine communication.

5. Is the system designed in such a way that it can be progressively built up and tested?
6. Have hardware and software monitoring facilities been provided?
7. Is use made of error-check software?
8. What is the traffic of data on links and the speed of links? Will the links handle the traffic in the required time? Will they give the required response rates?
9. Can the internal data highways meet their loading and timing requirements?
10. Will the system detect and tolerate operator error?
11. Are there facilities for recording system states in the event of failure?
12. Have acceptable degraded facilities been defined?

A1.7.2 Fault tolerance

1. Are detailed statements of reliability, degradation and recovery requirements of the system stated?
2. Are there any special characteristics or failure modes of the hardware that the software must protect against or avoid?
3. Are interfaces defined such that illegal actions do not corrupt the system or lock up the interface?

A1.7.3 Hardware aspects

1. Will the user configuration support the hardware?
2. Is there enough storage and is it of the required access time and degree of permanence?
3. Are the processors sufficiently powerful?
4. Are the following adequate:
   - electrical protection (mains and emc);
   - power supplies and filters.
5. Is memory storage adequate for foreseeable expansion requirements?

Appendix 2

Glossary of terms and abbreviations

The following is an explanation of the main terms used in software and systems engineering. There are many glossaries in the various documents described in Chapter 5 which address this subject and it could be argued that there is no need for yet another. However, this list attempts to combine the available glossaries in the author's words and to offer a comprehensive coverage of the terms. It is split into groups of words, and the words in each group are in alphabetical order. The final section of the glossary gives the meanings of some common abbreviations. The groups are:

- (A) terms connected with failure;
- (B) terms connected with software;
- (C) terms connected with software systems and their hardware;
- (D) terms connected with procedures, management, documents and quality assurance;
- (E) terms connected with test;
- (F) some abbreviations.

(A) TERMS CONNECTED WITH FAILURE

Availability
What is usually referred to as availability is the steady availability. It is the proportion of time that the system is not in a failed state.

Bit error rate
The rate of incidence of random incorrect binary bits. This usually refers to the effect of corruption in a communication channel.

Bug

A slang expression for a software fault (see *fault*).

Common-cause failure (common-mode failure)

Both terms refer to the coincident failure of two or more supposedly independent terms as the result of a single cause. This is especially relevant in systems incorporating redundancy where one event causes the coincident failure of two more normally independent channels.

Data corruption

The introduction of an error by reason of some alteration of the software already resident in the system. This could arise from electrical, magnetic or ionizing interference or from incorrect processing of a portion of the software.

Error

An error has occurred when the software in the system reaches an incorrect state – a bit or bits in the program or in data take incorrect values. This can arise as a result of outside interference or because of faults in the program. An error is caused by a *fault* and may propagate to become a *failure*. *Error recovery software* may thus prevent an error propagating.

Error recovery software

Sections of a program, involving redundant (*parity*) bits or checksums, which can recognize and correct some bit errors.

Failure

Termination of the ability of an item (or system) to perform its specified task. In the case of software the presence of an *error* is required in order for it to propagate to become a failure.

Failure rate

The number of *failures*, per unit time, of an item. Since software failures are path- rather than time-related this is not a particularly useful parameter except for hardware failures.

Fault

Faults may occur in hardware or in software. Whereas hardware faults are time-related, software faults are conditions which may lead to bit *errors* in the system. These faults may be ambiguities or omissions in the logic structure of the program or environmental/hardware conditions which can cause software corruption.

The presence of a software fault does not necessarily guarantee that an *error* and *failure* will ensue.

Fault tolerance
Hardware and software features (discussed in Chapter 13) which render a software system less likely to *fail* as a result of software *faults*.

Graceful degradation
A design feature whereby a system continues to operate, albeit at a reduced efficiency or with fewer functions available, in the presence of *failures*.

Integrity
The ability of a system to perform its functions correctly when required. The term 'integrity' is usually associated with safety systems.

Intrinsic safety
A degree of *integrity* designed into a system in order to meet defined safety criteria.

Maintainability
The probability that a failed item (or system) will be restored to operational effectiveness within a specified time and when the repair action is carried out according to prescribed procedures. The parameter is often expressed by reference to a mean down time (MDT) or mean time to repair (MTTR).

Reliability
The probability that an item will perform a required function, under stated conditions, for a stated period of time. System reliability is often described by reference to parameters such as failure rate and mean time between failures. Since software reliability cannot easily be quantified, these terms are better applied to hardware alone.

(B) TERMS CONNECTED WITH SOFTWARE

Algorithm
A set of logical rules for the solution of a defined problem.

Alphanumeric
A code or description consisting of both alphabetic and/or numerical characters.

Application language
A problem-oriented language whose statements closely resemble the jargon or terminology of the particular problem type.

Application software

The software written for a computer for the purpose of applying the computer functions to solve a particular problem. This is distinct from the resident operating software which is part of the computer system.

Assembler

A program for converting instructions, written in mnemonics, into binary machine code suitable to operate a computer or other programmable device.

Assembly language

A low-level language where the instructions are expressed as mnemonics and where each instruction corresponds to a simple computer function.

Basic coded unit (BCU)

Often referred to as a *module*, a self-contained manageable element of a program which fulfils a specific simple function and is capable of being completed and run. The BCU should be at a sufficiently simple level to permit its function to be described by a single sentence.

Baud

The unit of signal speed where 1 baud corresponds to 1 information bit per second. This is equivalent to the bit speed in a binary system where each bit can take either of two values (0 or 1). In multilevel signalling the baud rate will be higher than the bit rate.

Binary coded decimal (BCD)

A binary notation whereby each decimal digit is represented by a four-bit binary number (e.g. 1001 0011 represents 93).

Bit

A single binary digit taking the value 0 or 1.

Code

Any set of characters representing program instructions or data in any computer language.

Code template

A standard piece of proven code, for a particular function, which is used repetitively.

Compiler

A program which, in addition to being an *assembler*, generates more than one instruction for each statement, thereby permitting the use of a *high-*

level language. It consists of:

- lexical analyser (recognizes the words);
- syntax analyser (recognizes logical commands);
- semantic analyser (sorts out the meaning);
- code generator (generates the 0s and 1s).

Database
Any set of numerical or alphabetical data.

Data-flow diagram
The next stage after the requirements specification involves data-flow analysis. The data-flow diagram is a graphic (usually flow) diagram showing data sources and the flow of data within a program.

Decision table
The representation of a number of decision options showing the various outcomes. This is usually shown in matrix or tabular form.

Default value
The value of a variable which will be assumed when no specific input is given.

Diversity
One form of diversity is said to exist when the redundancy in a system is not identical. In software terms this would apply if redundant channels had been separately programmed. The disadvantages of this are discussed in Chapter 13.

Another form of diversity exists when an alternative means is available for a particular function to be performed despite the failure of the main function.

Dump
To transfer the contents of a store or memory to an external medium.

Global data
A major named group of data which serves as a common base between various tasks in a program. It will be accessible to all modules.

High-level language
A means of writing program instructions using symbols, each of which represents several program steps. High-level languages do not reflect any particular machine structure and can be compiled to any computer for which a *compiler* exists for that language.

Initialization

The process whereby a system, usually at switch-on, is put into the correct software state to commence operation.

Interpreter

A type of *compiler* which enables one instruction at a time to be checked and converted into machine code. This permits step-by-step programming at the VDU. Syntax errors are then announced as they occur.

Language

The convention of words, numerals, punctuation and grammar which enables programs to be written in a form comprehensive to a computer.

Listing

A printed list of the coded program instructions. A listing is usually of the *source code*.

Machine code

See *object code*.

Metrics

Parameters for describing the structure, size and complexity of a program. Attempts are made to relate these metrics, by regression techniques, to software quality (see Chapter 15).

Mnemonic

Characters used to represent a particular instruction. Low-level languages use mnemonics in their instructions.

Module

The basic testable unit of software (see also *basic coded unit*).

Multi-tasking

The ability of a computer system to carry out more than one task, apparently simultaneously.

Object code

The final machine code, probably the output from a *compiler*, which the computer can understand. Programming directly in machine code is now extremely rare.

Operating system

The machine-resident software which enables a computer to function. Without it, applications programs could not be loaded or run.

Parity
An additional bit or bits which are added to a segment of data or instruction to enable subsequent checking for error. The value of the parity bits is generated from the values of the bits which it is 'protecting'.

Procedure
An identifiable portion of a program which carries out a specific function. A procedure may be a module.

Program
A set of coded instructions which enable a computer to function. A program may consist of many modules and be written in assembly or high-level language. Note the spelling 'program', whereas 'programme' is used to describe a schedule of tasks.

Pseudocode
High-level 'English' language statements which provide an intermediate level between the module specification and the computer language.

Routine
A frequently used piece of code which is resident inside a program.

Software
The term software covers all the instructions and data which are used to operate a computer or programmable system. It includes the operating system, compiler, applications software and test programs. The definition also embraces the documents (specifications, charts, listings, diagrams and manuals) which make up the system.

Source code
The listing of a program in the language in which it was written.

Structured programming
Well-defined and standardized programming techniques which result in greater visibility of the program and less complexity.

Syntax
Rules which govern the use and order of instructions in a language.

Task
A sequence of instructions which together carry out a specific function.

Translator
A program which transforms instructions from one language into another.

(C)   TERMS CONNECTED WITH SOFTWARE SYSTEMS AND THEIR HARDWARE

Analogue/digital converter
A device which converts an analogue electrical value (voltage or current) into an equivalent binary coded form.

Applications hardware
A special-purpose unit designed, as a peripheral to the computer, to carry out some specified function.

Asynchronous
A timing arrangement whereby each event is started as a result of the completion of preceding events rather than by some defined trigger.

Bus
A digital signal path (or highway).

Configuration
A complete description, at a point in time, of a product and the interrelationship of its parts. This includes the hardware, software and firmware and is a description of its characteristics. Both physical parts and performance are described.

Configuration baseline
A specific reference point, in time, whereby the *configuration* is described. All changes are then referred to that baseline.

Configuration item
A collection of hardware and software which forms a part of the *configuration*.

Digital/analogue converter
The opposite of an *analogue/digital converter*.

Disc
See *magnetic disc*.

Diversity
An attempt at fault tolerance whereby redundant units are separately designed and coded in order to reduce common-mode software failures. See also section B of this glossary.

Ergonomics

The study of man/machine interfaces in order to minimize human errors due to mental or physical fatigue.

Firmware

Any software which is resident on physical media (e.g. hardwired circuitry, EPROM, PROM, ROM, disc).

Interrupt

The suspension of processing due to a real-time event. The program is so arranged that processing continues after the interrupt has been dealt with.

Large-scale integration (LSI)

The technology whereby very large numbers of circuit functions are provided on a single component. A programmable system may consist of one or more LSI devices.

Magnetic disc

A rotating circular lamina with a magnetic coating which can record binary bits by means of magnetic storage.

Magnetic tape

A tape with a magnetic coating which can record binary bits by means of magnetic storage.

Media

A collective term for the devices on which software programs are stored (e.g. PROM, EPROM, ROM, disc, tape).

Memory

Storage (usually binary) in a computer system.

Microprocessor

The central processing unit of a computer (usually contained on a single device) consisting of memory registers, an arithmetic and logic unit, program and instruction registers and some interface to the external world.

Modem

An acronym for MOdulator/DEModulator. It converts binary signals into frequency form for transmission over telecommunications channels and vice versa.

'N' version programming

See *diversity*.

Peripheral

Any piece of equipment, apart from the computer architecture of logic and memory, which provides input or output facilities;

PES – programmable electronic system

Any piece of equipment containing one or more components providing a computer architecture such that the functions are provided by a program of logical instructions. The term is increasingly used in the context of the control, monitoring and protection of plant.

PLC – programmable logic controller

A computer system with real-time inputs and outputs. It is provided with a special-purpose problem-oriented language and is increasingly used in the control of plant and processes.

Programmable device

Any piece of equipment containing one or more components providing a computer architecture with memory facilities.

Real-time system

A computer system (including PES, PLC) which operates in response to on-line inputs and stimuli.

Redundancy

The provision of more than one piece of equipment for achieving a particular function.

- *Active redundancy*. All items operating prior to failure of one or more.
- *Standby redundancy*. Replicated items do not operate until needed.

Safety-critical software

Software whereby one or more failure modes can have hazardous consequences.

Safety-related system

One or more systems upon which the safety of a plant or process depends.

Synchronous

An arrangement whereby logical steps or processes in a program are only initiated as a result of a reference clock rather than as a result of preceding events being completed.

Watchdog

A part of the system (may be hardware or software) which monitors the state of the processor and signals when tasks are not completed within a prescribed time.

(D) TERMS CONNECTED WITH PROCEDURES, MANAGEMENT, DOCUMENTS AND QUALITY ASSURANCE

Acceptance

The act whereby a user states to a supplier that the product is now satisfactory. This acceptance may be partial in that agreed outstanding modifications or rectifications are to be implemented.

Archiving

Storing programs, data and documents externally to the computer system either for security (in the event of corruption) or for later resumption of design.

Bureau

The facility where computer-processing facilities and software packages are offered for hire.

Code inspection

The design-review activity wherein members of the design team, other than the programmer/designer, examine a module of code against standards in order to reveal faults.

Code walk-through

The design review activity wherein the programmer/designer participates in leading other members of the team through a module of code. They then attempt to discover faults by questioning.

Configuration control

The discipline that ensures that all changes and modifications to the *configuration baseline* (see Part C of this glossary) are controlled and recorded and that, as a result, documents and firmware conform to issue status.

Configuration item

An aggregate of hardware and software which is designated for configuration control.

Design review

A formal comparison of the software and hardware with the specifications in order to establish conformance. Code inspections and walkthroughs are part of this process, which may be carried out at many stages in the design.

Feasibility study

A preliminary study of some proposed solution to requirements in order to establish viability apropos of cost, schedule, function, reliability, etc.

Flow chart

A graphical representation of the logic and data flow which satisfies a specification. Normally coding follows from the flow chart. Modern structured languages have much reduced the need for this technique.

Library

The formal documentation and software storage within an organization.

Life cycle

The complete series of activities from requirements specification, through design and test, to field use and modification.

Quality assurance

The total range of activities which attempt to ensure that a finished product, both in design and manufacturing respects, meets the requirement.

Quality system

A formal set of procedures, methods and standards whereby the management of design and manufacture seeks to operate *quality*.

Release

The issue of software after it has been formally validated by design review.

Requirement

A statement of the problem or function required by the user.

Safety integrity

The probability of a safety-related system satisfactorily performing the required safety functions, under stated conditions, within a stated period of time.

Specification
A document, at one of the levels in the hierarchy of design, which describes either requirements or solutions.

(E) TERMS CONNECTED WITH TEST

Acceptance testing
Testing carried out specifically to demonstrate to the user that the requirements of the functional specification have been met.

Development system
Usually a VDU, keyboard and computer equipped with appropriate support software in order to test and debug programs.

Diagnostic software
A program which assists in locating and explaining the causes of faults in software.

Emulation
A type of simulation whereby the simulator responds to all possible inputs as would the real item and generates all the corresponding outputs.

Endurance test
Extreme testing whereby the software is subjected to abnormal and illegal inputs and conditions and saturation levels which stress the program capabilities in terms of data volume and rate, processing time, response time, utilization of memory, etc.

Integration
The step-by-step process of testing where each module is tested alone and then in conjunction with others until the system is built up.

Load test
See *endurance test*.

Simulation
The representation, for test purposes, of a unit or system by hardware or by software in order to provide some or all inputs or responses.

Soak test
A test where a system is submitted to prolonged periods of operation, often at elevated temperature and humidity.

Static analyser

A suite of software which analyses code (see Chapter 11).

Stress test

See *endurance test*.

Test driver

See *test harness*.

Test harness

Specially designed hardware and software used to replace parts of the system not yet developed and in order to permit testing of available modules to proceed.

Test software

Any program used as a test aid.

Validation

The process of ensuring that the results of the whole project meet the original requirements.

Validator

A suite of programs which examines a computer program and determines if certain types of fault exist (see Chapter 11).

Verification

The process of ensuring that the result of a particular phase meets the requirements of the previous phase.

(F)   SOME ABBREVIATIONS

ACMH	Advisory Committee on Major Hazards
A/D	Analogue to digital
ALARP	As low as reasonably practicable
APSE	Ada project support environment
AQAP	Allied quality assurance programme
ASCII	American Standard Code for Information Interchange
ASIC	Applications-specific integrated circuit
ATE	Automatic test equipment
BCD	Binary coded decimal
BCS	British Computer Society
BCU	Basic coded unit

BSI	British Standards Institute
CAD	Computer-aided design
CASE	Computer-aided software engineering
CCDM	Conceptual database design methodology
CCF	Common cause failure
CCS	Calculus of concurrent systems
CCTA	UK government centre for information systems
CIMAH	Control of industrial major accident hazards
CMF	Common-mode failure
COMAH	Control of major accident hazards
CPU	Central processing unit
CRAMM	Computer risk analysis and risk methodology
CSP	Communications sequential processes
D/A	Digital to analogue
DOD	Department of Defense (USA)
DTI	Department of Trade and Industry (UK)
EC	European Community
EEA	Electronic Engineering Association
EEMUA	Engineering Equipment and Material User's Association
emc	Electromagnetic compatibility
EMI	Electromagnetic interference
ERA	Electrical Research Association
ESD	Emergency shutdown system
EU	European Union
EUROCAE	European Organization for Civil Aviation Equipment
EWICS	European Workshop for Industrial Computing Systems
FMEA	Failure mode and effect analysis
FRESCO	Framework for evaluation of safety-critical objects
HAZOP	Hazard and operability study
HSC	Health and Safety Commission
HSE	Health and Safety Executive
I/O	Input/output
IEC	International Electro-technical Commission
IEE	Institution of Electrical Engineers (UK)
IEEE	Institution of Electrical and Electronics Engineers (USA)
IGASE	Institution of Gas Engineers (UK)
IL	Intermediate language
IPSE	Integrated project support environment
ISO	International Standards Organization
IT	Information technology
JSD	Jackson systems development
LDRA	Liverpool data research associates
LSI	Large-scale integration
MALPAS	Malvern program analysis suite

MASCOT	Modular approach to software construction, operation and test
MOD	Ministry of Defence (UK)
MTBF	Mean time before failures
NCC	National Computing Centre (UK)
NIG	National interest group
NIHHS	Notification of installations handling hazardous substances
NPL	National Physical Laboratory
OODT	Object-oriented design technique
PC	Personal computer
PES	Programmable electronic system
PLC	Programmable logic controller
PROM	Programmable read-only memory
QRA	Quantified risk assessment
RAM	Random-access memory
RISC	Reduced instruction set computer
ROM	Read-only memory
RSRE	Royal Signals and Radar Establishment (UK)
SADT	Structured analysis and design technique
SaRS	Safety and reliability society
SEI	Software Engineering Institution
SPADE	Southampton program analysis and development
SSA	Structured systems analysis
SSADM	Structured systems analysis and design methodology
UKOOA	United Kingdom Offshore Operators Association
VDM	Vienna development method
VDU	Visual display unit
VIPER	Verifiable integrated processor for enhanced reliability

Appendix 3

Bibliography and references

A3.1 BRITISH STANDARDS

British Standards Institute
Sales Dept
Linford Wood
Milton Keynes MK14 6LE

BS 3527 *Glossary of Terms used in Data Processing.*
BS 4058 *Data Processing Flow Chart Symbols, Rules and Conventions.*
BS 4778 *Glossary of Terms used in Quality Assurance.*
BS 5476 *Specification for Program Network Charts.*
BS 5515 *Code of Practice for the Documentation of Computer Based Systems.*
BS 5760 *Reliability of Systems, Equipment and Components.*
BS 5783 *Code of Practice for the Handling of Electrostatic Sensitive Devices.*
BS 5887 *Code of Practice for the Testing of Computer Based Systems.*
BS 5905 *Specification for Computer Language CORAL 66.*
BS EN 61131-3 1993 *Programmable Controllers (Part 3, Programming Languages).*
BS 6238 *Code of Practice for Performance Monitoring of Computer Based Systems.*
BS 6488 *Code of Practice for Configuration Management of Computer Based Systems.*
BS 7750 *Environmental Management Systems.*
BS EN 9000 *Quality Systems.*

A3.2 UK DEFENCE STANDARDS

The Directorate of Standardisation
Ministry of Defence
Montrose House
187 George Street
Glasgow G1 1YU

EQD Guide for Software Quality Assurance.
IECCA *A Guide to the Management of Software-based Systems for Defence* (3rd edition).

JSP 188 *Specification and Requirements for the Documentation of Software in Operational Real-time Computer Systems.*

JSP 343 *MOD Standard for Automatic Data Processing.*

UK DEF STD 00-13 *Achievement of Testability in Electronic and Allied Equipment.*

UK DEF STD 00-14 *Guide to the Defence Industry in the use of ATLAS.*

UK DEF STD 00-16/1 *Guide to the Achievement of Quality in Software* (Withdrawn).

UK DEF STD 00-17 *Modular Approach to Software Construction Operation and Test (MASCOT).*

UK DEF STD 00-18 *Avionic Data Transmission Interface System* (5 parts).

UK DEF STD 00-19 *The ASWE Serial Highway.*

UK DEF STD 00-21 *M700 Computers.*

UK DEF STD 00-47 *Computer On-line Real-time Application Language – CORAL 66 – Specification for Compilers.*

UK DEF STD 00-55 *The Procurement of Safety Critical Software in Defence Equipment.*

UK DEF STAN 00-56 *Hazard Analysis and Safety Classification.*

UK DEF STAN 00-67 *Guide to Quality Assurance in Design* (Section 12 of this guide deals with computer software and quality assurance).

UK DEF STAN 05-57 *Configuration Management – Requirements for Defence Equipment.*

A3.3 US STANDARDS

A-DatP-2(B) *NATO Glossary of Automatic Data Processing (ADP) Terms and Definitions.*

DOD STD 2167 *Defense System for Software Development.*

MIL HDBK 344 *UK Military Handbook – Evaluation of a Contractor's Software Quality Assurance Program.*

MIL STD 1750A *Military Standard: 16 Bit Computer Instruction Set Architecture.*

Publication 78-53 *Standard Practices for the Implementation of Computer Software,* Jet Propulsion Laboratory, Pasadena CA 91103 USA.

US MIL-S-52779(AD), *Software Quality Assurance Requirements.*

IEEE documents

610.12 *Glossary of Software Engineering.*

730   *Standard for Software Quality Assurance Plans.*

828   *Standard for Software Configuration Management Plans.*

829   *Standard for Software Test Documentation.*

830   *Recommended Practice for Software Requirements Specifications.*

982.1 *Standard Dictionary of Measures to Produce Reliable Software.*

982.2 *Guide for the Use of IEEE Standard Dictionary Measures to Produce Reliable Software.*

990   *Ada as a Program Design Language.*

1002   *Standard Taxonomy for Software Engineering Standards.*

1003.1   *Information Technology – Portable Operating System Interface. Part 1 System Application Program Interface (C language).*

1003.1-1988/INT   *Interpretations for Portable Operating System Interface for Computer Environments.*

1003.2 Volumes 1 and 2   *Standard for Information Technology Portable Operating System Interface. Part 2 Shell and Utilities.*

1003.3   *Standard for Information Technology Test Methods for Measuring Conformance to POSIX.*

1003.5   *Standard for Information Technology POSIX Ada Language Interfaces. Part 1 Binding for System Application Program Interface.*

1003.5 INT   *Standards Interpretations for IEEE Standard 1003.5-1992.*

1003.9   *Standard for Information Technology POSIX FORTRAN 77 Language Interfaces. Part 1 Binding for System Application Program Interface.*

1008   *Standard for Software Unit Testing.*

1012   *Standard for Software Verification and Validation Plans.*

1016   *Recommended Practice for Software Design Descriptions..*

1016.1   *Guide to Software Design Descriptions.*

1028   *Standard for Software Reviews and Audits.*

1042   *Guide to Software Configuration Management.*

1045   *Standard for Software Productivity Metrics.*

1058.1   *Standard for Software Project Management Plans.*

1061   *Standard for a Software Quality Metrics Methodology.*

1062   *Recommended Practice for Software Acquisition.*

1063   *Standard for Software User Documentation.*

1074   *Standard for Developing Software Life-cycle Processes.*

1209   *Recommended Practice for the Evaluation and Selection of CASE Tools.*

1219   *Standard for Software Maintenance.*

2003.1   *Standard for Information Technology Test Methods for Measuring Conformance to POSIX Part 1 System Interfaces.*

A3.4   OTHER GUIDANCE

IEC International Standard: Functional Safety – Safety Related Systems (three parts).

Guidelines on Risk Issues, 1992. The Engineering Council, UK.

Engineers and Risk Issues, 1992. The Engineering Council, UK.

Safety Related Systems, Guidance for Engineers – The Hazards Forum. Available from IEE.

HSE Publication, *The Tolerability of Risk from Nuclear Power Stations.* HMSO, ISBN 0 11886368 1.

HSE Publication, *Guidance on the Use of Programmable Electronic Systems in Safety Related Applications* (1987).

ERA Technology Report SEMS PLC 9019/2D/ERA/0114/R/A *Study of the Application of Software Metrics to Software Development.*

Guidelines for Process Control and Safety Systems on Offshore Installations, UKOOA.

Out Of Control, A Complication of Incidents involving Control Systems, HSE.

TickIT Guide to Software Quality Management System Construction and Certification, BCS under contract to DTI.

Guidelines for the Documentation of Software in Industrial Computer Systems (2nd edition) IEE 1992, ISBN 0 86341 0466 4.

IGasE: IGE/SR/15 1994 *Programmable Equipment in Safety Related Applications*.

EEMUA: *Safety Related Programmable Electronic Systems*.

RTCA DO-178B/(EUROCAE ED-12B) *Software Considerations in Airborne Systems and Equipment Certification*.

DIN VDE 0801 *Principles for Computers in Safety-related Systems* (Germany) 1990.

EWICS TC7 Documents.

The EEA Guides:

- *Guide to the Quality Assurance of Software* (UK), 1978;
- *Establishing a Quality Assurance Function for Software* (UK), 1981;
- *Software Configuration Management* (UK), 1983;
- *A Guide to the Successful Start-up of a Software Project* (UK), 1985.

The STARTS Guide.

STARTS Purchaser's Handbook.

ElektronikCentralen: *Standards and Regulations for Software Approval and Certification* (Denmark).

Guidelines for the Nordic Factory Inspectorates.

A3.5 BOOKS

Anderson, T. (1985) *Software Requirements Specification and Testing*, Blackwell Scientific Publications, London.

Buckle, J. K. (1982) *Software Configuration Management*, Macmillan Press, London (paperback edition, 1994).

Dahl, O.-J., Dijkstra, E. W. and Hoare, C. A. R. (1982) *Structured Programming*, Academic Press, New York.

Humphrey, W. (1989) *Managing the Software Process*, Addison-Wesley, Reading, MA.

Kernighan, B. W. and Plaugez, P. J. (1978) *Elements of Programming Style*, McGraw-Hill, New York.

Musa, J. D., Iannino, A. and Okumoto, K. (1987) *Software Reliability Prediction and Measurement*, McGraw-Hill, New York.

Myers, G. J. (1979) *The Art of Software Testing*, Wiley, Chichester.

O'Connor, P. D. T. (1994) *The Practice of Engineering Management*, John Wiley, Chichester.

Smith, D. J. (1992) *Reliability Maintainability and Risk*, 4th edition, Butterworth, Oxford.

Smith. D. J. and Edge, J. S. (1991) *Quality Procedures for Hardware and Software*, Elsevier Applied Science, Barking.

Index